WHAT
CHABAD
REALLY   CHASSIDUS/MYSTICISM
BELIEVES

A MIDAIR DIALOGUE ON CHASSIDIC PHILOSOPHY AND ITS CLIMACTIC VIEW OF OUR CURRENT AGE

YOSEPH KOHANOV

CREATIVE LITERARY WORK

WHAT CHABAD REALLY BELIEVES

A Midair Dialogue on Chassidic Philosophy and its Climactic View of Our Current Age

Published and Copyrighted © 2016 by

Rabbi Yoseph Kohanov

10129 Haley Road
Jacksonville, FL 32257
whatchabadbelieves@gmail.com

Second Printing 2020

ISBN: 978-0- 9972060-0- 5

A glossary of terms can be found at the back of the book

Design: Meir Kahanov
Layout: Menachem Mendel Browd

A noted Chassid was once asked,
"how is it that you Chabad
Chassidim are so successful in
attracting so many people to Torah?
What is your secret?"

"We just tell them the truth…"
answered the Chassid.

"Chassidus is closer to the truth than
anything else; that is what people
want to hear nowadays.

"When people hear the simple
unvarnished truth, they respond to it.
It is as simple as that."

TABLE OF CONTENTS

A wise person observed that the day a Jewish child is born, he or she is 2000 years old. The product of 2 millennia of Jewish oppression and exile, the Jew enters the world shouldering this burden. The long and arduous exile has, indeed, left its mark, leading to our current religious crisis.

Perhaps the most revolutionary measure taken by the foremost Jewish leader of our time, the late Lubavitcher Rebbe, was to classify the non-committed Jew of today as a "Tinok Shenishba," literally, infant raised in captivity. These casualties of exile are, therefore, absolved of any misdeeds. G-d, in fact, loves these innocent souls. Their every Mitzvah is cherished, regardless of what was yesterday or what will be tomorrow.

The Jew of our generation—whose life is inconsistent with Torah—possesses an essential connection with G-d that is neither intellectual nor logical; it is above the confines of religion and Mitzvah observance.

The Rebbe proclaimed our generation, despite all its flaws and spiritual deficiencies, or perhaps because of them, to be the era heralding the coming of Moshiach-Messiah. It is we who are granted the good fortune of bringing an end to this dark and bitter exile, through the fulfillment of just a single Mitzvah.

Chabad sees a critical parallel between our unique age, dubbed, "Heel of Moshiach," and the recent emergence of the Chassidic movement and the proliferation of its ideology. In fact, Chassidim (particularly Chabad) perceive themselves as the army, and Chassidus as the armor, in this final foray.

This book offers a glimpse into the mind of the Chabad Chassidic movement.

PREFACE

Reared in the central Lubavitch community of Crown Heights, Brooklyn, I was introduced to Chassidic thought at a rather early age as part of my formal education.

Particularly significant were the thousands of hours of Chassidic lessons, presented by the preeminent Chassidic master—the late Lubavitcher Rebbe, Rabbi Menachem Mendel Schneerson OBM—to which I was fortunately exposed.

The Rebbe's teachings were shared, largely, during what were known as "farbrengens,"[1] which formed a major part of his legacy. These frequent events offered a window into the core and scope of the Rebbe's revolutionary approach to Judaism—a portal to his unique distillation of *Torah* in general and Chassidism in particular.

It was a true blessing to have been privy to these public proceedings throughout the formative years of my life.

It is expected of a Chabad Chassid to continue learning Chassidus well beyond the formal years of his education—as is the duty of every Jew regarding *Torah* in general—hence, by means of his ongoing study, the Chassid's familiarity with the discipline continues to grow and mature throughout his life.

Some Chabad Chassidim are fortunate to serve as "Shluchim" (plural for Shliach)-Chabad Emissaries.[2] As a Shliach, one's acquaintance with Chassidus must be particularly well maintained. This is due to the fact that the Shliach's responsibilities include the dissemination of this very discipline—it is part of his vocation, if you will.

---

[1] Chassidic gathering, including words of inspiration, some L'chaim and stirring Chassidic melody.

[2] A Shliach, in this context, is a member of the Chabad movement whose life is devoted to promulgate Judaism and Chasidism in locations around the world.

Finally, in addition to the academic and theological properties that constitute Chassidic thought, there is the practical outreach dimension associated with Chabad, whose origins is no doubt sourced in the works of Chassidus. The Shliach is intricately involved with the implementation of this practical component of Chabad Chassidism as well.

Hence, as a Chabad Chassid and Shliach (minor as may be), I come to the book's topic from both its intellective and pragmatic perspectives. Still, this renders me not an authority. Rather, I approach the topic as a student. The ideas offered in this work are my own understanding and distillation of the teachings.

Though much of the material is quoted and footnoted, some of the ideas and applications may be considered novel. I certainly make no claims to speak in the name of any Chassidic author, Rebbe or other authority on the matter.

It should be noted that this book is not your typical exposé on Chassidic philosophy. It is rather a creative literary work, or narrative, not common within the genera of Chassidic philosophy. This novel approach is meant to convey, with G-d's help, the concepts in a more palatable user friendly fashion.

By no means should this book be considered a comprehensive treatment of the subject matter. Chassidic philosophy is an extremely profound and voluminous theology. It would be a huge understatement to think that it could ever be condensed into a single book.

Interspersed throughout the book are several excerpted articles shaded in gray. They've been included, as they support the extraordinary value of Chassidic philosophy or speak to its various practical benefits.

On another note, this is an apolitical work. Its focus is the discipline of Chassidus and the tireless work of the Chabad movement in disseminating its teachings. Reference to any faction, movement, or organization—religious or secular—is without political intent.

I am profoundly grateful to the Almighty for granting me the opportunity and strength to complete this work. I pray that the book touch the heart of its reader and leave a positive impact.

I wish to express my thanks to all the distinguished Rabbis and good friends who graciously reviewed this book and made apt and instructive comments.

I'm particularly indebted to the following people for helping make this book a reality in one capacity or another: Chaya Benjaminson, Dr. Ronald Bernstein, Dr. Richard Bronowitz, Rabbi Mendel Duchman, Susan Horwitz-Editor, Rabbi Yossi Gansburg, Rabbi Zalman A. Grossbaum, Meir Kahanov, Debra Levine, Shaul Lugerner, Rabbi Yossi Schildkraut, Mathew Silverton, and Rabbi Sholom B. Wineberg.

I would like to acknowledge the kind support and assistance offered by my children in preparing this manuscript for print: Nechamie & Mendy Browd, Fraidy & Levi Vogel, Shaina & Shmuly Feldman, Leibel & Chana Stery Kahanov, Mushkie & Efraim Zimmerman, Chanie & Chai Kohan, Chavie & Sruly Shemtov & Velvil.

My heartfelt appreciation goes out to my wife Rivkie for her unfailing support in all areas of my life and particularly with this book. She, in her inimitable way, is always there.

Rabbi Akiva once pointed to his wife and told his students, "What is mine and what is yours, is hers." He recognized that his success and the success of his students were a product of his wife's support. This book would never have been without her unrelenting encouragement and assistance.

Yoseph Kohanov
18 Elul 5776
September, 21, 2016

INTRODUCTION

Ours is, in many ways, the lowliest and most degenerate of times. Yet, by the same token, it is the most fortunate and propitious moment in all of history. This bold assertion is predicated on Kabbalah-based Chassidic philosophy, known as "Chassidus," which is the primary theme of this creative literary work.

Shrouded in mystery throughout the millennia, Kabbalah has, at last, reached a state of broad elucidation, even fruition, in the form of Chassidic philosophy. Our generation is the beneficiary and remarkably the focus, to a large degree, of this potent wisdom.

Chassidus is an intellectual discipline that puts into perspective the mystery of the entire cosmos—its origins and existential purpose, as well as its relationship with its Creator in a logical and compelling order. Adding to all this is the human psychological, emotional, and spiritual enigma. What *Chabad Really Believes* is a book on Chabad Chassidic philosophy and its modern day application.

Penned as a dialogue between two friends during a plane trip on a Jewish Federation Mission, the narrative is drawn to the climactic nature of our present era. This occurs as Danni, the more religious of the two, shares Chassidic insights with his disenfranchised friend, Jay.

When Danni speaks out in Treblinka, it causes an inner shift in Jay. This leads him to a spiritual awakening, yet, at the same time he grows increasingly perturbed over his seemingly insurmountable religious predicament.

Danni eases his friend's distress by sharing the unique nature and potential of our current age, and how it relates to him personally. He assures Jay that, deficient as we may seem today, the measuring stick is thoroughly altered. No longer do we live by the incriminations of yesteryear—no longer do we bear the same stigmas.

This book defines the current condition of Jewry in context of the broader historical perspective. The latter is based on the premise that history is not merely a hodgepodge of random events, but, rather, a deliberate sequence with a beginning, middle and end.

The product of almost 6 thousand years of tumultuous history and 2 thousand years of continuous exile, ours is the final generation of exile, dubbed the "Heel of Moshiach."[3] Ours is the generation destined to usher the Messianic era, blemishes and faults notwithstanding.

Given the Kabbalistic axiom that the end is wedged in the beginning and vice versa, it follows that all of history serves as a systematic buildup and preparation for our age—the moments of the finishing act that brings definition to all history, indeed, to creation itself.

Though the founder of Chassidism is the saintly Baal Shem Tov (1698-1760), it was not until the first Chabad Rebbe,[4] Rabbi Schneur Zalman of Liadi (1745-1812) that the mysticism espoused by the Baal Shem Tov and his successor the Maggid of Mezritch was distilled into methodical philosophical articulation.

Rabbi Schneur Zalman named the Chassidic intellectual system—of which he served as the leading architect—"Chabad." The name Chabad reflects the Kabbalistic terms for the intellectual faculties that the doctrine targets, namely, Chochmah, Binah, Da'as—Wisdom, Understanding, and Knowledge.

According to Chabad Chassidism, knowledge of the intelligible characteristics of the Creator, found in the mystical dimension of *Torah*, is absolutely necessary in one's service of the Divine Creator.

The late Lubavitcher Rebbe, Rabbi Menachem M. Schneerson, summarized this mandate as follows:

---

[3] Isaiah; 59:2.

[4] Rebbe is a Yiddish word derived from the Hebrew word rabbi, which means "master, teacher, or mentor". Like the title "rabbi" it refers to teachers of *Torah* or leaders of Jewry. Since the founding of the Chassidic movement, the term Rebbe has been used primarily to refer to the leaders of Chassidic groups.

To serve G-d with the emotions alone or with faith alone, or even with intellect alone, is not enough, this would be an incomplete service. There must be a fusion of all of these elements. (See *Zohar* III, p. 224a. *Tanya*, chapters 12, 17, 30, 51) Rabbi Schneur Zalman of Liadi stressed that one must use his intellect and not be content with a service of G-d centered only in the emotions or in faith alone. The result is employing each and every one of our character traits and emotions in the service of the Supernal Being.[5]

The third Chabad Rebbe, R' Menachem Mendel (1789-1866)—known as the Tzemach Tzedek—once asked his grandfather, the first Chabad Rebbe, Rabbi Schneur Zalman of Liadi, to explain the purpose of Chassidus. R' Schneur Zalman replied, "The purpose of Chassidus is to transform the nature of one's personal traits."

In Chabad this transformation is achieved through the development of mind and character in accordance with Chassidic ideology. In fact, Chassidus revolutionized the way its follower views his or her inner self. Human identity, as articulated in Chassidus, parallels no other discipline.

Chassidus, in general, and Chabad Chassidus, in particular, casts a person's identity and hence, his or her very life mission, in a most lofty and critical context. Life in our world as perceived in the eyes of Chassidic discipline is nothing short of the playground of the Divine will.

That may sound peculiar. In what way is our seemingly Heaven-forsaken world considered, of all things, the "Playground of the Divine will?" There is no sound bite answer. This subject is precisely the focus of Chassidism and this book.

A key Kabbalistic principle, emphasized in this narrative, is that human anatomy reflects metaphysical cosmic structure. This means that an individual's own inner experience serves as an allegorical model to understand the deepest mysteries of creation.

---

[5] Talk given to Hillel Students March 7, 1960.

Consequently, through inner personal awareness of the human psyche, we can draw parallels to the macrocosmic order. Even the imagery of something as reticent as human intimacy is invoked in Kabbalah and Chassidus, as metaphoric of the supernal creative process.

Most notably, Chassidus stresses the analogy between the way human action develops from thought and emotion and the way the world came into being. There is a sequence by which a glimmer of thought develops into a full-fledged idea invested with emotion, and results in decision and action. Others only see the final stage of the process—the behavior. Yet, its essential meaning lies in the first flash of thought that sets the process in motion, and even beyond.

More important, however, is the notion that the process also works in reverse. Because, as humans, we are created in the Divine image, the celestial order serves as a mirror of our existential selves. Hence, not only is our comprehension of the cosmic process of creation crystallized through self-exploration, but our own psychological and emotional anatomy is increasingly revealed.[6]

In other words, analyzing the Divine process of creation, as depicted in Jewish mysticism and interpreted through Chassidic philosophy, results in deeper insight and understanding of one's own essential being.

This discipline, even if only indirectly, provides its student with the power and inspiration to remedy psychological perplexities and confusion, as well as to achieve his or her higher goals.

If we are unable to glean this type of practical information directly from Chassidus, likely, it is due to our own deficiencies. Still, Chassidus remains an important component of our metaphysical wellbeing. Psychology alone cannot take the place of Chassidus, because it is limited in its scope.

---

[6] For more on this subject, see *Likutei Sichos* Volume II, p. 363-371.

Psychology's answers rely largely on outside observance and educated guesses about what is happening inside one's mind and heart. This approach can lead to interesting ideas and techniques, mostly through trial and error. Chassidus, by contrast, holds the map of the human psyche.

The greatest advantage of the Chassidic system, however, is that unlike the scientific systems that begin their analysis with the brain, Chassidus' insight into human identity begins with the individual's unique soul. This distinction cannot be overstated.

Perceiving the brain as a person's highest essence is to perceive only half of the person and the smaller half at that. For, if a human comprises body and soul, the soul is certainly the more significant partner. Therefore, constructing a model of the human entity without the soul factor is like stabbing in the dark.

Thanks to the esoteric dimension of *Torah (Bible)*, as articulated through Chassidus, we are fortunate to know our human self in the context of our soul.

The revelation of the mystical teachings ended, by no means, with Rabbi Schneur Zalman. Attention is called in this book 1 to the continual expansion of the hidden dimension of *Torah*. It focuses on the living, breathing nature of Chassidus and its evolutionary process.

Through its articulation, in breadth and depth, by each generation of Chabad's dynastic leaders, this developmental process continues. The more recent the Rebbe, the greater and more lucid is the revelation.

The teachings have, by now, evolved to where even the uninitiated can grasp and internalize Kabbalistic teachings and their transcendent spirituality—to where one can perceive the realm of the physical in its higher mystical context.

1

FATEFUL REUNION

It is 7:00 a.m. I take out my Tallis (prayer shawl), the size of a small blanket, and drape it over my shoulders before wrapping it around my torso. I then reach for my Tefillin (Phylacteries)—two small black boxes with black leather straps that Jewish men are enjoined to place on their left or weaker arm and on the front part of their heads, at the hairline, during weekday morning prayers.

Sitting directly across me is my friend Jay Epstein, who is noticeably uncomfortable. In fact, Jay seems utterly ashamed to be associated with me.

To be honest, I am not really sure I could blame him. After all, we are in one of the busiest airports in the world during a layover on a Jewish Federation Mission to Europe and Israel.

By design, Federation Missions foster Jewish identity and community mindedness through firsthand impact of ineffaceable Jewish history and events. They serve as an opportunity for participants to deepen their collective connection to Jewish life and community.

Our particular mission is on its way to Poland to learn about the Jews of Eastern Europe and their lives before and during the Holocaust. Our group, including several Holocaust survivors, plans to visit sites from Warsaw to Krakow—including concentration camps at Treblinka-Birkenau and Majdanek—to learn about a lost Jewish world.

The mission is scheduled to continue on to Israel, affording participants a behind-the-scenes look at Israeli life. Some of the planned highlights include a solemn ceremony commemorating Israel's fallen soldiers, an affirmation ceremony atop Masada, and events at the Israel Museum and Beit She'an Archaeological Park. The itinerary also includes a spiritual Shabbos (Sabbath) in Jerusalem.

I don the Tefillin and complete my prayers just in time to board the next flight. When onboard, Jay finally gets his chance to psychoanalyze me over my "eccentric" behavior, a routine we have been through before.

Jay and I go back many years. We met in college 19 years ago and remained friends. Somehow, we both found our way into the lay leadership of our respective Jewish Federations. In our early days, Jay was the religious one. His family was traditional in their religious identification, while mine was not religious at all. For the first 39 years of my life, I knew next to nothing about my Jewishness.

"What's the deal with all that religious stuff," Jay ribs me, as we settle into our seats.

"What's the deal with all that religious stuff?" Jay ribs me, as we settle into our seats. "When we met, you were a nice, all-American, open-minded young man. When and how did all this come about?"

"Oh, Jay," I retort only half kiddingly, "is my religious observance upsetting you so badly? Why are you having such difficulty accepting my newfound growth? Are you the same open-minded guy you were when we first met?"

"C'mon Danni," Jay says somewhat defensively. "It's not like that, you know me better. I mean, a lot of my good friends are religious people."

"Man, I can't believe you would step headlong into that one, Jay."

"Oh stop it, Danni!" he cries. "I'm just curious about what has caused the change in you, that's all. What's the big deal?"

"Okay, bud," I tell my friend. "Let me see if I can help enlighten you somewhat. But, I'll need a little bit of time to gather my thoughts. I've never shared this before, you know." After some quiet contemplation, I begin my narrative.

"It all began when it dawned on me that almost half my time in this world is already behind me and that I have little to show for it. Truth be told, I hadn't the slightest clue as to what on earth I was doing here.

"I've experienced enough of life to know that most of its so-called pleasures and rewards are not what they are made out to be. It became increasingly apparent how easily life may be consumed by senseless aspirations and addictions that divert our attention from any kind of substantive purpose and accomplishment.

"Sure, like most people, I spent the majority of my time in output mode, running about like the proverbial 'chicken without a head,' with little opportunity to think about anything outside the many demands of the moment, let alone the luxury of exploring deeper existential purpose.

> I had a strong desire to connect with my own soul and family roots.

"But then, there were occasional moments of solitude, when, instead of pulling out my smart phone to check my emails for the 30th time that day or that morning, or instead of choosing to interact through one of the ever-growing social media platforms, I actually stopped and listened to myself. It was during such occasions that these subtle feelings of hollowness and lack of meaningful fulfillment crept up.

"The quip, 'Why did I ever bother to show up for my existence in the first place,' did not appear all that humorous. After all, the gnawing void, whose urgency seemed to keep pace with my biological clock, was ever demanding.

"Of course, like so many others, I easily could have blocked out these feelings in a million different ways. I actually played that game for some time but, in truth, I knew deep down that ignoring these feelings was tantamount to fooling myself. Worse even, I felt all along like I was somehow 'cheating' myself and it's only a fool who would willingly cheat himself.

"Having explored a range of different social and spiritual paths in life, I reached a point where I had a strong desire to connect with my own soul and family roots. It mattered a lot to me from where I came; the lives and sacrifices of generations whose name and DNA I shared.

"The irony of cheating oneself reminded me of an adage I had once come across. It was about a peasant who had an opportunity of making an exceptionally large business transaction. For practical purposes, it was decided that a coin would be placed on the table each time a bundle of merchandise was transferred from his wagon to the buyer's. Then, the buyer would pay the stipulated price, based on the number of coins on the table.

"Simple-minded as the peasant was, he became captivated by the coins on the table, finding it hard to resist the easy opportunity to increase his fortune. Instinctively, every time the buyer turned his head, he would pocket a few coins. The poor rustic did not realize that he was only cheating himself.

"Great story, Danni, and truly apropos," Jay notes. "Thanks for sharing."

"Sure thing," I return. "But you know, Jay, it really wasn't just about me, not cheating myself. It was as much about not cheating others—not dropping the ball and letting down the team. By 'team' I mean the tens of generations of our ancestors, who put their lives on the line to give me—to give us all—a sense of identity and purpose.

"I felt a sense of responsibility to all those who went through fire and hell to preserve and protect the precious heritage that belongs to every Jew, so that the privilege would not be denied them.

"I remember hearing a story, at some point during a lecture I attended, that left an indelible impact on me. It was about a United States Naval Academy graduate named Charles Plumb. The story stuck with me; I think about it all the time:

"After 75 combat missions, Charles, who flew jets in Vietnam, was shot down by a surface-to-air missile. Upon ejecting, he parachuted into the jungle where the Viet Cong captured him and held him prisoner for 6 years in North Vietnam. After the war, Charles Plumb lectured on lessons he learned from that extraordinary experience.

"One day sitting with his wife in a restaurant, a man came up to him and said, 'You're Plumb! I know you. You flew jet fighters in Vietnam from the aircraft carrier Kitty Hawk. You were shot down!'

'How in the world did you know that?' asked the former pilot in astonishment.

'Well, because I packed your parachute,' replied the stranger. Plumb gasped in surprise. The man pumped his hand repeating, 'I guess it worked!'

"Plumb assured him that, indeed, it worked. 'If your chute hadn't functioned sir, I wouldn't be here today.'

"That night Plumb couldn't sleep. He kept thinking about the stranger. He wondered how many times he might have seen the guy before, but had not paid him any attention. After all, he was a fighter pilot, and the man who packed his chute was 'just a sailor.'

"Plumb thought about the many hours the sailor spent perched over the long wooden table in the bowels of the ship, carefully weaving the shrouds and folding the silks of each parachute. Each time, he held in his hands the fate of someone he didn't know.

"Now, when Plumb lectures, he always asks his audience, 'Who's packing your parachute?'

"You see Jay, since then, I've been thinking about all those who packed my parachute. So, for a while, I've been primed and ready for something real and meaningful in my life. My break came when I met up with Chabad. My encounter with Chabad spurred my religious endeavor."

From Jay's perplexed expression, it was obvious that I had just opened the floodgate of curiosity. I hardly could finish my thought before Jay, with his blank stare, asked, "Chaba...who...?"

At that moment, it was clear how we would spend the rest of the time on the flight. "You sure you want to do this Jay," I asked. "It can get somewhat involved."

"You have a captive audience," Jay said. "I'm all ears."

"Let's see then, where do I start? It's always good to begin with something light. How about I give some humor a shot?

"A congregant once asked his Rabbi, 'why is it, Rabbi, that I always find you, a man of G-d, talking business, when I, a businessman, always talk about spiritual matters, when not at work?'

'Ahh', replied the Rabbi with a twinkle in his eye, 'you have just stumbled upon one of the fundamental principles of human nature.'

'And, what might that principle be,' asked the curious congregant.

'You see', replied the Rabbi sporting a wily grimace, 'people like to discuss things they know nothing about!'

"Hope I'm not describing myself here, Jay," I add.

"Okay, so where are we? Oh yes, Chabad. It is a brand within the diverse spectrum of organized Jewish expression and observance.

"One needs to be somewhat familiar with the dynamics of the Jewish world to truly understand where Chabad fits in; it's not a one-legged endeavor," I add. "But, a snapshot portrayal is not a bad place to start; let me give it a try.

"For the purpose of this discussion, it would be beneficial to keep the focus on the Orthodox branch of Judaism, though, there are others, of course. The Orthodox Jewish world is comprised of several general segments. There is the Lithuanian Yeshiva sector, to whose left is the modern or 'centrist' Orthodox branch. On the opposite end is the Chassidic movement. Then, there are the various Sephardic lineages.

"For the moment, we ought to, once again, narrow the focus of our conversation to the Chassidic bloc. This novel system of Jewish expression, which subscribes to a dynastic structure of leadership known as 'Rebbes,' began to take root during the 18th century in Jewish communities across Eastern Europe, in face of and as a response to the destitute state, in which the Jewish community found itself at the time.

2

BADGERED FLOCK

"During the late 17th century, European Jewry was still reeling from the devastation wrought by the Chmielnicki pogroms of 1648-1649. Chmielnicki led a revolt against the Polish nobility and at the same time, massacred and pillaged all Jewish communities that fell into his hands. The massacres left tens of thousands of Jews dead, and the grief-stricken survivors struggled to rebuild their broken lives and communities.

"Many agreed with Rabbi David ben Shmuel Ha-Levi[7] (1586-1667), also known as Taz,[8] that Poland was a place where 'Most of the time the gentiles do no harm; on the contrary, they do right by Israel.' However, at times, the elaborate legal and customary structures that were instituted to ensure a Jewish modus vivendi would break down.

"Jews were exposed disproportionately, due to the nature of their businesses, to the dangers of the generally poor state of law enforcement and lack of security, both in the towns and on the roads. They also were the victims of blood libels, host desecration charges, and other accusations that, from time to time, resulted in local attacks and pogroms.[9]

"The most widespread persecutions of Jews accompanied the combined peasant uprising and Cossack revolt against Polish hegemony in Ukraine. This began in the spring of 1648 under the leadership of Bogdan Chmielnicki and targeted Jews, in particular, as representative of Polish rule.

---

[7] Born in Vladomir, in the Province of Volhynia; his family was famed for scholarship. His father, Samuel, was the son of a famous scholar, Rabbi Isaac Betzalels. In addition to his scholarship, David's father was well to do; so, the young prodigy David, who had shown unusual talent for study, was fortunate enough to grow up in an atmosphere of both wealth and learning. His early happy youth was in marked contrast to his later years, when he suffered great hardships and poverty.

[8] Initials of his main work Turei Zahav ("Rows of Gold"), a major commentary on the Shulchan Aruch, written by R' David in Poland.

[9] Divrei David 1689.

"From a Jewish perspective, these events known as 'Gzeyras Tach Vetat'[10]—the persecutions of 1648-1649—consisted mainly of attacks by rebels against many Ukrainian, Belorussian, and Eastern Polish towns with large Jewish populations. As many as twenty thousand Jews were killed. A similar number became refugees, and some were forced to convert.

"The Muscovite and Swedish invasions of Poland in 1654-1656, likewise, brought death and misery to large numbers of Jews in the paths of the invading armies. In the 18th century, a series of Cossack (Haidamak) rebellions culminated in the well-organized 1768 revolt, centered on the city of Uman that resulted in the deaths of many Jews.

"In the wake of the attacks, the infamous Shabtai Zvi led thousands of despairing Jews to believe that he was the long-awaited Messiah destined to redeem them from exile. Many Jews were inspired with the hope that their suffering would soon end, but after Shabtai Zvi turned out to be a fraud—he converted to Islam under pressure from the Ottoman Turks—they were plunged back into the bitter reality of Shtetl life.

"A vast number of Jewish families lived in unspeakable poverty. Burdened by constant hunger, people began to neglect the most basic age-old traditions. Many families were left without a livelihood, and the vast majority of children were forced to abandon their *Torah* study at a young age—sometimes as young as 5 or 6 years old—to help provide for their families.

"Only the wealthy—far and few between—could afford a proper *Torah* education for their children. This resulted in a generation of largely ignorant, yet pious and devoted Jews, who were, for the most part, neglected and scorned by the learned elite—the Talmudists.

---

[10] According to the Jewish calendar, the Gzeyras Tach V'tat ("Evil decrees of 1648–1649") took place in 5408–5409. The acronym of these years is Tach V'tat (referring to the Hebrew letters that correspond to 408 [tch] and 409 [tt]). In the years 1648–1649, a large-scale uprising of Cossacks and Ukrainian peasants led by Bogdan Chmielnicki swept through much of today's Ukraine, then part of the Polish–Lithuanian Commonwealth. In the course of the fighting, there were many Jewish casualties and many Jewish communities were destroyed.

"Many felt that they had lost their guiding light and the timeless Jewish sense of a sacred duty in this world. A rift eventually developed between the learned and unlearned Jews, to the point that, in many towns, the two groups prayed at separate synagogues.[11]

"Adding to all this were the 'Maggidim' (plural for Maggid), referring to the traditional Eastern European Jewish itinerant preachers, who were skilled as narrators of *Torah* and religious stories. The Maggid served as a source of inspiration in the Jewish communities of that era. The Maggid's mission was to awaken the dormant spirit of Judaism in the hearts of the masses.

> Many felt that they had lost their guiding light and the timeless Jewish sense of a sacred duty in this world.

"In the beginning of the 18th century, however, a new school of Maggidim became popular. They preached of the terrible punishments on the Day of Judgment that awaited those who lacked in proper and complete observance.

"These Maggidim, who preached fire and brimstone, were sometimes referred to as 'Terror Maggidim.' It is said that Dante himself could not have described the horrors of hell and punishment that awaited the wicked, as preached by some of these Maggidim. The latter put further stress on an already broken and badgered Jewish flock. Such was the landscape against which the Chassidic movement took root.

---

[11] See Philosophy of Chabad, Volume II.

3

THE BA'AL SHEM TOV/CHASSIDISM

"Rabbi Israel Baal Shem Tov (1698-1760)—literally, 'Master of the good name'—was the Eastern European, 18th century founder of the Chassidic movement. Recognizing the despair and broken spirits of his brethren, the Baal Shem Tov set out to revitalize the beleaguered Jewish populace and breathe new life into a fainting nation.

> The Baal Shem Tov wiped away tears from the Jewish people.

"Traveling from village to village, he gathered Jews in the marketplace and anywhere he could find them and shared a message of hope and joy. He taught that joy, in itself, is precious before G-d and that the warmth with which they served G-d was dear to Him, despite—or even due to—their simplicity.

"The third Rebbe of Lubavitch, Rabbi Menachem Mendel, also known as the Tzemach Tzedek"[12] (1789-1866) said, 'The Baal Shem Tov wiped away tears

---

[12] Rabbi Menachem Mendel Schneersohn, third in the line of leaders of the Chabad movement, famed as the "Tzemach Tzedek" after his magnum opus on *Talmudic* law, was born on the eve of Rosh Hashanah in 1789 to Rabbi Shalom Schachne and Devora Leah. His maternal grandfather was Rabbi Schneur Zalman of Liadi.

Rabbi Menachem Mendel's father-in-law was his uncle, Rabbi Dov-Ber Schneuri, the "Mitteler Rebbe," whom he succeeded as head of the Chabad Chassidim on Kislev 10, 1827, until his passing on Nissan 13, 1866.

When Rabbi Menachem Mendel was 15, Rabbi Schneur Zalman instructed him to work with his uncle, Rabbi Moses, in communal affairs. This was in addition to his responsibility to study all inquiries on *Torah* matters and to submit responsa in outline to Rabbi Schneur Zalman.

After residing briefly in Haditch, where Rabbi Schneur Zalman had been interred in 1813, Rabbi Menachem Mendel settled in Lubavitch, Mogilev province in 1814 with his father-in-law. His assiduity in study was exceptional, and he continued to examine all *Torah* inquiries received by Rabbi Dov Ber. When Rabbi Dov Ber approved, he would answer the letters. This regime lasted about 12 years.

Already, by the age of 10, Rabbi Menachem Mendel had a swift and beautiful hand. He could write a page of 30 lines in 5 or 6 minutes. Every day he wrote for 3 hours and to make up for Shabbos and Holidays, he wrote the following evening.

Once his son complained about the excessive stringency of a teacher, R' Gershon. "Is that stringent?" Rabbi Menachem Mendel exclaimed. "It is nothing compared to the regimen I imposed on myself at the age of 9, regarding hours of study and writing."

In later years, he attributed his success at the Rabbinical Commission of 1843 to three merits. One was the 32,000 hours he spent during 30 years in profound study of Rabbi Schneur Zalman's works and the commentaries he wrote, then, 20 hours every week.

Rabbi Menachem Mendel was, throughout his life, an activist for his people. He intervened politically, economically, and spiritually to help his brethren.

from the Jewish people. He worked hard to ensure that every Jew would be happy, simply because of his Jewish heritage.'

"In place of the almost exclusive scholarly and legalistic genre of Judaism of that time, the movement he founded, which came to be called Chassidism, emphasized spirituality through the most fundamental aspects of faith. It stressed that the value of sincerity and pureness of the unlettered, common folk was as significant as the vast *Torah* knowledge of the scholarly elite.

"Through their self-effacement before the Omnipresent, taught the Baal Shem Tov, simple, sincere common folk actually could reach closer to G-d than elitist scholars, who were often burdened by pride. He asserted that the self-righteous scholars might envy and learn lessons in devotion from the uneducated community.

> Simple, sincere common folk actually could reach closer to G-d than elitist scholars.

"The effects of these teachings are felt today—both by its direct followers known as Chassidim and by followers of other streams of Jewish thought, who were deeply impacted by its teachings and philosophy.

"The Ba'al Shem Tov preached Chassidism over the Lithuanian Yeshiva approach of ethical discipline known as 'Musar,' which tends to focus on Heavenly retribution resulting from transgression. Chassidism typically avoids the subject of rebuke and punishment, emphasizing the joy and reward that stems from the immanent Divine presence in everything. It places prayer and deeds of kindness on par with the supremacy of study. Most important, Chassidism favors Simcha—joy, encouragement, and daily fervor.

"The Baal Shem Tov opposed methods of those who criticized and demoralized the Jewish masses, in an attempt to motivate them. Although such admonition may have had its time and place, as may be seen from the harsh rebuke that some Biblical prophets issued, the Baal Shem Tov taught that the Jew who suffered nearly two millennia of exile and persecution, need not be further broken by reprimand and the threat of unthinkable retribution.

"This was specifically true regarding that particular generation, which only 50 years before the Baal Shem Tov's birth, in 1648, was physically ravaged by the pogroms, intellectually humiliated by the elitist scholars, spiritually demoralized by the Maggidim, emotionally victimized by the false messiah Shabtai Zvi, and mentally intimidated by their neighboring gentiles.

"A captivating tale is related about a vivid encounter between one of these Maggidim and a well-known Chassid of Rabbi Schneur Zalman of Liadi (1745-1812),[13] which depicts the dissonance regarding this matter:

"A renowned Maggid arrived, one day, at the hometown of Reb Shmuel Munkes;[14] a noted disciple of Rabbi Schneur Zalman. After reading his letter of approbation, lauding him as a righteous 'Tzaddik' who was wont to wander from town to town for the sole purpose of inspiring fellow Jews, the townspeople invited him to preach.

"Throughout his sermon, the Maggid berated his simple audience,

[13] Rabbi Schneur Zalman was born in 1745 in Liozna (situated in the Vitebsk area of Byelorussia). He married at age 15 and following his marriage, joined his father-in-law in Vitebsk. Before long, he decided to leave his home in search of a deeper understanding of Torah. He already learned everything that Vitebsk could offer him. Eventually he reached Mezritch and Rabbi Dov Ber, the Maggid.
When Rabbi Schneur Zalman returned to Vitebsk one and a half years later as promised, his companions asked him what he had found in Mezritch that was not to be found in Vilna. His answer was, "In Vilna they teach the Torah; in Mezherich, the Torah teaches you."
For a number of years, the married couple lived in dire poverty. Finally, in 1767, Rabbi Schneur Zalman was offered the position of preacher in Liozna. From that time on, the authority of Rabbi Schneur Zalman steadily increased. Three years later, the Maggid of Mezherich entrusted Rabbi Schneur Zalman with the task of reediting the Shulchan Aruch—the Code of Jewish Law. This was an enormous task, requiring extraordinary knowledge of the Talmud and practical Halacha.
After Rabbi Dov Ber, the Maggid of Mezritch, left this world, his son Rabbi Abraham, known as the Malach, the 'Angel,' declined the role of Rebbe. Three of the Maggid's most prominent disciples—Rabbi Menachem Mendel of Vitebsk, Rabbi Abraham of Kaliska, and Rabbi Schneur Zalman—separated, each going to a different location with the pledge to spread the Chassidic philosophy, wherever possible.
Rabbi Schneur Zalman inherited the formidable undertaking of introducing Chassidism to Lithuania. The Rabbi's popularity and admiration for his righteousness and knowledge were so great that the number of people flocking to Liozna grew with each day, until he was compelled to issue 'The Liozna rule,' limiting the number of visits the Chassidim could pay to their Rebbe.

[14] R' Shmuel Munkes, one of the leading Chassidim of Rabbi Schneur Zalman of Liadi, was known for his wit and "Chassidic pranks."

accusing them of dreadful sins. He proceeded to describe in vivid detail, the severe punishment that awaited them as a result of their evil ways. When finished, the proud orator quickly retired to his room, leaving his crestfallen audience to wallow over the Divine retribution that was to befall them.

"As soon as he made himself comfortable, a man with a long knife and sharpening stone entered his room. To the Maggid's utter surprise, the armed visitor was none other than R' Shmuel himself. Bolting the door behind him, R' Shmuel proceeded to sharpen his knife. After a few tense and wordless moments, the Maggid broke the silence. 'What's this all about?' he asked with a look of astonishment on his face.

"His eyes still trained on the sharpening stone, R' Shmuel replied in mock sincerity: 'As the honorable Maggid knows, we simple folk never had the merit of having a righteous scholar in our midst. Who knows, likely it is due to our wanton sins.'

"Bemused as to where this was heading, the Maggid replied, 'yes yes, quite true, but what does any of this have to do with the knife?'

"'Well,' retorted R' Shmuel, 'tradition has it that before the High Holidays, it is proper for one to pray at the gravesites of our righteous and saintly ancestors.'

"'Of course, of course,' nodded the Maggid, 'but where is all this heading? Why the knife?'

"'It's rather simple,' explained R' Shmuel calmly. 'Most Jewish communities are blessed with the burial site of at least one Tzaddik. Because we never merited having a *Torah* scholar or saint dwell among us, it is no wonder that the closest such site is far from our town. It is extremely cumbersome for the townsfolk to make the yearly trek.'

"Now the Maggid was beginning to feel uneasy. 'But you still have not explained the reason for the knife,' he ventured, his temples evermore clammy.

"'What is so difficult to understand,' asked R' Shmuel. 'The reason for the knife is because it's high time that our community, once and for all, have its own righteous burial site!'

"As the grim reality began to set in, the Maggid adeptly switched course. 'Come to think of it,' he stammered, 'I am not all that righteous after all. I have committed some small sins here and there; they were, obviously, all inadvertent...'

"R' Shmuel dismissed the Maggid's confession in midsentence: 'Honorable Maggid, you are still a righteous and learned man. As for the transgressions? They are so minor, who would even know that these were sins? Your humility is nothing but proof of your exceptional righteousness.'

"'On second thought,' stuttered the Maggid, 'some of my transgressions were a bit more serious, such as...' R' Shmuel quickly dismissed these as well: 'To us, you are still a great Tzaddik. The fact is that you are far better than anything we have.'

"This strange dialogue continued for some time with the Maggid admitting to ever larger transgressions and R' Shmuel assuring him that he was still well qualified. Finally, the Maggid confessed to some rather ugly and embarrassing transgressions. He admitted that in reality, he was far from the great Tzaddik that he portrayed himself to be.

"Now, R' Shmuel no longer played the simpleton. Putting away the knife, he rebuked the Maggid for causing the simple, yet sincere, Jews so much anguish.

"When satisfied that the Maggid fully understood how to treat his coreligionists, R' Shmuel unbolted the door and sent the Maggid on his way, a much wiser and more sensitive man than the one who had arrived.[15]

---

[15] Based on Early Chassidic Personalities: Reb Shmuel Munkis, by Rabbi Sholom D. Avtzon.

4

MYSTICAL REVIVAL

"The Baal Shem Tov reached out to two groups of people, the simple unlearned masses whom he encouraged and invigorated and the great *Torah* scholars who formed a close circle of saintly mystics around him. He taught both groups using short parables, stories, and ideas, whose meaning alluded to the inner Kabbalistic dimension of *Torah*.

"To the simple masses, this was the first time Jewish mysticism was conveyed in a way that they could grasp. To his close circle, these parables illustrated the profound nature of the Kabbalistic ideas he alluded to. This 'Holy Society' of saintly followers later became Chassidic Masters themselves, in the second and third generation, diversifying into many branches across Eastern Europe, under the leadership of R' Dov Ber (the Maggid) of Mezritch.[16]

"The Baal Shem Tov and later Chassidic Masters made Dveikus[17] (fervor) a central principle of Jewish spirituality. They taught that sincerity of heart, of even the most artless Jew, reflected essential Divine simplicity. 'A soul may come into the world for 70 or 80 years, in order to do a single deed of kindness to another person,' the Baal Shem Tov would preach.

"Chassidic thought gained admirers from outside its immediate following as a result of its charismatic inspiration and Kabbalistic insights. According to the 1906 Jewish Encyclopedia, 'Chassidism should, in Jewish history, be classed among the most momentous

---

[16] The disciple of the Baal Shem Tov and the teacher of Rabbi Shneur Zalman of Liadi, the Maggid (1772) strengthened the Chassidism of his master, anchoring it firmly in Jewish thought and practice.

[17] Chassidism teaches that Dveikus, or bonding with G-d, is the highest form of Divine service and the ultimate goal of all *Torah* study, prayer, and the 613 Mitzvos. The highest level of Dveikus is Hitpashtus Hagashmius, which is an elevated state of consciousness, in which the soul divests itself of the physical senses of the body and attains a direct perception of the Divine in all things. The very act of striving toward Dveikus is meant to elevate one's spiritual awareness and sensitivity and add life, vigor, happiness, and joy to one's religious observance and daily actions.

spiritual revolutions that have influenced the social life of the Jews, particularly those of Eastern Europe.'[18]

"Hence, a revival of Judaism was underway by means of the new access and interpretation of Jewish mysticism, contained in Chassidic philosophy. Whereas, the Baal Shem Tov had an inner circle of 60 students, his successor, the Maggid, doubled his inner student base to 120.

"Chassidism reached beyond physical borders. It is difficult to describe any type of Chassidism as belonging to a particular geographical region or to ascribe to it a particular set of distinctive local characteristics. Chassidism, after all, was a religious revival movement that transcended both communal and national boundaries.

Chassidism, was a religious revival movement that transcended both communal and national boundaries.

"While geographic proximity and ease of access generally facilitated adherence to a particular Chassidic court and its own style of Chassidism, some Chassidim lived a great distance away from their leaders and even needed to cross political frontiers to reach their courts.

"By now Jay sports a visible expression of concentration, or is it confusion?

"You with me, Jay," I ask.

"So far so good," he says, "But where does Chabad come into all this?"

"Good, so you are keeping track," I reply.

---

[18] "HASIDIM—HASIDISM:" The unedited full text of the 1906 Jewish Encyclopedia. JewishEncyclopedia.com. Retrieved 9 September 2013.

5

CHABAD MOVEMENT

"Chassidic Judaism," I continue, "is not a single homogenous movement, but rather an amalgamation of numerous distinct dynasties that share a common ancestry and measure of underlying principles.

"With the spread of Chassidism throughout Ukraine, Galicia, Poland, and Russia, divergent schools emerged within Chassidism. Currently, there are at least 30 to 50 larger Chassidic dynasties and perhaps as many as several hundred smaller groups that often share common worship practices, dress, and song. This brings us to Chabad.

"Founded by Rabbi Schneur Zalman of Liadi,[19] Chabad—also known as Lubavitch because of its base in Lyubavichi (Lubavitch) for over a century—is one of many ethnic Chassidic sects to sprout from the early teachings of the grand patriarch of Chassidism, the holy Ba'al Shem Tov and his successor the Maggid of Mezritch. Yet, the Chabad faction has grown increasingly unique from its counterparts, charting a course all its own. It has evolved into a category and class for itself.

"Chabad was organized in White Russia and Lithuania more than 2 hundred years ago. Over the past 50 years, it has grown into one of the world's largest and best-known Chassidic movements. Chabad boasts an important global network of 'Emissaries' and spiritual practitioners devoted to the promotion of Jewish ideals and practice in every conceivable format and context.

"This network—consisting of nearly 4,000 institutions in over 1,000 cities, spanning 70 countries—provides outreach to Jews of all backgrounds, including the unaffiliated. Chabad-run community centers, synagogues, schools, and camps serve as centers of enrichment for Jews of all ages, by means of religious, cultural, and educational activities."

---

[19] See footnote 13.

"So, you were taken-in by all their popularity and hype," interjects Jay. "This is all an emotional trip, isn't it? You've always been somewhat of a sucker that way. You were forever searching for a deeper purpose, a blissful cause in life that would make it meaningful, exciting, and worthwhile.

"You were willing to buy into anything that held out hope, or at least maintained that appeal. Still, I would have never thought you would find the answer in religion, let alone in a religious cult."

"Hold on a minute Jay," I interrupt, "things seem to be getting somewhat personal here. Don't ye' think? First, I haven't joined or committed to anything. Second, can't you be a bit more discriminate about what you call a cult? Do you even know what the word means?"

"Oh c'mon Danni, everyone knows those Chassidics are a cult."

"Well" I say, "in that case I guess, I'm flat out of the loop. But, just for curiosity sake, can you share with me your definition of 'cult'? Or do you prefer the pejorative definition: 'Any religion or religious interpretation that you don't subscribe to?'

"Allow me one more question," I continue, "It's a personal one and you obviously don't have to answer. The question is rather simple: Do you believe in G-d, Jay?"

"Now that's a loaded question, Danni," Jay retorts in almost knee-jerk fashion. "Well," he adds, "I guess it depends on what you mean by 'G-d' and what you mean by 'believe.' Besides, what on earth has this got to do with anything," he cries.

"Oh, I think it's got everything to do with one's perspective vis-à-vis the definition of cult," I assert. "The nature of one's belief in G-d, speaks volumes as to what or who, he or she perceives to be a cult. Regardless," I persist, "Isn't the question simple enough? Why would you refer to it as 'loaded'?"

"Okay, okay Danni," Jay hastily retreats, "We're getting way off track.

Forget that I ever mentioned it. Let's get back to where you left off. You were talking about Chabad's unique status as a Chassidic organization. Isn't that right?"

"Good idea," I concur, seeking to rub it in somewhat. "We'll leave this cult talk for another time. As for now, we'd best resume with our discussion as you say.

"Chabad is not only distinguished from other Chassidic strands, as a result of its extraordinary worldwide outreach campaign, but even more so as a result of its deep theological weltanschauung. Unlike other branches of Judaism, even Chassidic, Chabad's scope is well beyond the human's emotional dimension. Its focus is uniquely intellect oriented.

Interesting comparisons to cognitive behavioral therapy recently have been advanced.

"In fact, this branch of Chassidism is armed, for lack of a better term, with a well-structured contemplative theology, based on Kabbalah (Jewish mysticism). Its ideology consists of a comprehensive intellectual approach to G-d, creation, and human purpose, designed to transform its committed follower.

"The term Chabad, itself, is a Hebrew acronym for 'Chochmah, Binah, Da'as'—Wisdom, Understanding, and Knowledge—which represent the human cognitive faculties targeted by the discipline.

"Rabbi Schneur Zalman of Liadi formulated the Chabad School in his classic work *Tanya* which, systematically and comprehensively, lays out the principles of Chabad-Chassidic thought. Chabad emphasizes the need for in-depth study of Chassidic philosophy, in order to gain any degree of familiarity with the higher celestial reality.

"Chabad's scholarly disposition inspired wider modern Jewish denominations. It caught the interest of Neo-Chassidic thinkers and influenced contemporary academic study.

"Interesting comparisons to cognitive behavioral therapy recently have been advanced. Active contemplation of paradoxes, like Divine immanence and transcendence, helps fill the mind of its students with sublime light. This could offer lasting transformation of the human thought process and, ultimately, of human practice, as well as existential condition."

REKINDLING THE FLAME: NEO-CHASSIDUS BRINGS THE INNER LIGHT OF TORAH TO MODERN ORTHODOXY

Barbara Bensoussan, "Rekindling the Flame: Neo-Chassidus Brings the Inner Light of Torah to Modern Orthodoxy," Jewish Action, winter 2014.

A prince once lay dying, and seeing that the doctors could do no more for him, the frantic king sent for a Tzaddik known to be a master of medicine. The Tzaddik told the king, "There is one cure that might help him. There is a rare precious gem that, if crushed and mixed into a potion, might cure your son. The gem can be found on a faraway island, but there is also one in the center of your crown."

'What good does my kingship do me if my only child dies,' cried the king. 'Take the gem from my crown and cure him!'

This parable, which comes from the Ba'al Ha*Tanya*, the first Lubavitch Rebbe, Rabbi Shneur Zalman of Liadi, was offered in response to those who opposed teaching the Peninim—inner dimension—of *Torah* in the open. The dying prince represents the Nation of Israel languishing from lack of inspiration; the gem represents the inner light of *Torah* that can revive him.

'From the middle of the eighteenth century, masters like the Ramchal [Rabbi Moses Chaim Luzatto] and the Ba'al Shem Tov began bringing forth the deeper secrets of the *Torah*,' says Rabbi Moses Weinberger, Mashpia—mentor at Yeshiva University's Rabbi Isaac Elchanan Theological Seminary (RIETS) and the Rabbi of Congregation Aish Kodesh in Woodmere, New York. 'Halachah—Jewish law constitutes the physical life of the Jew, but the soul of the *Torah* is the potion, needed to infuse life with. The Almighty saw that the Jewish people were suffocating, so He sent the Besht [the Ba'al Shem Tov] to revive them and give them a taste of the light of Mashiach.'

Despite the fact that the Orthodox world brims with Minyan factories, Glatt kosher vacation packages, Yeshivos and Kollelim and a thriving print media, Rabbi Weinberger is concerned. 'One thing is missing,' he says: 'The soul.' As he wrote in an essay that appeared in the online journal Klal Perspectives in 2012, 'Our communities—spanning the entire spectrum of Orthodoxy—are swarming with Jews of all ages and backgrounds who have little, if any, connection to Hakadosh Baruch Hu'—the Holy one blessed be He.

Many of the off-the-path youth, he says, are not running away from authentic Yiddishkeit; they simply 'Never met it.'

'There are many out there who may have been shown or taught a version of Yiddishkeit that is dry, that is cold,' agrees Josh Weinberg, an YU musmach (ordained rabbi) who considers himself a neo-Chassid and is one of many who look to Rabbi Weinberger for inspiration. 'They may practice Judaism in their communities, but inside, there's a lot of apathy and rote. "Chances are they were never exposed to this deeper and joyous side of religious observance," says Josh, who lives in Riverdale, New York, and works as a photographer and videographer.

Rabbi Weinberger's outspoken encouragement of a deeper engagement with what he calls 'The inner light of *Torah*' has caused others to describe him as the captain of a growing trend among the Modern Orthodox to reconnect with the spiritual vision of the Ba'al Shem Tov and his disciples and others who delved into this dimension of *Torah*.

THE INFLUENCE SPREADS

Rabbi Weinberger's appointment as Mashpia at YU indicates just how deeply the neo-Chassidus movement has impacted the Modern Orthodox world. 'I myself went to YU forty years ago,' Rabbi Weinberger says. 'Today, it's a different world. There's still the same strong learning, but so many of the boys are thirsting for the life of inner *Torah*.'

Rabbi Judah Mischel, a former Rabbi at Yeshivat Reishit Yerushalayim and a popular teacher of Chassidus in Israel, maintains that the rediscovery of Chassidic teachings in the Modern Orthodox world is 'Changing the face of the community.' YU traditionally embraced a more intellectual or Litvish approach to *Torah* study. Now YU offers weekly Shiurim – classes – in Chassidic thought, monthly Farbrengens with Rabbi Weinberger, which represent a dramatic shift for YU.

Rabbi Mischel, a resident of Ramat Beit Shemesh, Israel, who is a current student of Chassidic master Rabbi Avraham Tzvi Kluger, defines neo-Chassidus as 'people trying to live Yiddishkeit from the inside out, to live more deeply and fully .... People today are refusing to be put into boxes. God is One, and His truth can be refracted in many different ways.'

Rabbi Weinberger may be the movement's senior spokesman, but most of the followers are young. 'The majority of the people involved with neo-Chassidus are under thirty,' says Rabbi Dovid Bashevkin, an avid follower of the movement who lives in Teaneck, New Jersey.

Noting the trend, even some Modern Orthodox high schools have begun offering courses on Chassidus. *Torah* Academy of Bergen County in New Jersey offers an elective called 'Introduction to Chassidus.' This past year, the Rae Kushner Yeshiva High School in Livingston, New Jersey, held a school-wide day-long program on Chassidus which stimulated so much interest in the subject the school decided to offer an ongoing course on Chassidic thought.

Nor is this surge of interest in Chassidus limited to Modern Orthodox Jews in the New York tri-state area. Rabbi Shlomo Einhorn, dean of Yeshiva Yavneh in Los Angeles, says that every few months, a few Shuls in the Pico-Robertson neighborhood, a solidly Modern Orthodox part of town, classes on Chassidic thought are sprouting all over.

In the darkest days of Jewish history, Chassidism brought a new hope, a new happiness to millions of people. It brought Judaism to life again, making it meaningful to the masses. The radiance that illuminated two centuries of Jewry may yet have another great purpose to serve.

I was once at a conference where it was discussed what kind of Judaism we will have in America 100 years from now. Some people said the trend would be toward Reform. Others said it would be toward the middle, conservative movements. The pessimists said that there would be no problem, given the current rise in intermarriage, for in 100 years, there would be no Judaism at all in America. But one person suggested that 100 years from now, Chassidic Judaism would dominate the American Jewish scene.

I would agree. The Chassidic spirit, the Chassidic philosophy, is certainly the up-and-coming thing. Perhaps this is our answer, the missing ingredient which will provide our coming generation with a new kind of Judaism, a turned-on Judaism ... Maybe we have to get involved in this love affair of the Chassidim, this love affair with G-d. Classes on Chassidic thought are in fact sprouting all over, such as a class on *Tanya* at Netivot Shalom and classes offered in the Boca Raton Synagogue.

AN ALL-ENCOMPASSING APPROACH

Joey Rosenfeld, a twenty-six-year-old enthusiast who used to give lectures on Chassidus in New York (he recently moved to St. Louis), says that many of his friends found spiritual support in Chassidus when they returned from a year or two of learning in Israel and transitioned back into American life. 'They come back after a year of inspiration and increased piety, which was easy to maintain in the bubble of the Beis Medrash, and find themselves among an affluent, modern lifestyle,' he says. 'It creates cognitive dissonance: Either you go back to your old lifestyle, or you find new ways to cling to authentic Judaism. Chassidus offers an all-encompassing approach to Jewish life. It includes not only life in the Beis Medrash—hall of study— but dealing with struggles and failures and connecting to G-d even through mundane activities.'

Rosenfeld adds that Chassidus also offers an alternative to the Litvish— Lithuanian—Yeshiva tradition, which emphasizes intense learning above all else. 'Chassidus encourages people to connect to G-d in their own unique ways,' he says. 'It's less elitist.

Rabbi Moses Tzvi Weinberg, who teaches at YU's Irving I. Stone Beis Medrash program (SBMP), agrees that the Chassidic approach promotes a balance sometimes missing in the Yeshiva world, 'he says. 'It's liberating for them to find other means of connecting to Hashem that are authentic. The Litvish and Mussar approaches emphasize Yirah—awe—and the Shulchan Aruch— Code of Jewish Law, but that can be damaging. The Chassidic approach is softer, more positive. It emphasizes Simchah— joy, Simchah Shel Mitzvah— joy of a Mitzvah, Simchah Shel Chaim— joy of life. It's a different vision of what it means to be an ideal Jew.'

Rabbi Weinberg came to Chassidus through his brother Josh, mentioned earlier in this article, who studied in Israel about a decade ago under Rabbi Mischel. 'Chassidus has an energy I haven't seen elsewhere,' Rabbi Weinberg says. 'I had no connection to Chassidism as a child in Philadelphia, beyond their image; I had no idea it could be a language of spirituality, of communication with Hashem.'

Rabbi Moses Weinberger says that even those raised in Chassidic homes are coming to his lectures, seeking to reconnect. 'For some of them, Chassidus became a way of life, not a fire. Now they're seeking a new spirit of Chassidism, a rekindling of the fire of the Besht.

ROOTS OF A REVIVAL

Providing sociological context to the neo-Chassidic trend, Dr. Chaim Waxman, professor emeritus of sociology and Jewish studies at Rutgers University notes that: 'American Jews are brought up around the particularly American idea that religion is something that should be meaningful. Spiritual seeking is something that has always been a part of the broader American culture. In the past couple of decades, there has been an increased emphasis on the question, 'What does religion do for me?''

Dr. Waxman says that Lubavitch Chassidism, which he claims is the fastest-growing movement within American Judaism, resonates particularly well among the Modern Orthodox because it has traditionally encouraged participation in the wider world, the pursuit of higher education, and reaching out to less-affiliated Jews.

'Today, you have well-regarded intellectuals like Rabbi Adin Steinsaltz and Rabbi Joseph Telushkin producing biographies of the Lubavitcher Rebbe,' he points out. In general, the Modern Orthodox as well as unaffiliated Jews are more likely to connect with more outward-focused Chassidic groups such as Lubavitch and Breslov than with more insular groups.

Some young people are aware that their own family trees include Chassidic branches, which generates curiosity about Chassidism that leads to involvement. 'People are moved by sports and movies,' explains Rabbi Einhorn. 'They want to be moved emotionally by religion too.'

Thus, it should come as no surprise that women also find neo-Chassidus appealing. Yehudis Golshevsky of Jerusalem, a product of a Modern Orthodox home who considers herself Breslov today, has been teaching Chassidic *Torah* for nearly twenty years in Israel. Her popular classes attract women from across the religious spectrum. Why do they come? 'Oxygen,' she says. 'The Jewish world is in serious need of oxygen.... There is nothing sadder to me than Jews going through the motions of observance without feeling the passion. Chassidus instills in a lot of people that passion, that fire, for serving G-d. It's not that you can't have the fire without Chassidus, but it sure is harder.'

According to Rabbi Bashevkin, there's also a lighthearted side in the movement determined to put the Geshmack—enthusiasm back into Jewish practice. 'There's a sweetness and a rich sense of humor in the movement, a component which goes back to Rabbi Nachman of Breslov,' he says.

Josh notes that this exuberance has a broad appeal. 'A Jew is looking to be connected and the soul needs to be filled with something,' he says. 'In a world where there's so much excitement in non-kosher venues, the movement gives one the ability to fill the soul with holy things, giving young people an exciting way to connect to Judaism.'

PROCEED WITH CAUTION

Rabbi Moses Weinberger cautions against leaping into the fire of inner *Torah* without taking certain precautions. 'If people jump in too quickly, without proper teachers, it can lead to imbalance and confusion,' he says. 'There are many broken people out there looking for a fix. This is a less expensive high than drugs, but if it's not grounded in Halachah and connected to a living master, it won't succeed.' Without guidance, the mix of youthful high energy and Chassidic practice can be volatile.

'Young people are still finding themselves,' says Rabbi Moses Tzvi Weinberg. 'If there's nothing grounding Chassidic practice can degenerate into trendy, even silly New Age-style practices.' Activities such as going to Uman or meditation shouldn't replace traditional learning, but rather add a deeper dimension to it.

Rosenfeld similarly believes that it's easy for some to pervert Chassidic concepts of joy, prayer and Tikkun Olam to the detriment of Halachic observance. 'As much as it's a problem to be a vessel with no light, you can't be light with no vessel,' he cautions. Another adherent, Yitzchak, adds that it's simplistic to view Chassidic practice as all about prayer and kabbalah, and not about serious learning. 'Parts of the *Zohar* are very dry and technical!' he points out. '*Tanya* is very complicated—it requires tremendous Zitzfleisch—patience. While on the one hand you have these Chassidic stories about people sitting and reciting the Aleph Bet to show that it's possible to connect to Hashem on a simple level, the intellectual tradition of Chassidus is very deep and sophisticated.'

He adds that it can be just as challenging to be Matzliach— successful in prayer as it is to succeed in learning.

Many of the movement's adherents mention that Chassidic writings predict that in the days before Moshiach there will be an explosion of meaning in the Jewish world. 'Rav Kook, who came from one Chabad and one Litvish parent, wrote that at the end of days there will be a conversation between the followers of the Vilna Gaon and the followers of the Ba'al Shem Tov,' Rosenfeld says. 'He said that the students of the Besht will herald the coming of Moshiach.'

Rabbi Mischel likewise tells a story that the Besht interacted with Moshiach in the upper chambers of Heaven and was told that Moshiach will come when the wellsprings of inner *Torah* spread to the outside. 'Rav Kook wrote that ours would be a 'Wondrous generation,' in which many things will begin happening all at once,' he says. 'Ours is a postmodern reality in which there are many options, and many spiritual options.'

Until Moshiach comes, we can look to this generation's revival of Chassidus as a way to comfort and warm the Jewish soul in the trying times before his arrival. Rabbi Weinberger relates that a Misnaged once challenged the Chassidic master, the Tzemach Tzedek (Rabbi Menachem Mendel Schneersohn, the third Lubavitcher Rebbe): 'What's the difference between you and me? We study the same *Torah* and observe the same mitzvos.'

'It's like two chicken soups,' the Tzemach Tzedek replied. 'The ingredients are exactly the same. But one is cold—and one is hot.'

6

ULTIMATE DISCIPLINE

"Wow," says Jay, "quite a presentation. Did anyone ever tell you that you could run for public office? Perhaps now you can tell me, in lay terms, what this all means and how it pertains to you and your religious trip?"

"Trip," I ask, "there you go again. Why do you insist on using condescending terms? Don't you think that for an open-minded guy like you, you're being a bit judgmental here? Cynic that you may be, I can hardly remember you acting this way for as long as I know you."

"Well," Jay remarks sheepishly, "I guess I'm somewhat of a religion-phobic. You know, religion has been known to press a person's hot buttons, every now and then. Perhaps, there's a subconscious part of me that perceives your embrace of religion as a threat; as a subtle indication, if not an outright statement, that you are better than me and that I'm not good enough."

> Perhaps, there's a subconscious part of me that perceives your embrace of religion as a threat.

"Perhaps there is a subconscious issue here," I affirm, "but whose fault is that? Is there anything I can do about it? I mean, no one can control what's in another person's mind. I can only tell you that judgmentalism is not part of the Chabad program. In fact, it goes against the very grain of its core beliefs and objectives. As for myself, to the best of my knowledge, I've never judged you, or anyone else, on the basis of their religious observance or philosophy."

"I guess you are right," Jay concedes. "A person is entitled to his or her beliefs regardless of how it rubs the other person. One may even harbor a superior attitude, say for example, consider oneself wiser, more pious, or better-looking, for that matter, than the next individual. That is his prerogative, irrespective of whether it is true or false. The only recourse there is with such an individual, is to adjust the friendship in accordance with the reality of his or her attitude, and how it makes you feel.

"Perhaps this is what's bothering me. Our friendship, after all, predates your new found religious... what should I call it... journey? Yet, it is apt to somehow impact our relationship so, I'm kind of at a disadvantage here. Still, I agree that it's really my problem, not yours. Sorry for the attitude, but I'm still interested in what you see in all this religion stuff. I hope you are still willing to share the secret."

"Now please Jay, don't make me feel bad," I reply. "I didn't intend to put you on the defensive. Of course I'm willing to share my secret. Well... I wouldn't call it a secret exactly, how about my attraction or fascination?

"Let me put it to you this way, if you were to discover an intellectual discipline that puts into perspective the mystery of the entire cosmos— its origins and existential purpose, as well as its relationship with its Creator in a logical and compelling order—would you not be attracted? If I added the secret to the human psychological, emotional, and spiritual enigma would you not be fascinated? Well there's your answer."

"Do you mean to tell me Danni that your religious ideology has answers to all of life's mysteries," Jay retorts incredulously.

"Well, it depends on what you mean by that," I reply. "Does it present the answers as a matter of empirical scientific fact? Of course not, but does it set forth a logical and highly plausible theorem; one that is far more complex, sophisticated, comprehensive, and superior to anything that may exist out there? The answer is a resounding yes. There's nothing that even holds a candle to it.

"I know this may be hard for you to believe Jay, but it shouldn't really be that surprising," I note. "There are scores of contenders that profess to do the very same thing. There are an untold number of books, by authors of every one of life's walks and backgrounds, that profess to hold the answer to life's meaning and existential purpose and that they can deliver it in a single book.

"In fact, the claim is so common that no one even thinks twice when they hear it made. Just browse the shelves of the nonfiction section of your local library or book store, and you will see what I mean.

"So you ought not to be all that shocked when the oldest monotheistic religion in the world professes to hold answers to the above questions by virtue of an intricate and voluminous string of profound writings and discourses, based on teachings dating back thousands of years."

"That was well put Danni," says Jay, "Even I cannot argue with that point. If there are answers to life's existential mysteries, they are likely found in an ancient religious canon, whose writings date back to the beginning of recorded literacy. This is far more likely than finding the answers in the thoughts and machinations of some contemporary guru, who claims to have figured it all out on his or her own, whether a philosopher, psychologist, mathematician, engineer, anthropologist, or any other professional practitioner."

> If there are answers to life's existential mysteries, they are likely found in an ancient religious canon.

"I'm beginning to like the way you think, Jay," I utter in jest. "There must have been a reason for our friendship, after all. There had to be something I saw in you, and you know it was not your looks."

"Here's a question for you Danni," Jay interjects. "Did you suggest that the evolutionary process that transforms celestial property into physical creations is somehow reflective of the human psychological order, that is to say, the development of an individual's emotions and behaviors from his or her higher essence? What does that mean? In what way is Divine creative energy indicative of mortal human's psychological structure?"

7

The World He Placed in Their Hearts

"Well, congratulations to you Jay," I exclaim, "you actually hit upon one of the first principles of Chassidic philosophy—the correlation between the cosmic celestial order and the human psychological anatomy. This phenomenon is based on the opening portion of the *Torah*, Genesis, where it states that a human was created in the image of G-d. Did you ever wonder what that means? In what way are we created in G-d's image? Are we miniature G-ds with G-dly powers? Obviously, not."

> The microcosmic order of human behavior mirrors, the Divine system of creation and vice versa.

"Speak for yourself, Danni," interjects Jay, never having lost his raw sense of humor. "Okay, sorry for interrupting, back to your point please," he prompts.

"The meaning of the statement," I continue, "is that the microcosmic order of human behavior mirrors, as it were, the Divine system of creation and vice versa. Chabad philosophy, in particular, stresses the analogy between the way human action derives from thought and emotion, and the way in which the universe is spawned into existence. When one studies the human behavioral progression, one gains unprecedented insight into the descending order of the Divine creative energy.

"There is a sequence by which a fleeting idea is nurtured into a fully-fledged thought invested with emotion and, eventually, turns into decision and action. Others only see the final stage of the process, the behavior. But, its essential meaning lies way back, in the first flash of thought that set the process in motion.

"The same is true on a cosmic scale. The world that we see with our eyes is only the last stage in the chain of descent-Hishtalshelus. Like human action, the macrocosmic 'World of Action'-'Olam Ha'asiyah'— tends to mask the preceding worlds, from where it stems and to which it owes its very origins. The latter includes a series of contractions and concealments, known as Tzimtzum, something we'll get to in due time.

"But, if we were to travel backwards and inwards, we would reach the originating reality—the four metaphysical worlds described in Kabbalah: Assiyah (Action), Yetzirah (Formation), Beriah (Creation), and Atzilus (Emanation). Perhaps we would even reach back beyond the first thought to the personality that conceived it—Ein Sof—which is, of course, infinitely wider than any specific intention into which it is directed.

"This macrocosmic reflection of the Divine order of creation is the meaning of King Solomon's cryptic words in Ecclesiastes: 'The world He placed in their [mans'] hearts...'[20]

Chassidic discipline reveals insights into the human psychological and emotional dimension

"By contrast, analyzing the Divine process of creation, as depicted in Jewish mysticism and interpreted through Chassidic philosophy, one acquires deeper insight and understanding of his or her own essential being and modus operandi."

Our intense conversation is brought to a halt as a flight attendant interrupts with beverage service. Both of us were lost in the discussion, forgetting for a moment where we were. "That's actually profound stuff, Danni," says Jay. "I mean I didn't understand everything you said, but the little that I did, makes a lot of sense.

"As a psychologist, I'm particularly fascinated with the idea that this Chassidic discipline would reveal insights into the human psychological

---

[20] Ecclesiastes 3:11.

and emotional dimension. I'm curious how it treats the subject. Psychology, as you know, is basically the science of 'self,' the awareness of how we humans operate. I am forever amazed how little the average person learns and knows about this critical subject.

"Isn't it odd that just about every product, with which we come into contact, comes with an instruction manual that teaches us how to use and care for it? These instructions are included in everything from the most sophisticated mechanical or technological device to the simplest junk toy or kitchen utensil. Yet, for the human being, the most complex creature in the world, there is no such guidebook.

"Is it not strange that, in our schools, we teach about almost every essential topic in life, from literacy to mathematics to history, science, biology, geography, economics, and so forth, and, now, even sexuality; yet, there is next to nothing about the most important thing of all, our very selves—our human emotions?

"Even within religion, we find little emphasis on psychology. Yes, I know that the *Torah* is filled with narratives that contain psychological lessons, regarding most every subject that pertains to a human's character, but those are selective and anecdotal. There isn't, to the best of my knowledge, and correct me if I'm wrong, Danni, a structured, comprehensive religious curriculum on the psychology of humans. I've always thought that this is a shame. From the little that you've described, this material sounds fascinating. It gives me new hope."

"Jay," I note, "I don't know you to be that passionate. You obviously have strong feelings about this. Well, then, let me assure you that this might be exactly what you've been waiting for. I say this because Chassidus has revolutionized the way we view and analyze the inner self. Our human identity and operating system, as articulated in Chassidic text, is paralleled by no other intellectual discipline, religious or secular.

"Despite the great strides made in the field of psychology, in its attempt to understand the mystery of human nature and personality, the science pales in comparison to the insights held by Chassidus vis-à-vis the nature of human thought, emotion, and behavior.

"In fact, Chassidus introduced a vocabulary all its own regarding human's inner mental and emotional dimension. This lexicon, which is woefully deficient in secular psychology, allows Chassidus to identify key elements of the human psyche."

8

The Soul Factor

"The greatest advantage of the Chassidic system over other psychological disciplines is that it perceives and depicts a human's psychological existence in the context of his or her soul. Whereas scientific systems begin their analysis with the brain, Chassidus' insight into human identity begins with the human's unique soul. In fact, Chassidus identifies no less than five different levels within a person's Divine soul.

Chassidus' insight into human identity begins with the human's unique soul.

"The difference as to whether we commence our assessment of a human's identity with the brain or with the soul is huge. It hardly can be overstated. It may be compared to the examination of a person's internal organs by prodding and probing in the dark with one's hands, versus the benefit of a CAT scan or MRI.

"To perceive a person's essence as beginning with the brain is to perceive only half the person, and the smaller half at that. For, if an individual comprises body and soul, the soul is certainly the more significant part. Hence, to construct a model of the human entity without the soul is stabbing in the dark.

"Most important, however, are the contrasting places to which these divergent approaches lead. The secular psychological system, inevitably, leads to selfishness. For, the more we follow the trail of that system back, the closer we get to our physical core. Logic dictates that the more attuned we are with our physical core, the more corporeal we become.

"In other words, if our own intellect and feelings represent the highest essence of our existence —cogito ergo sum—then, it only makes sense to do everything to enhance and vindicate that essence. So, we end up serving ourselves, which is the definition of selfishness.

"This path has but one eventual outcome: Emptiness and disillusionment. As our lives begin to appear feeble and fleeting, we find ourselves struggling for deeper definition and purpose: What is life's true meaning and where does the individual—a tiny speck in time and space—fit into the scheme of things?

"In order to withstand the dread that our lives will soon be covered by eons of time, blotting out the fact that we ever existed at all, we frantically seek lasting impact and definition. But, in lack of essential purpose, where do we turn? Our desperate search for self-definition and realization is often satisfied by trivial attention-seeking and vain popularity.

"Thanks to the esoteric dimension of *Torah*, as articulated through Chassidus, we have the ability to know our essential human self in the context of our soul. Cognizance of our Divine soul, which is a sliver of the Sublime existence, leaves us humbled. For 'Who am I and what am I, in face of the all-powerful and all-pervading core on whom I depend for every breath?' The obvious conclusion of this outlook is a state of selflessness and awe.

> Our desperate search for self-definition and realization is often satisfied by trivial attention-seeking and vain popularity.

"This state inevitably leads to true self-contentment. It spawns new channels for joy and serenity. Joy that stems from being part of something infinitely greater than one's feeble self; from being part of the ultimate and eternal truth.

"Only through an overriding, all-encompassing relationship with a Higher Eternal Existence, can a person achieve the blessing of inner satisfaction and fulfillment in this world, and secure the highest memorialization for the afterworld. In the words of R' Schneur Zalman:[21]

---

[21] *Tanya*, Chapter 33.

'When one's life centers on one's relationship with the Almighty, the person will soar far above all obstacles.' Meaning that if a person works at achieving mindfulness of the Divine presence, he or she will gain deep contentment."

"I've got to tell you Danni that, as a psychologist, I fully relate to what you say regarding the human need for self-actualization," interjects Jay. "The inexorable need to feel as if our life matters— as if we matter—is, in fact, at the center of every value system.

"Your observation," he farther notes, "Regarding our tendency to reach for an empty cause to fill the gap is, likewise, on the mark. This explains our culture's woeful embrace of social media. It is our way of gaining self-worth and satisfying the gaping void.

The inexorable need to feel as if our life matter is, in fact, at the center of every value system.

"Our desire to gain fulfillment by means of hollow pursuits, such as social media, is not unlike the Greeks' fixation on cultural achievement. If there is a difference, it is that the Greeks sought to fill the human void with substantive cultural and philosophical accomplishments. But, in the end, that fell short as well. After all, where are they today? Their empire collapsed and few are remembered for their great secular triumphs.

"Compare that to the vain popularity and imaginary attention that comes from today's social media culture to which we cling, and what are you left with? The answer is nothing but artificial fulfillment, and purpose that is insubstantial and short-lived.

"Yet, while I recognize the innate human need for immortality and its many pitfalls, I never quite thought of religion as an effective response to the void. I certainly have not considered it the only answer, but it's clearly food for thought, especially because off-hand, I cannot think of another way to fill the void.

THE SOUL FACTOR

"So, Danni, now that you've piqued my interest how do I go about accessing this material?"

"Well, I suppose that there are many ways," I reply. "There is a plethora of books, many translated into English. There also is a variety of audio and video materials out there and of course, there is always the web."

"Is there a course that teaches this stuff?" Jay persists, trying not to sound overly curious.

"There are many Yeshivos—Jewish religious schools—that include this subject as an integral part of their curriculum," I point out, "but those are designed for young adults. Occasionally, there might be a retreat, here or there, geared towards adults, but those only offer a light sample tasting. To get a true feel for the ethos, one must study it methodically, preferably with a qualified Rabbi or instructor."

"Is that how you became so wise, Danni?"

"I don't know about wise, but I actually attend a daily study group," I affirm. "We call the sessions, which meet 6:30 a.m. every weekday— 'Mornings with the Rabbi.'"

"So that's the secret," remarks Jay, "Very interesting. I would love to hear more about those sessions; you think you're up for it?"

"Let's see, there are still another 5 hours left to the flight," I muse, "How about we catch a little snooze, an hour or so, and continue afterwards?"

"Good with me," says Jay.

We close our eyes and relax to the white noise generated by the powerful jet engines and the garbled voices of the soft cabin chatter.

9

THE ORCHARD

I never actually fell asleep. I hardly ever could on a plane, but Jay had less of a problem. Eventually, he wakes up, with the help of some jarring turbulence caused by a patch of rough air, a tad disoriented. He asks what time it is. I look at my watch and tell him that it's 11:10 a.m. "I got almost an hour of sleep," he marvels in surprise. "Not too bad," he adds rubbing his eyes.

"For the sake of accuracy," I interject, "it was more like 2 hours, but who's counting?"

"Well, it seems like you are," he retorts with a twinkle in his eye, "but I guess accuracy is a virtue."

"Now, Jay, that reminds me of an old joke:

"A young man takes a seat next to an elderly Jew riding a train in old Europe. The young man turns to the older gentleman and asks him 'What time is it, sir?' The old chap does not answer. A few minutes later, he tries again, but is ignored all the same. After several attempts to get the older fellow to give him the time, the young man gives up. Nevertheless, he is curious why the man with the watch refuses to respond to him; so he asks the old fellow, 'Can you at least tell me why you won't give me the time?

"After some hesitation, the man replies: 'You don't understand the obvious, do you? If I answered your question, then you would ask me where I'm from, and I would have to tell you that I am from Slutsk. Then the next question would be where I'm going, to which I would have to reply that I am going to Slabodka to visit my daughter Lea.

"Upon hearing that, you are certain to inquire if she is single, to which I would have to indicate that, indeed, she is single. Then, certainly you would ask to meet her for a Shiduch—date (match)—and the last thing I want in my life is for my Lea to marry someone who doesn't even have the money to buy himself a watch!"

"Ha-ha... So, you ready to kill some more time chatting," Jay asks. "I'm prepared to hear about those morning study sessions."

"You're acting like you're on a mission or something," I quip.

"I'm sorry, didn't mean to be pushy," Jay offers, somewhat contritely.

"There is no need to get all defensive," I remark. "Just chill a little and we'll get started."

"The morning study sessions are held in the Synagogue library on weekday mornings at 6:30 a.m. Five in the group attend regularly. Osher Chaimson, a bearded be-spectacled middle-aged Chabad Rabbi, is the instructor. The format of the lessons is text-based from the original Hebrew. Despite the group's varying ability to follow the Hebrew, Rabbi Osher Chaimson does a good job translating.

"As an introduction to the subject, Rabbi Osher imparted critical background regarding the nature of the school of Chassidic thought and its place within the body of sacred *Torah* teachings. He prefaced these remarks with the observation that all of *Torah* and its evolutionary developmental process is based on a firm foundation of prior *Torah* knowledge and fundamental principles.

"Rabbis and scholars of previous generations established this foundation, in turn predicating their works on even earlier generations, going back all the way to Moses and the Divine revelation at Mount Sinai.

"Rabbi Osher then elucidated the four basic levels in which the *Torah* converses: P'shat, Remez, D'rash, and Sod—the first letter of each of the words P-R-D-S. Adding vowels for pronunciation, this spells the word

Pardes, meaning 'orchard.'[22] Each layer, he asserted, is deeper and more intense than the last, like the layers of an onion.

"Despite the varied forms in which these bodies were preserved and transmitted, they all trace back to the Divine communication of the *Torah* and the Sinaitic experience.

"P'shat (pronounced pi-shat), stemming from the root that means simple, is the straight forward interpretation of the text—understanding the words in their natural and customary meanings based on literary style and context. P'shat is the keystone of understanding the text. If we discard the P'shat, we lose the fundamental understanding and end up with a subjective reading into the words. Hence, the *Talmud* states that no passage loses its P'shat: 'A verse cannot depart from its plain meaning.'[23]

"Remez (pronounced reh-mez) is where the text alludes to an additional 'implied' meaning, revealing something deeper. Remez in Hebrew means hint. Traditionally, Remez refers to methods such as Gematria— word number values, codes, and the like.

"D'rash (pronounced deh-rash), from the same root as '*Midrash*,' is an interpretation that is not explicit in the text, but rather, an interpretative meaning derived homiletically, as well as, through analogy.

"Finally there is Sod (pronounced soa-d) meaning 'hidden.' This method reveals the spiritual and mystical truths that are couched within the *Torah* text. These secrets are usually gathered under the term 'mystical Kabbalistic interpretations' and appear in a variety of works, including the *Zohar* (Book of Splendor),[24] *Sefer HaBahir* (Book

---

[22] The English word Paradise is derived from the same Persian root.

[23] *Talmud* Shabbat, 63a.

[24] According to all Kabbalists and, as the beginning of the book writes, The *Zohar* was written by Rabbi Shimon Bar Yochai (Rashbi), who lived in the 2nd and 3rd centuries CE. There are views in scholastic circles stating that The *Zohar* was written in the 11th century by Kabbalist Rabbi Moses de Leon, who contradicted this view, saying that Rashbi wrote the book. In the Kabbalistic approach, the question of why The *Zohar* was written is far more important than the question of who actually wrote it. The purpose of The *Zohar* is to be a guide for people to attain the origin of their souls. This path to the origin of one's soul consists of 125 stages. Rabbi Yehuda Ashlag writes that a Kabbalist, who passes these stages and shares the same perception as the book's author, sees that its author could be none other than Rashbi.

of Illumination),[25] *Sefer Yetzirah* (Book of Creation),[26] as well as, the works of mystical commentators such as Rabbi Isaac Luria[27] and Rabbi Chaim Vital.[28]

"While D'rash generally adheres to the narrative or to the subject that is being raised in *Torah*, the Sod material may drift far in scope and enter into topics, content, issues, or ideas that seem to be only loosely related to the portion itself.

"Rabbi Osher closed the circle by identifying Chassidic philosophy with the mystical esoteric dimension, whose source is in the deepest core of

---

[25] Kabbalists ascribed authorship of the Bahir to R' Nehunya, a rabbi of the Mishnaic era, who lived around 100 CE. Medieval Kabbalists wrote that the Bahir did not come down to them as a unified book, but, rather, in sections found in scattered scrolls and booklets. The scattered and fragmentary nature of the Bahir's text, which sometimes ends discussion in mid-sentence and which often jumps randomly from topic to topic, supports this claim.

[26] Sefer Yetzirah "Book of Formation" or "Book of Creation," the title of the earliest extant book on Jewish esotericism, is devoted to speculations concerning G-d's creation of the world. The ascription of its authorship to the biblical patriarch Abraham shows the high esteem that it enjoyed for centuries. It may even be said that this work had a greater influence on the development of the Jewish mind than almost any other book after the completion of the *Talmud*.

[27] Rabbi Isaac Ben Shlomo Luria (1534-1572) 16th century Kabbalist, renowned as the greatest Kabbalist of modern times, revolutionized the study of Jewish mysticism through Kabbalah before his passing at the young age of 38 in an epidemic. R' Luria, also known as Isaac Ashkenazi, attracted a large number of followers, who gave him the title of "HaAri," the Lion, because of the initials of the phrase "Haeloki Rabbi Yitzhak"—the divine Rabbi Yitzhak. No other master or sage ever had this extra letter prefaced to his name. This signifies what his contemporaries thought of him. (Later generations, fearsome that this appellation might be misunderstood, said that this alef stood for Askenazi, indicating that his family had originated in Germany, as indeed it had). He is also referred to as the Arizal. It was only in the last 2 years of his life that he met his foremost disciple, Rabbi Chaim Vital. While the Arizal himself never wrote any books, Rabbi Chaim Vital faithfully recorded all his words and compiled them in Kitvei Ari, the "Writings of the Arizal." By the 17th century, Luria's ideas and the unique vocabulary, in which they were expressed, had not only spread throughout European Jewry; they became a central pillar of traditional Jewish thought, a position they occupy to this day. The Ari also authored the liturgical poems, "Azamer Bishvachin," "Asader Lisudata," and "Benei Heichala," sung at the three Shabbat meals, respectively, and included in nearly every Chassidic and Sephardic prayer book.

[28] Rabbi Chaim Vital (1543-1620) was unquestionably the leading disciple of the Holy Ari, Rabbi Isaac Luria. In fact, Rabbi Chaim transcribed the Ari's teachings. Within a year of his initiation into the Ari's teachings, Rabbi Chaim became famous throughout Israel and the Diaspora, as one of the great Kabbalists. When the Ari passed on in 1572, a mere 2 years after Rabbi Chaim began studying with him, Rabbi Chaim was almost universally regarded as his successor. The Ari was not accustomed to recording his teachings in writing; he had given only Rabbi Chaim permission to record his teachings. After the Ari's passing, Rabbi Chaim gathered all the manuscripts and began editing and organizing them. He began teaching the Kabbalistic insights that he received from his master to his many disciples, and, thus, he became the revered leader of a significant group of Kabbalists. He also gained a reputation as a miracle worker, a healer, and a master of practical Kabbalah. He was able to discern the nature and history of the souls of humans.

Torah. Chassidism or Chassidus, the teachings revealed by Rabbi Israel Ba'al Shem Tov, was intended to awaken the Jewish People to their own inner selves, through the inner dimension of the *Torah*, thus, preparing the way for the advent of the Messianic era."

> Chassidus was intended to awaken the Jewish People to their own inner selves.

"Fascinating thought," says Jay, "It sheds important light on how the greater comprehensive body of *Torah*, including that revealed in later generations, is all part of the one *Torah* and the original Divine revelation. This is the case, even though hundreds, even thousands of years may have elapsed before it came into full blossom. What I'm curious about, however, is how Chassidic philosophy actually differs from Kabbalistic teachings?"

"That's actually an important question," I admit. "But, I cannot really satisfy that query at this point in our conversation, because there is a lot more to establish regarding the nature of both Kabbalah and Chassidus."

"So let me ask you another question, Danni," continues Jay, exuding more interest than I could have ever imagined. "Why did it take so long for the Sod dimension and, particularly, the Chassidic element to come to fruition?"

"Another excellent question," I acknowledge. "But now we're really starting to get ahead of ourselves. Now that we've established the origins of Kabbalah and Chassidism, we probably ought to focus first on the substance and purpose of these mystical theologies."

10

KABBALAH

"Most people's perception of Kabbalah, if they have any, derives from pop culture. Indeed, Jewish mysticism is perceived by the masses as a mixture of self-help and pop psychology. Needless to say, however, what's portrayed in secular and social society as Kabbalah is not even close to the actual thing.

"Kabbalah, literally 'receiving' or 'tradition,' refers to Judaism's mystical strand and related literature. It is an esoteric discipline and school of thought meant to define the existential nature and purpose of the universe and its human inhabitants.

"Kabbalah is, first and foremost, part of *Torah*. It constitutes the 'hidden' dimension as compared to its 'revealed' realm—such as the 24 books of *Tanach*, the *Talmud*, and their related commentaries.

> Kabbalah is, first and foremost, part of Torah. It constitutes the 'hidden' dimension.

"The mystical tradition is also known as the 'soul' of *Torah* in contrast to its 'body.' Much as with a person, the body performs actions, but the life and meaning behind the actions stem from the soul; Judaism likewise consists of body and soul.

"*Torah* and its commandments are like bodily actions; Kabbalah, on the other hand, gives life and meaning to the *Torah* and Mitzvos. Hence, the study of Kabbalah is crucial, like the soul is to the body. Just as you can't separate the soul from the body without catastrophic consequences, similarly, you can't separate Kabbalah from *Torah*.

"Before we continue, Jay, I ought to make you aware that some of the material in this particular dialogue may be slightly deeper than the usual. Yet, I find it unappealing to present a watered-down semblance of the ideas. I prefer that you get a good feel for the concepts, in this case, a few actual examples of Kabbalah's application. However, rest assured that you will find the conversation rather comprehensible.

"If something feels unclear, you ought not to fret or give up. I assure you that the concepts will become increasingly intelligible. In fact, *Torah* is acquired, largely, through perseverance. Truth be told, if you comprehend but half the discussion, you will learn a whole lot.

"As stated, Kabbalah was developed entirely within the realm of Jewish doctrinal thought. Kabbalists used classical Jewish sources to expound and define the inner concealed meaning of both the *Torah* and traditional rabbinic literature, as well as to explain the significance of Jewish religious observances.

"This esoteric system is based on the axiom that every word, letter, number, and even accent contains mysteries, interpretable by those who know its depth. The esoteric or 'hidden' dimension of Judaism described in Kabbalah, thus, is an extension of the mainstream tradition or 'revealed dimension,' but explains it on a deeper and more spiritual level.

"We can use the reasons given for the Biblical commandments and the purpose of creation as illustrations of the significant contribution that the school of Kabbalah offers, beyond the other dimensions.

"The Five Books or Pentateuch—the foundation of *Torah*—for example, outlines the numerous acts that comprise the Sublime commandments; yet, it provides little rationale regarding the purpose of these Mitzvos and their function.

"Scriptures similarly encourage the observance of the Biblically-ordained commandments. They invoke prophetic admonishment and the use of poetry, but still offer little by way of reasons or direct advantage gained from these Divinely prescribed acts.

"The *Talmud* codifies the law, and the *Midrash* describes how it relates to G-d in abstract metaphysical terms, but still, the benefits to creation, humans, or even the Almighty are not part of their purview.

"The commentators, codifiers, and masters of Musar offer a limited degree of explanation for the laws on various symbolic, psychological, and ethical levels. Yet, while they tend to awaken within the individual an assortment of sensitivities and responsibilities towards G-d and fellow religionists, from a strict analytical perspective, these explanations have meaning only because they are Divine decrees.

"Kabbalah discloses how the Mitzvah brings about personal and cosmic elevation, refinement of the secular domain, and the revelation of the spiritual dimension. Within the framework of the mystical teachings alone, the *Torah* commandments are understood as utterly consequential and indispensable to life and its Sublime objectives, including the ultimate objective—the Messianic redemption."

Unlike the esoteric dimension, the classical texts render the Mitzvos neither entirely indispensable nor critically consequential, outside of the Divine will.

"The upshot of it all is that, unlike the esoteric dimension, the classical texts render the Mitzvos neither entirely indispensable nor critically consequential, outside of the Divine will. Only the mystical teachings, as depicted in Kabbalah, provide profound insights how the revelation and energy-flow of the worlds actually depend on the performance of Mitzvos by mortal creatures of our lowly temporal world.

11

REVELATION OF THE EIN SOF

"The nature of the materialistic world is to conceal its mystical properties, far more than to reveal them. In fact, the word 'Olam'—world—stems etymologically from the word 'Helem,' hidden or concealed. Indeed, the corporeal world disguises and withholds its internal workings and inner soul. Its innermost heavenly mysteries lie far beyond the wall that meets the raw senses.

> Much as the soul fills the body, infinite unperceivable Divine energy inhabits the limited physical world.

"Yet, much as the soul fills the body, infinite unperceivable Divine energy inhabits the limited physical world. This ephemeral energy constitutes the soul of the world, whose presence is hidden even from its possessor. Still, elements of this Divine soul were made known to and through the Jewish Mystics.

"According to Kabbalah, we humans, despite our finite composition, are capable of achieving a modicum of knowledge of the ontological structure of creation and its Divine Architect. This phenomenon is based on the verse: 'Know the G-d of your fathers, and serve Him with a complete heart.'[29] This command, as we shall determine later, implies that it is possible to know G-d and that such knowledge is a prerequisite to serving Him with 'a complete heart.'

"Kabbalah essentially ventures to explain the connection between the unified, eternal, unchanging, and mysterious Ein Sof Light—literally 'without end'—a Kabbalistic term describing the infinite nature of

---

[29] Chronicles I 28:9.

the Divine creative energy and the temporal finite universe. The ever-present tension between Divine immanence and Divine transcendence is its central focus.

"While the energy is infinite and intangible, it permeates the finite world. A paradox indeed, but one with which we learn to live, for the Sublime Creator we're taught, contains opposites. Thus, despite all the camouflage, beneath all appearances, lies the reality of the infinite Ein Sof.

"Consequently, the mystical task is to take a journey into the interior and reveal the truth within its coarse encasement. Much as, on a microcosmic level, the mystic tries to move a student closer to the roots of his or her soul, on a macrocosmic level, Kabbalah seeks to reveal the infinite soul that gives life to the world.

"No wonder it has been said that Kabbalah is to *Torah* what philosophy is to science. Like science, *Torah* gives us facts that we perceive, sensually and rationally. Like philosophy, Kabbalah gives us the grander abstract picture about what the facts actually mean.

"In order for creation to occur, asserts Kabbalah, the powerful Ein Sof creative energy must undergo a series of contractions, reductions, compressions, and abbreviations. These occur by means of sundry worlds, attributes, vessels, and processes that serve the purpose of distilling and filtering the energy to conceal its source.

"Kabbalah holds the map to the structure of this hidden progression and the laws by which it influences us. More important, Kabbalah reveals how we could influence it. It teaches us how to develop a sense for the progression and discover its very purpose—to bring about the revelation of the Creator into the physical world.

"Interpreting the verse 'G-d is your shadow, at your right hand,'[30] the Baal Shem Tov comments: A shadow follows the movement of one's limbs. Similarly, every action that we perform spirals upward to the spiritual

---

[30] Psalms 121:5.

49

realms, generating intense light, or Heaven forbid, the opposite, in those realms. [31]

"The effects of our conduct are not confined to the spiritual worlds. Rather, the energies aroused above are then drawn down into this world, modifying the future. Divine revelation equals Supernal blessings, which equals a better world in every conceivable way.

"Briefly summarized, albeit extremely simplified, Jay, there are three basic states vis-à-vis the Sublime energy. The first is the state of infinity, where G-d's boundless, all-pervasive, and essential light shines, as it were, without limit, filling all space. There is no place devoid of it and, therefore, nothing could exist aside from it.

> The effects of our conduct are not confined to the spiritual worlds.

"The second state entails the concealment of His infinite light in order to create an apparent 'empty space.' In this state, it becomes possible for a myriad of finite creatures and perspectives to exist, each with its own limited parameters.

"In the third state, the finite and infinite merge. As the finite inhabitants of the universe transform, through the fulfillment of the Divine will, they raise themselves and the surrounding world from a state that conceals their Divine source to a state that expresses and reveals it.

"It is us earthlings who are endowed with this mission. A human alone, through his or her Divine service, is capable of uncovering the truth, or better, mistruth, about the universe's physical essence. It is, indeed, nothing but a reflection of the all-pervading infinite reality of G-d; its formidable mass is but a facade to a deeper spiritual existence.

---

[31] Kesser Shem Tov, p. 344; Kedushas Levi, Parshas Beshalach. Also see Hayom Yom, Iyar 13: The Alter Rebbe once said during those years that he would say short maamarim (Chassidic discourses): "Know what is above you" (Avos 2:1). Know that everything "above" in the supernal sefirot and partzufim (Divine emanations and configurations), all derives "from you"; it all depends on man's service.

"Like a game of hide and seek, the Creator conceals Himself in our finite world and waits for us to find Him. Through this process, He can bestow us with the greatest gift there is—to exist as finite individuals and yet experience a truly intimate relationship with the infinite Creator. A story told about Rabbi Dov Ber of Mezritch underscores this point:

"R' Dov Ber once encountered a weeping child. 'Why are you crying,' he asked.

"The child replied that he and a friend were playing the game 'hide and seek.' He hid and waited for a long time, only to discover that his friend ran off to some other amusement, leaving him curled up in his hiding place and waiting in vain to be searched out.

"Rabbi Dov Ber lifted his eyes heavenward and cried, 'You, too, have hidden your face from us only because you want us to seek you. But your children have tired of the game and have run off...'

"Chassidus associates this phenomenon with a Talmudic story: Rabbi Chanina was so poor that he would survive on a kav[32] of carobs from Friday to Friday. One day his wife said 'How long must we suffer such poverty? Pray that we should be provided with sustenance.' Rabbi Chanina prayed and from heaven came a table leg of solid gold.

> An individual's mission in life entails a more difficult accomplishment than the act of creation itself.

"That night, his wife saw the righteous in the world-to-come in a dream. Everyone was sitting at three-legged tables of gold, while she and her husband sat at a table with two legs. When she awoke, she begged her husband to once again pray, this time for the gold to be taken back. So, again, Rabbi Chanina prayed and the golden leg was retrieved.

---

[32] A measurement used in the *Talmud* translating to approximately 47 ounces.

"The second miracle, concludes the *Talmud*, was greater than the first; for while things are often given from heaven, they are not readily taken back.[33]

"The inner meaning of this Talmudic passage, explains the late Lubavitcher Rebbe, Rabbi Menachem Mendel Schneerson, is that an individual's mission in life entails a more difficult accomplishment than the act of creation itself. G-d's creation of the universe consists of the formation of physical matter out of utter nothingness (creation ex nihilo). On the other hand, a mortal's role is to reverse this process, to prove the true Divine essence of material matter.

"Spiritual reality finds expression in physical form more readily than the converse. For something to be divested of its materiality and revert to a purer elevated state is a more difficult accomplishment, hence the Talmudic axiom: Things are more readily given from heaven than they are taken back.

"This is the true purpose of Mitzvos; through the Mitzvah, a person elevates the world and brings its intended purpose into fruition. At the same time, one becomes in tune with his or her spiritual essence that, in turn, creates a deep sense of satisfaction and fulfillment."

[33] Taanis, 25.

12

MATTER OF PERSPECTIVE

"If the latter is not enough," I tell Jay, "Judaism gives us the demanding task to not only grasp the sublimity of the Divine, but also to comprehend the definition of existence itself. Indeed, we are called upon to understand that the very 'I' that is making the observations is a matter of perspective. While created matter perceives itself as real, there is a higher more truthful reality; namely, that essentially 'there is none else beside Him.'[34]

"As with all physical matter in this world, our ego masks the light of our true essence. Therefore, we are able to think of ourselves as independent, with a personal life, perspective, and experience. In absence of the ego, we're simply a part of a larger whole, a part of the greater Divine reality.

> Our ego masks the light of our true essence.

"Given the masking properties of the physical, we are allowed, indeed compelled, to perceive the existence of the universe as separate and detached. The intrinsic connection with the Omnipresent and His essential oneness with the universe is disguised.

"So, we perceive our own existence and the existence of the myriads of objects and forces that we call 'universe,' but this is our finite and subjective perception of reality. If we could observe reality from the all-transcendent perspective of the Creator, we would see a world devoid of selfhood and being. In the words of *Tanya*:[35]

> If the eye were allowed to see the life and spiritual content flowing
> from the utterance of G-d's mouth into every creation, we would not

---

[34] Deuteronomy 4:35.
[35] Shaar Hayichud Veha'emunah, p. 3.

see the materiality, corporeal tangibility of the creation, for it would be utterly nullified in relation to this Divine life-force...

"To achieve this tremendous leap of mind, we can use the fitting analogy of the glow of the 'sun,' compared to its luminous body. From here on earth, the observer perceives both the sun and the light that extends from it; accordingly, both the terms 'sun' and 'sunlight' are part of our vocabulary. But, the perspective from within the sun, itself, is certainly different. Obviously, the sun would not perceive its light as an existence distinct from itself.

"If sunlight is defined as 'the sun's luminescent expression,' it cannot be said to exist within the sun, where the very notion of 'expression' is not relevant or applicable. Light exists only insofar as it serves its function to carry the effect of its emitter to that which lies outside of it. Being that the sun's ray has no function within its emitter, it lacks all context of existence and, therefore, cannot be said to be present therein."

The questions couldn't come out of Jay's mouth fast enough. "When you say that our existence is our own finite and subjective perception of reality, is this realm meaningless in the absolute sense? Is it just for the sake of keeping our minds occupied, because we can't ever grasp the real Divine perspective?"

"You'll have to take it slowly" I tell Jay. "One cannot eat a whole cake at once. It's one slice at a time."

"Now," I tell Jay, "because we have a better understanding of the nature of Kabbalah, is a good time to broach your original question regarding the difference between the Kabbalistic teachings and that of Chassidic philosophy or Chassidism.

13

CHASSIDUS

"At first glance, both Kabbalah and Chassidus—also known as the inner dimension of *Torah*—focus on the same mysteries of the Divine and its various manifestations. How then does Chassidus differ from Kabbalah, which was initially revealed millennia prior? What does Chassidus add to the equation?

"The answer to the question is that, while Chassidus is indeed based upon the ancient Kabbalistic teachings, they are, nevertheless, different in many ways.

"Kabbalah's focus—from its very inception and throughout its development in the 12th century and the newer formulations of the 16th century—has been on the more technical side of the metaphysical system. Kabbalah addresses the various components and categories of Jewish mysticism, rather than its practical application.[36]

"Kabbalah provides little tangible transformation in one's experiential relationship with G-d. Indeed, the wisdom of the Divine ontology that Kabbalah strives to reveal remains somewhat vague and intangible, too lofty for the ordinary person, even one with high intellect, to fully internalize.

> How then does Chassidus differ from Kabbalah, which was revealed millennia prior?

"It is noteworthy that the mystics never engaged in attempts to disseminate Kabbalah, nor encouraged the widespread study of it. Their negative attitude towards any formal or organized study of Kabbalah is widely known. In fact, they strongly discouraged even the individual

---

[36] See also Toras Shalom that Kabbalah reflects the "Tziur Odom (human matrix), but Chassidus is beyond that.

study of Kabbalah. Only a 'fitting vessel,' someone of exalted spiritual stature—due to a particularly lofty soul from birth or through an advanced level of self-refinement as a result of extraordinary effort—is able to properly grasp and internalize these esoteric concepts.

"One of the reasons the study of Kabbalah has been discouraged is because it lacks elucidation. This renders it vulnerable to coarsening and misinterpretation, especially regarding the Divine essence. That can have a detrimental effect on the student.

> Chassidus takes abstract principles of classical Kabbalah and distills them into a practical medium.

"In contrast, Chassidus de-emphasizes Kabbalah's abstract focus on the anatomical structure. Instead, it looks at its inner meaning and soul, as it relates to a person and his or her service of G-d in this world. Chassidus, then, reveals accessible Kabbalistic ideas regarding intellectual, emotional, and practical human experience within the service of the Divine Maker.

"This represents a profound change in expression, because it leaves aside the technical focus on Kabbalistic mysteries, which require enormous intricacy and subtle esoteric nuance that is only accessible to great scholars.

"Chassidus, by contrast, takes the abstract and often impenetrable principles of classical Kabbalah and distills them into a practical medium, or interface, to use in one's service of the Heavenly Creator.

"While Kabbalah stresses the transcendent ontology and structure of the cosmos, Chassidus focuses on a person's relationship with G-d. While Kabbalah tends to be intellectual, objective, and factual, Chassidus tends to be more emotional, personal, and yearning—permeating the person as a whole.

"Hey Danni, it seems like you're beginning to repeat yourself," says Jay.

"I might be kind of thick, but not quite that thick."

"I'm sorry, Jay," I apologize. "I didn't realize that I was being repetitive; nothing personal, I just wanted to be sure that I was making myself clear. I guess you don't believe in the maxim, 'Anything worth saying is worth repeating a thousand times.' Okay, I'll try not to be so repetitive. Seriously, Jay, if it becomes too repetitious just stop me.

Why have the critical Chassidic teachings been kept sealed until the most recent few decades?

"Getting back to our discussion, by focusing on palpable experience, Chassidus identifies aspects of Divinity that the abstract system of Kabbalah leaves unexplored. The above stated distinction between Chassidus and Kabbalah actually addresses your earlier question: Why, you mused, have the critical Chassidic teachings of *Torah* been kept sealed until the most recent few decades and revealed only to a select group of supra-scholars? The answer is captured in an analogy related by the sixth Chabad Rebbe, R' Yosef Yitzchak Schneersohn:[37]

---

[37] Rabbi Yosef Yitzchak Schneersohn (1880-1950), the sixth Rebbe of Chabad-Lubavitch, was one of the most remarkable Jewish personalities of the 20th century. He was the only son of Rabbi Sholom Dovber, the fifth Rebbe of Chabad, whose devotion to the child's education is lovingly chronicled in Rabbi Yosef Yitzchak's voluminous writings. While still in his teens, the young Yosef Yitzchak served as the right hand of his father. As the personal secretary of the Rebbe, Yosef Yitzchak's responsibilities included administrating the many civic and communal activities in which the Rebbe was involved. The young Rabbi Yosef Yitzchak, in full-length Chassidic garb, was a familiar figure in the receiving rooms of the government officials, ministers, and nobles of Moscow and Petersburg. In 5655 (1895), the young rabbi participated in the great conference of religious and lay leaders in Kovno and again, in the following year in Vilna. At times soft-spoken and with words coming from the heart, but always fearless and determined, he demanded the repeal of anti-Jewish decrees, the stopping of pogroms and the cessation of the government's program of forced "enlightenment" of traditional Jewish life. In his 70 years, he encountered every conceivable challenge to Jewish life: the persecutions and pogroms of Czarist Russia, Communism's war on Judaism, and melting-pot America's apathy and scorn toward the *Torah* and its precepts. The Rebbe was unique in that he not only experienced these chapters in Jewish history—as did many of his generation—but that, as a leader of his people, he actually faced them down and, often single-handedly prevailed. From early childhood, an almost painful yen to write nestled in Rabbi Yosef Yitzchak's heart. He kept a diary, from the age of 11, often writing in it for several hours a day. He also wrote an estimated 100 thousand letters during his lifetime—some 4 thousand are amassed in a 12-volume collection, many letters containing dozens of pages of Chassidic teachings and lore. This is in addition to thousands of pages of discourses, essays, and impressions that he penned in the course of his life.

In the summer you don't turn on the heat and during daylight hours you don't need to turn on a light. However, when winter arrives and it gets cold, or at night when it becomes dark, one turns on the heat and the light. Obviously, no one will argue, "I was fine during the summer without turning on the heater, so obviously now too I'll manage without."

"The meaning of this analogy is that the purpose of Chassidus is to imbue life and meaning into the ritualistic commandments of the *Torah*; it is meant to infuse passion, warmth and light into those who seek the service of G-d and to follow His ways.

> Baal Shem Tov brought the Kabbalistic idea of Divine immanence into the daily life of the common folk.

"In days of old, when we were close to the revelation at Sinai and the Holy Temple Era, Judaism was in a state of summer and daylight. Its followers were steeped in spirituality and inspiration; but we've traveled away from those spiritual days of glory.

"As the exiles intensified in breadth and depth, as our challenges proliferated in quantity and intensity, Judaism lapsed into a state of cold winter darkness. Due to a constant stream of debilitating circumstances and the fog of exile, spirituality slipped into a state of decline.

"As a result, religious observance has lost much of its joy and fervor. It became increasingly parched and lackluster. At this point in time, it was crucial to (re)introduce the life, light, and warmth inherent in the teachings of Chassidus.

"The revelation of Chassidus helped open the heart and mind of the ordinary person to realities of G-d's presence and greatness. Indeed, the Baal Shem Tov brought the Kabbalistic idea of Divine immanence within creation into the daily life of the common folk. Its psychological qualities and emotional effect on one's Dveikus (fervor) turned the mystical dimension of Judaism into a powerful asset in the Divine worship of the masses and their spiritual pursuit, resulting in its immense popularization.

"Simply put, Chassidus transforms abstract Kabalistic beliefs into new, attainable modes in one's service of G-d. This was expressed in new admiration for sincerity, joyful spirit, meditative prayer, and deeds of loving-kindness. Cherished and encouraged for their sincere simplicity, the unlettered folk found their suitable niche within Jewish observance, while the elite scholars sought to emulate the simple folk's negation of ego by engaging in Chassidic exegetical thought themselves.[38]

"The followers of the Baal Shem Tov and later Chassidic Masters are granted the ability to perceive the Divine here, in this world, through sensitivity of heart and grasp of mind. Through the teachings of Chassidism, the Ba'al Shem Tov brought Kabbalistic thought to its historical apex, both in terms of its conceptual refinement and its degree of influence upon the lives of the populace.

Chassidus ponders the essential mysteries of life.

"Chassidus ponders the essential mysteries of life, including purpose for creation; humankind's unique place among all other creations; the human mind, heart, and soul; Divine Providence; nature and miracles; personal and collective destiny; exile and redemption; good and evil; and faith and reason.

"Significantly, however, the Ba'al Shem Tov did not introduce any 'innovations' or changes in *Torah* or Judaism. The concepts of caring for one's neighbor, loving one's fellow Jew, as well as serving G-d with great joy and with one's entire heart and depth of emotion, are deeply rooted in Judaism since time immemorial.

"Even regarding his incredibly profound philosophical ideas, the Ba'al Shem Tov did not deviate a single iota from the traditional *Torah* viewpoint. It's just that the ideas—though deeply rooted in *Torah*—

---

[38] See Philosophy of Chabad II.

were not sufficiently emphasized and thus, not fully integrated into mainstream Jewish philosophy.

"The Ba'al Shem Tov merely shifted the emphasis, highlighting the importance of certain concepts and bringing them to their full fruition and applied meaning. In addition, he identified practical ways to make these concepts the joy and cornerstone of everyday Jewish life.

"The distinction between Kabbalah and Chassidus is succinctly summarized in the following adage: 'Kabbalah attempts to bring a person up to Heaven, while Chassidus seeks to bring Heaven down into the person.' A familiar teaching of Kabbalah, according to R' Levi Yitzchak the Rebbe of Berditchev (1740-1809),[39] asserts: 'With ten emanations does G-d continually sustain the universe.' A familiar teaching of Chassidus, he adds, is the dictum: 'The most important thing to remember is that G-d created all and that He is all.'

"Another way to phrase the differing emphases of Kabbalah and Chassidus is to note that Kabbalah focuses on the Keilim (vessels of creation), while Chassidus deals with the Ohros (lights) that fill these vessels. This distinction is apparent even in the names attached to these two mystical traditions: The word Kabbalah in Hebrew is derived from the root Kabel—to serve as a receptacle or vessel, while the word Chassidus is constructed from the root Chesed (loving kindness).

"Here's how I personally would sum up the difference between Kabbalah and Chassidus, Jay: 'Kabbalah is about G-d's relationship with creation, while Chassidus is about a person's relationship with G-d.'"

"I think I get the general drift of what you've been saying here," Jay remarks, "although I definitely do not really understand all the terms and nuances, especially the statement about the vessels and the lights. I'm not sure that I understand what light means in this context, although

---

[39] Rabbi Levi Yitzchak of Berditchev is one of the most beloved of Chassidic leaders. Hundreds of stories, plays, and poems highlight his fiery service of G-d, his love for the Jewish people and his characteristic role of advocating before the heavenly court on behalf of the Jewish nation.

I assume it's referring to energy. I'm also unclear as to what vessels mean, where these vessels come from, and how they differ from light..."

"That's not a big deal," I reassure Jay. "Every field has its own axioms, terminologies, and methodological system; and Chassidus is no different. It's perfectly normal to struggle with the finer aspects of any new discipline, especially one as complex as this. Perhaps, I may be sharing more information than is necessary, but that's the way you learn. As long as you're following the basic theme of the various different concepts, you're doing just fine."

Torat Chaim Ve'Ahavat Chesed by Ysoscher Katz

Excerpted with permission from The Book of Doctrines and Opinions (blog) posted by Alan Brill May 31, 2015

I was raised in the chassidic community of Satmar. I should make it clear from the outset: I am modern but not Orthodox. Do not get me wrong, I am observant and my practice is orthodox but that is not who I am. In other words, I am orthodox-my practice is halakhic and my belief orthodox-but Orthodoxy is not me. It is not an integral part of my identity. My orthodoxy is merely a means towards a religious end. Keeping halakha and accepting orthodox faith-claims provides me with the infrastructure which allows my soul to strive and pursue perfection. Orthodoxy enables me to be who I really am: a Modern Chassidish Jew.

As I mentioned, my identity is comprised of two parts, Modern and Chassidish. I inherited these identity markers from my parents, the modernity from my mother and the Chassidus from my father. Here, I mean real Chassidic, and not Neo-Chassidic. How my chassidic, homemaking and sheitel-wearing mom made me modern is a conversation for another time. At the moment I wish to focus on my dad.

My father is the most non-chassidish Chassid. He does not study "chassidus," nor does he want to "understand" it. The few times I tried to explain to him Moses Idel's distinction between theosophy and theurgy, his eyes glazed over. Chassidus is what he does, not what he learns. From his perspective, *Torah* is for learning, Chassidus for practicing.

His aversion is not limited to the study of academic mysticism. He also stays away from traditional Kabbalistic or Chassidic texts. He never studied the *Zohar* nor did he ever read any of the Arizal's writings. Not only would he not read them, he also would not touch them. He is so intimidated by their sacredness; he fears that his touch would contaminate them. Yet, despite never having formally studied Chassidic texts, he still is the quintessential Chassid. Chassidus is his essence, part of his religious DNA, but it is a Chassidus that is behavioral, not intellectual. Chassidus is how he lives his life. It is the prism through which he encounters the world and the ethos by which he lives by.

He adores his wife, loves his children, cherishes his community and reveres and respects his neighbors and fellow human beings, Jew and non-Jew alike. While this practice is not special, many people love their family and surroundings, its flavor is unique. It is Chassidic love, deriving its passion from the Chassidic teachings he has absorbed throughout his life. These teachings have filled his being with a deep religiosity, which, in turn, infuses his actions and emotions with a deep and robust spirituality. His love of humanity is, therefore, a love that is sensualized by its spiritualized valance.

Chassidus does not just spiritualize my father's interpersonal relationships; it also enhances his religious practices, particularly the yearly calendar. Chassidus allows him to infuse the annual cycle with a sensuous spirituality.

Satmar is a Hungarian/Romanian Chassidus (The broad strokes difference between Hungarian Chassidus and the Polish and Russian versions is that the latter were intellectually inclined while the former was not.

Hungarian Chassidus was predominantly behavioral. This is, of course, a generalization; the nuances are far more complex but outside the parameters of this presentation.)

Hungarian Chassidim are nourished by an elaborate "sacred calendar." They have more days of note than the conventional Jewish calendar, and their holidays tend to be richer than your typical modern Jews' chag experience. A Satmar Chasid's year is thus replete with days of deep joy and periods of intense reflection. While the Jewish calendar has several biblical holidays and two Rabbinic ones, the Chasid's calendar records additional dates of importance.

Every winter, the Hungarian Chasid has six to eight weeks of "shovavim," a period that usually falls sometime between Chanukah and Purim, which is dedicated to repentance and introspection, largely focusing on sexual impropriety; the days of awe continue through the end of Chanukah, the potential for repentance lasts for them for two more months; Purim celebrations begin three days earlier than usual; and (a modicum of) Pesach extends all the way to Shavuot (based on Nachmanides' notion that the interim weeks between Pesach and Shavuot are somewhat akin to a chol ha'moed of Pesach). Combined these add up to a significant number of additional days of awe and periods of celebration.

Qualitatively, chassidic holidays are different as well. Although many things distinguish a chassidic chag, there is one distinction that is particularly noticeable to the keen observer: chassidic religious celebrations are comprised of a dissonant blend of joy and contemplation...

Growing up, this is exactly what Shabbat looked like for me. My dad's Shabbat was intense and complex. While the day began upbeat, it gradually shifted into the contemplative...

But, my father's Shabbat, like his Chassidus, is adamantly experiential, text and study play a minor role in the development of his religious persona.

Kegavna (a section from the *Zohar* which Chassidim recite during Friday night prayers), is one of the most powerful kabbalistic liturgical texts. Utilizing the connection between Shabbat and the number seven, a prominent kabbalistic trope, it succinctly articulates the mystical value of Shabbat. It emphasizes that Shabbat is a day of heightened divine intimacy and advanced mystical union. I have begged my dad on many occasions to read this *Zohar* text with me. He refused each time. Sacred mystical texts are for the elite. The lay receive their nourishment residually, from the spiritualized environment created by those qualified to access those recondite sources.

While he will not study Kegavna, he does recite it every Friday night as part of the Kabbalat Shabbat service. Notwithstanding that he does not fully grasp its meaning, he reads it with the pathos and passion it deserves. Kegavna's power for him is metaphysical, not intellectual...

While I am nourished by my dad's behavioral Chassidus, personally it is not enough. Behavioral Chassidus gladdens my heart but does not stimulate my mind nor sufficiently satisfy my soul. I personally seek a religiosity which nourishes both pillars of my being, the mind and the heart. My personal journey is, therefore, informed by a combination of my father's passion and the academic's sophistication.

Chassidus resonates with both of them, sometimes simultaneously, when the intellectual engagement and behavioral spiritual encounter complement one another, and sometimes separately, when I religiously shift back and forth between the intellectual and the experiential.

Ultimately, the attraction to Chassidus is the fact that it can operate in different modes at different times, in the process offering up a variety of mechanisms to help spiritualize my life.

It is precisely this multifacetedness which convinces me that Chassidus is the proper theology for us moderns. Its theology is perfectly situated to offer meaning and spirituality to the contemporary modern seeker. I feel strongly that it is our only hope. Chassidus today is not a luxury, it is a necessity. If the *Torah*-u'Madda project is to succeed Chassidus needs to become an integral part of its curriculum.

Chassidus is of course a vast discipline, teaching all of it would be a daunting task. For the moment there are three aspects of chassidic theology that stand out as particularly suited for the world we live in today.

1) Truth. We live in a post-modern world where objective truth is rejected and absolute claims are frowned upon. I would go as far as to say that rationalism (in the general and colloquial sense) as a source for Emunah is bankrupt, it increasingly speaks to fewer people. It, therefore, behooves us to come up with alternative models. Chassidus could very well be that alternative model.

Facts and empirical truth is not Chassidus's primary currency. While it does a priori accept the biblical theological faith statements, its goal is not to argue or prove the scientific veracity of the Bible's claims. Truth is not of primary concern for these thinkers. Chassidic theology has two main features. It is a-rational and a-historical. It is apathetic about Jewish historicity as a proactive theological stance. The *Torah* for Chassidim is there to teach us how to live life and serve God, the narrative qua narrative (the origin story) is mere background music. The narration parts of the *Torah* are, therefore, not of much theological significance to them, they are a-historical.

However, during those rare occasions when they do pay attention to the biblical "stories," their orientation is a-rational. They absolutely "believe" those stories, but their belief is internal: it is true because it happened in the *Torah*. That is where these events transpire and that is where these stories matter. Asking about their historicity is, as far as they are concerned, foolish and missing the point.

At the same time, to the extent that the biblical narratives have religious and theological significance, they read those stories through the Rabbinic lens. So, for example, while Moses's historicity is not historically relevant to them, his persona carries theological and ethical significance.

The same is true for God's attributes. Chassidim are, by choice, apathetic about God as a scientific reality, his attributes and characteristics, however, are theologically highly significant to them. For that they did turn to the Bible, but the encounter with the *Torah* is filtered through Chazal [Talmudic Scholars].

They see Chazal as essential to the understanding of the *Torah*. As believers in immanence they actually see the Sages as much more integral to the experience of the written *Torah* than the rationalists did. They did not think that the presence at Sinai (mamad har Sinai) ended at the giving of the *Torah* (mattan *Torah*). For them the *Torah* is perpetually and continuously revealed. The modern reader of chassidic texts would, therefore, not have to decide whether they scientifically accept these postulates in order to engage with them.

Chassidus's goal is instead to describe an immanence which provides spiritual and emotional transcendence. Chassidus (informed, of course, by kabbalah) promotes a sophisticated immanence which results in a dramatic shift in Judaism's orientation towards God and His commandments...

The emphasis in Chassidus on meaning and sacredness, are perfectly suited for our community. These are exactly the things our culture needs more of; holiness and meaning. This emphasis in Chassidus on immanence also generates a move towards spiritualization.

2) Spiritualization. As scholars have pointed out, chassidic teachings contain elements of spiritual psychology. They provide us with a language which helps us infuse our lives with meaning. One can point to many examples where this psychological spiritualization occurs in Chassidus, I will mention two of them.

Everybody sometimes has a bad hair day, when we wake up feeling less than optimal. Chassidus has a term to describe that mood; it calls it mochen de'katnus. While it technically means the same as a "bad hair day," the language is mystical. Mochen de'katnus describes a less than stellar spiritual state, a low energy level which does not allow us to engage in the usual religious pursuits we crave to pursue.

Another example is Kabbalah's elaborate taxonomy of love and awe: Kabbalah and Chassidus talks about superior and inferior love (ahavah ela'e'e and ahavah tata'a) or superior and inferior awe (yirah ela'e'e and yira tata'a)While these terms primarily describe nuanced stages in our engagement with the Divine, they have traditionally been imported into the colloquial arena. They are used to describe varied emotional states which we experience in our interactions with our friends and loved ones.

Contemporary life does not provide us with that many opportunities for encountering the Divine in our daily lives. Chassidus allows us to bring God in.

Sprinkling our conversations with mystical and Chassidic terminology allows us to spiritualize our daily routines and infuse our mundane pursuits with meaning and spiritual significance.

Besides enriching our personal encounters, adopting a chassidic ethos could also enhance our communal experiences.

3) Social Change. One of the most pressing tensions in the community is how to reconcile our values with our convictions; what to do when halakha points us in one direction and our values in another direction. We are tempted to follow our values but pulled to abide by our halakhic commitments. A proper resolution requires an emboldened stance towards tradition, one that allows us to cajole the tradition to reconcile itself with our modern sensibilities [Using, of course, legitimate halakhic mechanisms developed by our predecessors when they were confronted with similar challenges].

Our values are so emboldened because they derive their power from Chaissdut. A chassidic life is a spiritualized life which infuses our values with powerful theological significance, and it allows us to aggressively challenge the tradition to reevaluate its assumptions and attempt to accommodate itself-when halakhically possible- to a changed modern reality.

Such change is actually an integral part of Chassidic social history. When one looks at recent major changes in traditional Jewish society it is hard not to notice that the forerunners were often Chassidim. The last sixty years have seen far reaching social and political change.

The two most dramatic changes that have happened is that Jews are now sovereign and women have made significant progress in their pursuit of religious equality. The pioneers of both these changes were driven, at least in part, by a chassidic ethos. R. Menachem Mendel Schneerson, the Rebbi of Lubavitch, was one of the first orthodox scholars to champion female *Talmud* scholarship, while R. Avraham Yitzchak Kook, a serious student of Chassidus, was an outspoken early proponent of a Zionist state.

There is no doubt that their chassidic worldview, at least partially, informed their proactive stances towards these changes. Their adherence to a spiritualized religiosity allowed them to explore new religious vistas. Their unique theological outlook changed the religious and legal equation for them, simultaneously making their decisions more complex, but also more progressive. Their spiritualized worldview allowed them to see divinity in the ostensibly secular state or the seemingly illegitimate request of women for greater equality.

Granted, this hybrid of chassidic spiritualization and robust religious creativity would be a 21st century concoction, traditionally, these two do not go together. Chassidism, for the most part, frowns on change and rejects innovation. As a matter of fact, nineteenth century Hungarian Chassidim were vociferously opposed to any accommodations to modernity. Further, the contemporary thinker is not going to intuitively embrace spiritualized non-rational thought. It is, nevertheless, a match pregnant with immense potential and could go a long way towards reviving a dormant Modern Orthodoxy.

Contemporary Modern Orthodoxy is struggling; a significant number of its adherents are abandoning yiddishkeit and many who stay no longer find it meaningful; inertia has set in. I suspect that Modern Orthodoxy's rationalist ethos is partially to blame.

Current Modern Orthodox theology is Litvish and hyper-Maimonidean, it lacks a native spiritual core, and does not satisfy people's search for meaning. We are due for a change.

Chassidus could be that change agent. I strongly believe that a chassidic theology combined with a sophisticated modern overlay could be the elixir for the dispassion and disinterest that ails our community. It will provide our community what it so desperately needs: a torat chaim ve'ahavt chesed; a *Torah* that stimulates our minds but at the same time also gladdens our Neshamah.

Rabbi Ysoscher Katz received ordination from Rabbi Yechezkel Roth, dayan of UTA Satmar. Rabbi Katz studied in Brisk and in Yeshivat Beit Yosef, Navaradok for over ten years. He is now the director of the Lindenbaum Center for Halakhic Studies at YCT and Rabbi of the Prospect Heights Synagogue.

Rabbi Ysoscher Katz is affiliated with a new movement called "Open Orthodoxy," which has become a subject of controversy. Its Orthodox status has been called into question.

The inclusion of this article here is not an endorsement of any person or movement.

14

CHABAD CHASSIDUS

"Great scholars followed the Baal Shem Tov as they beheld the powerful message of his profound teachings. The first few generations of the Chassidic movement established the various approaches of its different schools. R' Dov Ber, the 'Maggid of Mezritch'—the Baal Shem Tov's immediate successor—served as the architect of the Chassidic movement. He elucidated the underlying meanings of the Baal Shem Tov's teachings, parables, and stories to his close circle of disciples.

> R' Schneur Zalman composed a markedly unique approach to Chassidic philosophy.

"The disciples of the movement's third generation—great students of R' Dov Ber, who spread out across Eastern Europe—became the leaders of Chassidism in Ukraine, Poland, Hungary, and Russia. Among them was R' Schneur Zalman, who composed a markedly unique approach to Chassidic philosophy. The Chabad movement, which he went on to establish, initiated the search for philosophical investigation and intellectual analysis through Chassidic *Torah* exegesis.

"Chabad emphasizes the mind as the route to fostering spiritual arousal, in contrast to the general approach of Chassidism at the time, which promoted faith-based enthusiasm. Consequently, Chabad Chassidic writings are typically characterized by their systematic academic structure, while classic texts of general Chassidic mysticism are far less voluminous and usually more anecdotal.

"The Chassidic lessons of the Baal Shem Tov and subsequent Chassidic masters focus on emotions such as Dveikus (cleaving to the Omnipresent) as the expression of Chassidic, mystical faith. On the other hand, the scholarly Chabad approach of R' Schneur Zalman—developed and perpetuated by successive Lubavitch Rebbes—emphasizes the mind as the path to the inner heart. This intellectual approach allowed R' Schneur Zalman to attract Lithuanian Jews from nearby White Russia to his Chassidic School of thought.

"According to R' Schneur Zalman's seminal work *Tanya*, the intellect consists of three interconnected processes: Chochmah (wisdom), Binah (understanding), and Da'as (knowledge). While other branches of Chassidism focus primarily on the idea that 'G-d desires the heart,' R' Schneur Zalman argued that G-d also desires the mind, and that the mind is the 'gateway' to the heart. With the Chabad philosophy he elevated the mind above the heart, arguing that 'understanding is the mother of fear and love for G-d.'

R' Shneur Zalman argued that G-d also desires the mind.

"In R' Schneur Zalman's system, Chochmah represents the creation in its earliest potentiality; the idea of a finite world as was first born in the Divine mind. Binah is the idea conceived in its details, the result of contemplation. Da'as is, as it were, the commitment to creation, the stage at which the idea becomes an active intention.

"So in reality—according to the Chabad analogy—Chochmah is the birth of an idea in the mind, Binah is the contemplation, and Da'as is the beginning of the actualization of an idea. This is an important advance because it bridges the gap between spiritual insight and daily behavior, which had always been a problem for Jewish mysticism.

"Chabad is often contrasted with the Chagas[40] school of Chassidism. While all Chassidim have a certain focus on the emotions, Chagas sees

---

[40] Polish Chassidism, which traditionally stresses the emotive attributes—(Chesed (kindness), benevolence, Gevurah (strength), Tiferes (compassion) (ChaGa"S), serving G-d through emotions)— in contrast to Chabad Chassidism that places greater emphasis on the mental faculties—(Chochma, Bina, Da'as (ChaBa"D)).

emotions as a reaction to physical stimuli, such as dancing singing or beauty.

"R' Shneur Zalman, on the other hand, taught that the emotions must be led by the mind, and thus the focus of Chabad thought is *Torah* study and prayer rather than esotericism and song. As a Talmudist, R' Shneur Zalman endeavored to place Kabbalah and Chassidism on a rational basis. In *Tanya*, he defines his approach as 'the brain ruling the heart.'

Chabad requires knowledge of G-dliness, drawn from Chassidic philosophy.

"As such, the Chabad School requires knowledge of G-dliness, drawn from Chassidic philosophy, in order to establish the ultimate bond with the Almighty-One.

"As said, the school of Chabad Chassidism seeks to articulate Chassidic philosophy in an intellectual structure. The Fifth Rebbe, Rabbi Sholom Dovber Schneersohn,[41] had in fact established that his Yeshiva academies should teach Chassidic thought methodically, through intense textual analysis, traditionally used in Talmudic study.

"This approach was used by each Chabad Rebbe in his public discourses and talks, with each successive leader aiming to bring down the philosophy of Chassidism into greater detail and articulation. The seventh leader,

---

[41] Rabbi Sholom Dovber Schneerson, Rebbe RaShab (1860-1920). A mystic of the highest order, the Rashab authored the most comprehensive documents on mysticism to date, elegantly outlining the mystical infrastructure and its application to our lives. He wrote over 1500 discourses ('maamorim'), totaling over 50 published volumes of teachings and responsa. Rabbi Sholom Dovber was a Rebbe—a leader—to thousands. He worked tirelessly on behalf of the Russian Jewish community during the difficult period of transition from Czarist Russia, through World War I to the Russian Revolution. Recognizing the coming turmoil of the 20th century, in 1887, the Rebbe Rashab established Yeshiva Tomchei Temimim, dedicated to educating a new generation of young leaders to launch a spiritual revolution.
He was born in Lubavitch on 20 Cheshvan 1860, the second son of Shmuel Schneerson, the fourth Chabad Rebbe. In 1882, when his father died, he was not quite 22 years old, and his brother Zalman Aharon was not much older. A period followed, when they both fulfilled some tasks of a Rebbe, but neither felt ready to take on the title and responsibilities. Over this period, he gradually took on more responsibilities, particularly in dealing with the impact of the May Laws and, on Rosh Hashanah 5643 (September 10, 1882), he accepted the leadership of the Lubavitch movement.

Rabbi Menachem Mendel Schneerson,[42] typically addressed Chassidic philosophy in informal, analytical talks called 'farbrengens'. This approach to Chassidic mysticism enabled the integration of Chassidic interpretation into other aspects of Jewish thought.

"To its students, the systematic articulation of the inner depths of Chassidic thought is the most profound source of mystical fulfillment. Therefore, in Chabad, the Baal Shem Tov and R' Schneur Zalman, who share the same birthday, are called the 'two great luminaries,' representing heart and mind—a reference to the account of the installation of the sun and the moon in Genesis."

---

[42] Rabbi Menachem Mendel Schneerson, of righteous memory (1902-1994); seventh leader of Chabad-Lubavitch, lived in Nikolayev and Dnieperptrosk (Ukraine), Leningrad, Berlin, Warsaw, Paris, and New York; built upon and expanded his predecessors' work to revolutionize Jewish life across the globe. Known simply as "the Rebbe," he is widely recognized as one of the foremost Jewish thinkers of the 20th century. His teachings include ideas in Jewish philosophy and theology; commentary on Biblical, *Talmud*ical, and Kabbalistic texts; perspectives on world events; and moral and practical directives.

15

To Know G-d

"Biblical and rabbinic teachings target the attributes of love and fear (awe) of G-d and their offshoots, as the foundation of ritual observance and Heavenly service. But how is this possible? How are we expected to love an infinite Deity? G-d, as it were, is vastly more removed from our mortal sphere than an insect is from the human species, as the insect and the human are both finite entities.

"In light of this vast expanse, the entire notion of love and fear of G-d appears counterintuitive. Surely, there is a basic requisite that a minimal degree of knowledge and recognition of the direct cause precede an emotional expression. But, as stated, such knowledge appears unimaginable. In turn, this leaves love and fear of the heavenly Creator in the realm of the impossible.

"So what is meant by the various biblical and rabbinical statements, extolling the human emotional attributes toward the Heavenly Maker as an integral component of our Divine service?

"For example, what is meant by Moses' statement in Deuteronomy: 'And now, Israel, what does the Lord your G-d ask of you but to fear the Lord your G-d, to walk in obedience to Him, to love Him, to serve the Lord your G-d with all your heart and with all your soul?'[43] In absence of personal knowledge, how are we meant to fear and love Him?

> In absence of personal knowledge, how are we meant to fear and love Him?

"Surprising as it may be, the answer is yes; indeed, it is possible to know the Maker of heaven and earth and, hence, to love and fear Him.

---

[43] Deuteronomy 10:12.

"Chassidus is predicated on the principle that, despite our finite restrictive nature, we humans indeed are capable and even enjoined to intellectually grasp the ontology of the transcendent macrocosmic structure, as well as its primordial architect.

"This phenomenon is based on the verse: 'Know the G-d of your fathers, and serve Him with a complete heart.'[44] The implication: It is possible, at least to some degree, to know our Creator and that one's knowledge of Him is a prerequisite to serving Him with 'a complete heart.'

> It is possible, at least to some degree, to know our Creator.

"A similar assertion is found in the opening words of the renowned codifier and philosopher Maimonides,[45] in his magnum opus *Yad Hachazaka*:[46]

> The foundation of foundations and pillar of wisdoms is the knowledge that there is a Primordial Being who brings into being all existence; all that exist in heaven and earth and between them, exist only by virtue of His existence. ...This knowledge is the positive commandment included in the first words of the Ten Commandments, 'I am the Lord your G-d.'

"The words, 'I am the Lord your G-d,' embody the duty of faith. Yet, even here, Maimonides uses the term 'knowledge.' Thus, Maimonides espouses an obligation to know G-d, as far as it is

---

[44] Chronicles-I 28:9.

[45] Rabbi Moshe ben Maimon, (acronymed Rambam, for "Rabbeinu Moshe Ben Maimon", "Our Rabbi/ Teacher, Moses Son of Maimon"), *Talmud*ist, Halachist, physician, philosopher and communal leader, is one of the most important figures in the history of *Torah* scholarship.
Maimonides was born in Cordoba, Spain, on the 14th of Nissan (the eve of Passover) of the year 4895 (1135). He passed away on the 20th of Tevet of the year 4965 (1204) and was buried in the city of Tiberias in the Holy Land.
He was a preeminent medieval Sephardic Jewish philosopher and astronomer, and became one of the most prolific and influential *Torah* scholars and physicians of the Middle Ages.
Rambam was posthumously acknowledged as among the foremost rabbinical arbiters and philosophers in Jewish history, and his copious work comprises a cornerstone of Jewish scholarship. His fourteen-volume *Mishneh Torah* still carries significant canonical authority as a codification of *Talmud*ic law.
On his gravestone were inscribed the words, "From Moses to Moses, none arose as Moses."
Today, many hospitals and schools across the globe are named after Maimonides; and to this day, students worldwide pore over his scholarly works.

[46] Also known as *Mishne Torah* (1180).

intellectually possible, and only beyond that ability, does one's faith begin. This knowledge is found in the teachings of Chassidus.

"When one studies Chassidic mysticism, the individual learns about the Supernal Sefiros—attributes about continual creation of the universe, ex-nihilo, simultaneous Divine immanence and transcendence, miracles and nature, the special relationship between G-d and humans and G-d and the Jewish nation, to mention a few.

"As one studies these hallowed concepts and the host of other topics of Chassidus, one gradually comes to know the Holy One—blessed be He—to the fullest extent possible, as enjoined by the above verse in Chronicles.

"Furthermore, in Chassidic terminology the word Da'as or knowledge, is more than just knowing something in the ordinary sense of the term. Da'as implies conclusive knowledge, whose truth is felt and recognized. Da'as, then, is to know something so intimately that one becomes completely united with the subject. It is the type of knowledge that leads to personal commitment to 'serve Him with a whole heart,' with love and fear.

> Chassidic teachings of how to 'know' G-d enable the tangible expression of love and awe.

"In the above light, the verse 'Know the G-d of your fathers and serve Him with a whole heart' instructs us to use both our mind and heart, so that the whole person is engaged in the service of G-d. The intellect guides and controls the emotions and, simultaneously, is enlivened by them, thereby yielding a comprehensive impact on its student's personal life.[47]

"With Da'as, everything one does is imbued with sincerity, earnestness, and wholeheartedness because he or she is entirely immersed and subservient to the subject matter at hand.

---

[47] See *Hayom Yom*, 19 Shvat.

"Consequently, the Chassidic teachings of how to 'know' G-d enable the tangible expression of love and awe of the Heavenly Maker, as well as, one's essential service of the Divine Creator."

"I think you're losing me here, Danni," says Jay, "or perhaps I'm losing you. But I still don't get how it can be that we, who are finite creations, should be capable of understanding the infinite. In other words, how is a mortal being able to relate to an omnipotent G-d or His primordial energy through any familiar human experience or occurrence? Such an occurrence would inherently be limited and partial.

> True infinity should also find expression in the finite.

"It seems to me that no amount of comparison, illustration, or metaphor could logically bring His reality closer to our understanding, because He is called 'Ein Sof'—simply indefinable."

"I have to hand it to you, Jay, you raise an excellent point," I admit. "You are starting to give me a run for my money. But, we also have to think about the other side of it. Can it be that the human mind—one's most important and G-d-like faculty—has no place in the service of our Creator? Is it possible that we are to only employ our lower human faculties, our actions and emotions, but not our intellect? It is obviously not a plausible position. And, what about those Biblical verses that explicitly enjoin us to 'know' G-d?

"It appears that the finite mind should not be capable of grasping the infinite. However, on the other hand, true infinity should also find expression in the finite. A paradoxical phenomenon perhaps—similar to G-d's imminent, yet transcendent, relation with creation—but true nonetheless. Shackling G-d with the limitation of infinitude is just as limiting as denying Him the reverence of infinitude.

"The term 'infinite' defines a property no less restrictive than its antonym 'finite.' The concept of properties or characteristics is inapplicable to G-d. He is neither infinite nor finite, nor is He bound by any other restriction."

"Your point is well taken, but how does it change the fact that it is not possible for a finite being to grasp an infinite existence?" Jay refuses to relent.

"The answer," I insist, "is that the Almighty imbued humankind with a unique ability to perceive Him through a number of means. If not for those distinctive dispensations, we humans, indeed, would lack the capacity to 'know' G-d and, by extension, to love and fear Him.

"The special provisions include such matters as unique intelligence, the capability of deduction via the process of elimination, so one may apprehend a modicum of intimate knowledge of His ways and means. These properties exist, precisely, so a person can serve Him with proper love and awe.

"Additionally, the Creator provided a traditional mystical code, known as Kabbalah. The purpose of this body is to allow humans a further glimpse into His otherwise unknowable characteristics. Chassidus, essentially, is an extrapolation of Kabbalah.

> He allows us to know Him through the knowledge of our own inner psychological workings.

"The approach that Chabad developed over 7 generations of leaders, each Rebbe explaining the teachings of Chassidus, in ever greater elucidation and clarity, plays an important role in drawing down the Supernal intellect into comprehension and allows it to become truly assimilated into human thought.

"Most of all, however, the Almighty allows us to know Him through the knowledge of our own inner psychological workings. We talked about it at the outset of our conversation. We established, at considerable length, how to use the human psychological anatomy as a mirror to achieve a better understanding of the inner Divine workings and vice versa.

"Allow me to quickly review this idea because it constitutes a major principle within Chassidic dogma. Most important, it comprises a large part of the answer to your question: How finite human beings are able to grasp an infinite Divine reality.

ROUNDTABLE: THE REBBES AND HOW THEY SHAPED CHABAD

Excerpted with permission from Lubavitch.com, November 10, 2013

Chabad-Lubavitch traces its roots back to the last decades of the 18th century with its founding by Reb Schneur Zalman of Liadi. Many traditionalists within the Jewish community resisted R. Schneur Zalman's boldness in introducing a new approach to Divine Service. But many more were drawn to his creative, spiritually empowering teachings. With his authorship of the *Tanya*, Chabad's foundational source text, the Alter Rebbe set an intellectually and experientially innovative Chasidic movement on a trajectory that would gain momentum, attracting Jews worldwide to a deepened spiritual engagement with Judaism.

Rabbi Dovid Olidort, Senior Editor of Kehot Publication Society and Rabbi Nochem Grunwald, Editor of the periodical Heichal HaBesht, participated in a roundtable discussion with the editor on the leadership and scholarship of the Chabad Rebbes over the course of the last 200 years, and how they have shaped Chabad-Lubavitch.

Baila Olidort: We generally accept the view that each Rebbe followed his predecessor's teachings and that they were all dedicated to the continuity of Chabad as a discipline of Divine service. And yet, each Rebbe was distinct in personality, temperament and intellectual thrust. In some way, Chabad itself has evolved over the generations, no doubt as a result of the leadership of its respective Rebbes.

But it is also true that in Chabad, we tend not to really engage in comparative studies of the Rebbes, their scholastic output and leadership styles. We rather think of the Rebbes in terms of their place along the continuum in Chabad's long history.

Dovid Olidort: Chabad has shifted its focus at various points in its history, but its doctrine has not changed. It is true that in the works of our Rebbe (Rabbi Menachem Mendel Schneerson), the Rebbes are generally regarded as "one leader." But the idea of considering the distinctions between the Rebbes in terms of their personalities and their foci, that was something that the Frierdiker Rebbe (R. Yosef Yitzchak) himself observed. He described their personalities as corresponding to the different sefirot (emanations). The Alter Rebbe, he said, corresponded to Chochma, his son Reb Dovber, the Mitteler Rebbe, to Binah, and the Tzemach Tzedek, Reb Menachem Mendel, to the sefirah of Daat and so forth.

And then our Rebbe drew distinctions in describing each one as corresponding to another one of the Ushpizin of Sukkot. So while the Rebbes were all committed to advancing Chabad Chasidism as a pathway to Divine Service, it is true that each one contributed to this differently. You need only peruse their correspondences and their writings and this becomes plainly evident.

The Rebbes themselves constantly referred to their predecessors, but they gave themselves a lot of liberty to chart their own path. Look at our Rebbe: on the one hand he saw himself as no more than an extension of the Frierdiker Rebbe, and yet his works do not really bear much resemblance to his father's-in-law teachings. Compare a Sefer haSichos of the Frierdiker Rebbe to a Likuttei Sichos of the Rebbe. They are almost two distinct worlds. The Frierdiker Rebbe's Sefer haSichos are a collection of stories, inspirational thoughts and ruminations, with intermittent philosophical discussions delivered in free-style. The Rebbe's Likuttei Sichos, by contrast, is text-based, analytical and Talmudic in style, constructed with argument, counter-argument and resolution.

If we wanted, in general terms to lay out the differences, you might say that the Alter Rebbe (1745-1812) was the originator and innovator, the Mitteler Rebbe (1773-1827), the major expounder of Chabad and the one who dedicated himself to perpetuating Chabad as founded by his father; the Tzemach Tzedek (1789-1866), was the Rebbe who situated Chabad's ideas in classical Jewish sources; his son, Reb Shmuel, [the Maharash] (1834-1882) essentially carried on his father's style, introducing a quality of boldness and fearlessness to the Chabad character; Reb Sholom Dovber [the Rashab] (1860-1920), was a major innovator who culled from both the Mitteler Rebbe and the Tzemach Tzedek, but also gave new life to Chabad by establishing its flagship yeshiva; the Frierdiker Rebbe (1880-1950) carried on his father's legacy, but in the spirit of personal sacrifice, mesirut nefesh.

With our Rebbe, (1902-1994) the last in the dynasty of Chabad Rebbes, Chabad underwent a profound paradigm shift. The Rebbe reframed the focus and application of Chabad's philosophy and ideology, interpreting its most esoteric teachings in a way that made them widely and personally relevant.

BO: As the founder of Chabad, what was the AR's leadership model?

NG: At first the Alter Rebbe saw himself only as a teacher. He was averse to the idea of himself as a "charismatic" Rebbe. (This was one of the key differences between Chabad and the other Chasidic masters of his time—"Polish Chasidim" as they are known in Chabad parlance). The Alter Rebbe did not see himself as the miracle worker, or the inspirational conduit, the one who closes the gap between heaven and earth, or even the one who acts on behalf of the people.

In his famous letter (that is printed in the *Tanya*), the Alter Rebbe presented himself as a teacher, a mentor or a guide to bring people—observant Jews— closer to G-d, and not a prophet. The famous Chasidic Master R. Shlomo Karliner, by contrast, a contemporary of the Alter Rebbe, was the ultimate charismatic leader. But the Alter Rebbe tried to develop a Chasidic system that would be independent of the Zaddik. At the center of his system was a doctrine, and not only a doctrine, but a guide book—the *Tanya*—so that Chabad Chasidut would serve as a tool for those who didn't have a Rebbe.

BO: Let's talk about the Mitteler Rebbe and how he expanded and expounded on his father's teachings. In issue 8 of Heichal Habesht, in the review of the book Torat Chaim by the Mitteler Rebbe you treat this issue.

DO: Yes, in that article I looked at the history of the MR's involvement in publishing Chabad Chasidic works, and reviewed Torat Chaim, his last book, an anthology of Chasidic discourses on the *Torah* (which went as far as the middle of Bereishit when he passed away, was then continued later by his son, and in more recent times, by our Rebbe). The MR devoted himself to elucidating his father's work, and he developed Chabad Chasidut in both greater depth and more detail. In his introductions to his books on Chasidut, recently published in the new edition of his letters, he reflects a very intense interest to communicate the contemplation of Divine unity, which is really at the core of Chabad's theology.

NG: The Mitteler Rebbe was highly analytical and very philosophical in his approach to Chabad. He took the Alter Rebbe's methods and his Chasidic teachings and developed them into what we know today as the philosophy of Chabad. He dedicated himself to an intuitive analysis of the Alter Rebbe's main ideas—themes such as yesh m'ayin, creation ex nihilo, cause and effect, light, essence and emanations, potential vs. actualization--creating complicated structures and substructures.

He did not refer to other sources or texts beyond the Alter Rebbe's, and in that sense he was a Chabad Chasidic purist. His son-in-law the Tzemach Tzedek would say that if you cut his vein, he'd bleed Chasidus. I see in this expression an allusion to the fact (not only that his physical life was irrelevant to him, but also) that he saw Chabad Chasidus as kind of exclusive to everything else.

In a way, the Mitteler Rebbe embodied the Chabad of the Alter Rebbe. If you want to know what Chabad is, you need to study the Mitteler Rebbe. In terms of personality he was very intense and demanding of his disciples. In some ways you might say he was uncompromising in his single-minded commitment to Chabad. He was very focused on avodat hatefila, contemplative prayer, and was very invested in ensuring its continuity. He saw it as his responsibility to grow and to perpetuate the vision of Chabad, and he wanted Chasidim to be fully engaged in this cause.

BO: He passed away relatively young, and was succeeded by his nephew and son-in-law, Rabbi Menachem Mendel, known as the Tzemach Tzedek. He was also the grandson of the AR.

DO: The Tzemach Tzedek was very different from his father-in-law (who was also his uncle) In Chabad terms, you can say they are as different as Binah and Da'at. He contextualized all the Alter Rebbe's teachings, reconciled many scattered contradictions, and ordered and organized them giving us a better understanding of the Alter Rebbe. Our Rebbe used to say that the Tzemach Tzedek was unique in connecting the esoteric and exoteric parts of *Torah*, and illustrating the unity between them.

NG: Yes, and he was quite the opposite in almost every way from the Mitteler Rebbe. He was the quintessential Talmudic scholar as expressed in his responsa, Tzemach Tzedek and all of his other writings. This fact in itself naturally transformed Chasidut Chabad from its peculiar particularity into a much broader mainstream persuasion. He had such supreme mastery of Talmudic and Jewish legal and scholarly texts and traced all of the AR's teachings to earlier texts, locating the whole corpus of the AR's teachings within the rest of classical Judaism, the *Talmud*, *Tanach*, etc.

The Rebbe characterized the style and the era of the Tzemach Tzedek as the era of "peace." It was indeed a new era of mutual recognition and coexistence. One of the simple reasons being that a new generation was born on the misnagdic side for whom the Chasidic movement was an existing thriving movement. The Rebbe saw the reconciliation as a result of the TT's style of leadership.

BO: The Fourth Rebbe, Reb Shmuel, known as the Maharash, was leader of Chabad for a short time (1866-1883), and was probably, in his lifetime, the least known of the Chabad Rebbes.

DO: After the TT passed away, his five sons became Rebbes each in their own court. The youngest, the Maharash, became Rebbe in Lubavitch. He coined the concept of "Lechtchila Ariber," which became axiomatic in Chabad—this is the idea of a kind of holy chutzpah that empowers the Chasid confront challenges with courage and a boldness of spirit so that they don't become obstacles on his path in avodat haShem.

The Maharash continued in his father's path, but with new emphasis on certain ideas and themes that were not until then closely considered. One idea that was explicitly stressed by Maharash but wasn't that central before is the perspective of reality despite the absolute belief in acosmism.

Originally, Chabad taught that relative to Divine reality, our own reality is not authentic. In his discourse Mi Kamocha 5629 (1869) the Maharash argued that notwithstanding Chabad's attitude until now that all existence was perceived as null, the world in fact does have an authentic reality, even from a Divine perspective. Our Rebbe would frequently pick up on this theme and employ it in his own talks and discourses to support his call to engage with our environment and effect change in the world as we know it.

BO: When the Maharash passed away in 1883, his son, Reb Sholom Dovber was only 23 years old. But his leadership lasted until 1920.

DO: The Rashab was a major innovator. First of all, as far as Chabad teachings are concerned, he organized Chasidut in a formal, systematic way. This is why he's referred to "The Rambam of Chasidus"—Maimonides was of course the one who ordered and organized the entire body of Jewish law. The Rashab's contribution is also significant because he distilled many abstruse concepts in Chasidic thought.

In many ways, he was very similar to the Mitteler Rebbe. He was more textually and contextually focused than the Mitteler Rebbe, but as we see in his talks (in the collection Torat Shalom) he saw the Mitteler Rebbe as the paradigmatic

Chabad Rebbe. He, too, like the Mitteler Rebbe felt a sense of urgency about disseminating Chabad's work, was intense in his leadership, and saw himself as reviving Chabad. His famous booklet Etz Hachaim, as well as Kuntres haTefila and Kuntres ha'Avoda, reflect this clearly.

NG: Yes, although he was similar to the Tzemach Tzedek in terms of his concern with text, the dedication to the conceptualization of Chasidut mirrors much more closely the method of the Mitteler Rebbe. In his view, the MR was the conduit between the Chasidim and the Divine. In fact it was the Rebbe Rashab who analyzed for us the difference between the Mitteler Rebbe and the Tzemach Tzedek.

In his two largest works, known as 5666 and 5672, as in others, he reorganized in a clear and distinctive way the major themes of Chabad, such as Dirah B'tachtonim, and the mystical meaning of prayer, study and action.

In some ways, much of Chabad of today is an outgrowth of the Rashab's activities. He opened Yeshiva Tomchei Temimim, he set up our "constitution" so to speak, so Lubavitch as we know it today is rooted in the Rashab. After the Maharash, Chabad dwindled, losing Chasidim to the allure of Zionism and the Haskala at that time and also because Chabad itself was less vigorous. So the Rashab worked to revive the Chabad spirit as it existed in the time of the Mitteler Rebbe, when Chabad was at its peak, and his influence and inspiration were very enduring.

BO: In 1920, his son, Rabbi Yosef Yitzchak, or the FR became Rebbe. Was he similar in style to his father, the Rashab?

NG: People outside Chabad are more familiar with the talks of the Frierdiker Rebbe and his heroic leadership, and less so with his profound Chasidic discourses. His discourses are generally based on his father's discourses that dealt with highly abstract levels of the Ein Sof. You might say that the Frierdiker Rebbe dedicated himself to further developing his father's teachings in much the same way as the Mitteler Rebbe did to his father's works.

But the Frierdiker Rebbe lived in one of the most tumultuous eras in Jewish history, when communism, the Holocaust, and finally, secular America, each presented its own significant challenges to Jewish continuity.

Mesirut nefesh, the idea and virtue of personal sacrifice, was an important and central theme in his discourses and his leadership, and in the way he succeeded to transplant Chabad from one culture to another, ultimately relocating it to the US.

BO: Our Rebbe's leadership was often studied and scrutinized for the balance he struck so successfully and creatively between tradition and innovation. His teachings are firmly rooted in *Torah*, Jewish law and tradition, yet he was keenly attuned to contemporary life, to the challenges and the blessings of modernity.

NG: The Rebbe was surely the most innovative leaders since the Alter Rebbe, if not de jure, then de facto. While the focus of prior generations was contemplative prayer and meditation, the Rebbe used the same Chasidic concepts, such as dirah b'tachtonim—the creation of a divine dwelling place in this world—in establishing a new focus on action. He took classic Chabad ideas from the *Tanya* and used them in transforming Chabad into an action oriented movement, giving that priority above all else, in the avoda of the Chasid.

DO: Traditionally, Chabad taught contemplation and meditation as a function of the individual's self-refinement. But the Rebbe felt that in the current climate of Jewish assimilation, the contemplative model would have to take second place to outreach and activism. My good friend, Rabbi Feitel Levin explored this in his book, Heaven on Earth.

In the Rebbe's reconceptualization of Chasidic terms, the idea of "bittul" or self-nullification, also took on a new resonance: rather than engaging in meditative exercises such as pondering the insignificance of the self relative to the Divine, the Rebbe wanted Chasidim to turn their focus toward the other. Similarly, he reframed the idea of mesirut nefesh, which was in its plainest sense, necessary for the survival of Judaism in its long history of oppression as Nochem mentioned before.

In our times, with the freedom to live and practice as Jews, mesirut nefesh denotes a different expression of personal sacrifice. As the Rebbe explained in his Ve'ata Tetzave discourse, today mesirut nefesh requires that we become more aware of and sensitive to the existential condition of our reality, to the point where we are disturbed by it and motivated to focus not on our personal needs—even if they are spiritual—but to devote ourselves generously to others, and in that way transform society so that the Divine presence is felt and noticed in its midst.

16

From My Flesh...

"In the years 1884-1885, medical science discovered an artery in the brain that facilitates memory and concentration. The brother of the Fifth Rebbe, Rabbi Sholom Dovber, known as the Rashab, came to tell the Rebbe about this discovery. The Rashab went into the next room and came back with a small manuscript of Chassidus written by the Mitteler Rebbe.[48]

"He showed him that there were six or seven lines in the discourse, where the Mitteler Rebbe refers to a certain artery in the brain that is mobile, its movement facilitates memory and concentration. When the artery is facing the part of the brain that houses Chochma (wisdom) and Binah (understanding), it helps to remember. When it is facing the part of the brain that contains Da'as (knowledge), it helps concentration. That's why when one wants to remember, one tilts his or her head upwards, and when one wants to concentrate, one tilts his or her head downwards.

"After seeing this, the brother remarked that the Mitteler Rebbe must have been a great medical scientist. The Rebbe Rashab rejected the notion saying: "The Mitteler Rebbe knew how the spiritual Supernal being functions, and therefore he could predict how the physical human

---

[48] Dovber Schneuri (1773–1827), the second Chabad Rebbe, was the first to live in Lyubavichi (Lubavitch, now in present-day Russia), the town for which the Chabad dynasty is named. He is also known as the Mitteler Rebbe ("Middle Rebbe" in Yiddish), being the second of the first three generations of Chabad leaders.

His father, Reb Schneur Zalman, the first Chabad Rebbe, named him after his own teacher, the famous Rabbi Dov Ber of Mezritch, the disciple and successor of the Baal Shem Tov.

As a boy, Dov Ber was a very eager student, with a brilliant mind and exceptional memory. Soon after he started to attend "Cheder," his teacher complained that the little boy plied him with so many questions and demanded so much attention, that it was difficult for the teacher to conduct the classes. Little Dov Ber was far advanced for his age, and had to be put together with older boys.

At the age of sixteen, Rabbi Dov Ber attained great scholarship and maturity, that his father appointed him to instruct the young men who were students in his Yeshivah.

Rabbi Dov Ber was a true and worthy successor to his great father. He continued to teach the Chabad Chassidic way of life, and to enrich its literature by many volumes. He established a Yeshivah in Lubavitch, which attracted exceptionally gifted young scholars.

being works as well. He worked his way from the reality of the spiritual to a truth reflected in the physical."[49]

"The notion that human metaphysical or psychological anatomy reflects the cosmic structure is an axiom in Chabad Chassidic doctrine. It is a key component in achieving the mandate of 'know the G-d of your fathers and serve him with a complete heart.'

"The Biblical source for this phenomenon is a quote from the book of *Job*: 'From my flesh I shall perceive my Lord.'[50] Chassidus understands this to mean that, through inner personal awareness; by examining the process of the human psyche on a microcosmic level, we can draw parallels regarding the macrocosmic order. This process provides an intrinsic understanding of both our human metaphysical properties—'my flesh'—and the macrocosmic anatomy of the sublime creative process—'perceive My Lord.'

> By examining the process of the human psyche, we can draw parallels regarding the macrocosmic order.

"By using the individual's own inner experience as an allegorical model for understanding the deepest mysteries of creation, Chassidus both elevates human inner consciousness and expands the conceptual range of Kabbalistic thought."

"The thought of knowing G-d," interjects Jay, "brings to mind an amusing episode:

"The kindergarten children were having fun expressing themselves during drawing time, as the teacher moved about inspecting their skills. Chancing upon a little girl diligently at work, the teacher asked, 'What are you drawing?'

---

[49] See footnote 20.
[50] Job: 19:6.

'Why,' the girl replied, 'I'm drawing a picture of G-d.'

'But no one really knows what G-d looks like,' mused the teacher.

'True' replied the girl, without lifting her head from the page, 'but that's all about to change!'

"I hope you share my appreciation for the humor and don't find it too trivial, Danni," says Jay.

"I got to admit it, Jay, that was actually quite funny," I concur. "As far as triviality is concerned, there's nothing trivial about humor. To the contrary, Judaism considers humor rather useful, most notably, in education and pedagogy.

"The Talmudic sages share the benefits of humor in the following statement: 'Prior to beginning his lecture in Talmudic law, Rabbah always opened with a humorous remark. As a result, his students laughed, causing their "hearts to open." Afterwards, he continued with a serious presentation and in-depth analysis of Jewish Law.'[51]

"Another Talmudic legend has it that the prophet Elijah appeared in the presence of a sage named Rabbi Beroka. In this rare opportunity to address Elijah, R' Beroka poses the following question: 'Who here in the marketplace is assured a place in the World to Come?' Elijah looks around and points to two men. He says, 'these two have attained a place in the World to Come.' The rabbi walks over to the two men and asks, 'What is your occupation?' They replied, 'We're jesters. When we see people who are feeling down, we cheer them up.'[52]

"Okay, back to our discussion regarding the person's ability to grasp the infinite. Because our psychological anatomy mirrors the cosmic structure of creation, it allows us insight into the Divine process of creation. This, among the other factors, helps us humans achieve our religious responsibility to 'know' G-d and love and fear Him.

---

[51] *Talmud* Shabbos, 30b.

[52] Taanis, 22a.

"Let me further reiterate the flip side of this ethos that quite captivated you during our original discussion, Jay. The study of the cosmic order of creation, as depicted in Chassidus, helps us better understand our inner selves, psychologically, emotionally, and behaviorally.

"Arguably, this would make Chassidus the ultimate source of human psychology. Hence, when properly applied, Chassidic thought could and should take the place of most psychological therapy.

"In other words, because Chassidus is replete with genuine guidance, inspiration, and empowerment based on the Kabbalistic supernal model, its engagement provides the power and know-how to eliminate depression, build better relationships, and achieve one's goals."

"Danni, are you actually suggesting that Chassidus could take the place of a shrink," Jay queries in surprise.

"Theoretically, yes," I maintain. "I realize not everyone is able to glean this type of practical information directly from Chassidic teachings. This is because of their own deficiencies and not a lack on the part of Chassidus.

"Here's an example of what I mean: In order to derive one's guidance directly from the Chassidic discipline, one would have to be brutally honest in his or her self-evaluation for the sake of proper diagnosis. Yet, how many people are capable of that? The deficiency, here, is not on the part of Chassidus but, rather, on the part of one's ability to access it. Hence, says R' Schneur Zalman in *Tanya*, 'Not everyone is privileged to recognize their specific instructions in the *Torah*.'[53]

"Still, psychology alone cannot take the place of Chassidus, because it is limited in its scope. At the core of every issue lays the 'you'—your personality, your connection to your soul and self, and your awareness of your thoughts and your feelings. But, who is the actual 'you?' In other words, when one says 'I' or thinks about 'oneself,' who or what is he or she referencing? The tragic fact is that psychology has no clear

---

[53] Compilers forward-Tanya.

understanding of who is that 'you.' This could make it difficult to fix the problem with the 'you' or the 'I.'

"Mostly, psychology's answers are based on the outside observance of the individual and educated guesses about what's going on inside of his or her mind and heart. This process leads to interesting ideas and techniques, derived mostly through trial and error, but there is no real comprehension of the 'person'—what makes one tick, why a person is experiencing specific issues, or why a particular technique works.

"In contrast, Chassidus holds the map of the human psyche. In fact, one of the more innovative and fundamental assertions of Chassidic thought is that we have two souls, which constantly battle each other over control of our thoughts, speech, and actions. Our conscious experience of self—our personality—is the balance between these two forces.

"Chassidus contains a broad vocabulary, used to depict fine nuances within the human psyche that no other psychological discipline has the capacity to recognize. For example, the *Tanya* contains several terms describing a downtrodden, low, and depressed spirit: Nemichas Ruach (lowness of spirit), Lev Nishbar (contriteness of heart), Atzvus (depression), and Merirus Hanefesh (bitterness of the soul). Each of these refer to, if only slightly, different emotive expressions.

"Because of its direct knowledge of the human psyche, essentially, Chassidus is the best source of psychology and should be integrated, in whatever way possible."

"You know Danni," declares Jay, "everything you say so far is rather interesting. You present a unique way of seeing the person and life as a whole. It gives me a lot to think about. But this last thing that you mentioned about the two souls, I find exceptionally fascinating. You know, as a psychologist, this is right up my alley. If I'm not mistaken, Freud's philosophy regarding the id, ego, and superego is somewhat similar in nature."

"This phenomenon," I tell Jay, "is actually a fundamental aspect of Chabad theology. Let me just point out that, from my limited understanding of Chassidus and my even more limited knowledge of Freudian psychoanalysis, it seems that Freud may have gotten some of it right, particularly regarding the id and the ego. Who knows? He may even have taken it from Chassidus. Where he seemed to miss the mark is the superego, which he attributes to extenuating causation."

"Oh, I have a question Danni," says Jay. "What do you mean when you say Freud may have taken it from Chassidus? Is there any reason to believe he might have had access to this type of information? I mean, I know that he was Jewish, but I don't believe he was religious. In fact, if I'm not mistaken, he may have been an atheist, let alone someone who would be in the habit of studying Chassidic philosophy. Are you just saying this tongue in cheek or there is something more to it?"

"By golly, Jay, you don't intend to let anything get by, do you? It's really interesting that you would pick up on that. While I don't have any hard evidence that he was exposed to the Chassidic school of thought, there is ample reason to believe he may have been.

"In a paper published by Dr. Joseph H. Berke[54] and Professor Stanley Schneider[55] of the Hebrew University in Jerusalem, there is an account about a meeting that took place in 1903 in Vienna between Rabbi Sholom Dovber Schneersohn, the fifth Lubavitcher Rebbe, also known by his acronym the Rashab, and Professor Sigmund Freud. According to the paper, the Rebbe was at the time under great pressure from the Czarist police and Jewish anti-Chassidic antagonists—Misnagdim. Although

---

[54] Dr. Berke studied at Columbia College of Columbia University and graduated from the Albert Einstein College of Medicine in New York. He moved to London in 1965, where he worked with R. D. Laing in the 1960s, when the Philadelphia Association was set up and was resident at Kingsley Hall, where he helped Mary Barnes, a nurse diagnosed with schizophrenia, emerge from madness. Barnes, later, became a famous artist, writer, and mystic. A stage play based on the book that Berke and Barnes wrote together (Mary Barnes, Two Accounts of a Journey through Madness) was adapted as a stage play by David Edgar. He is also completing: The Highgate Haggadah of Tu B'Shevat (forthcoming, Teva Publications, London) and is also working on Freud and the Rebbe (forthcoming, Karnac Books, London).

[55] A senior professor at Hebrew University.

he already had extraordinary accomplishments in the exposition of Chassidus, he expressed great dissatisfaction with himself.[56]

"The paper further relates that 'Freud came from a long line of Chassidim, who for several generations lived in and around Galicia, a center of Chassidic life. We know his great grandfather, Ephraim, was a Chassid and that Freud was named after his paternal grandfather, Shlomo, also a Chassid and Rabbi. Sigmund is the German version of Shlomo or Solomon. His father, Jacob, was a Chassid until his adolescence, when he was affected by the Haskalah or enlightenment. Although he denied it, recent research shows Freud had an extensive Jewish upbringing, knew Hebrew, and was knowledgeable about Jewish practices. There is even a possibility that Freud was familiar with Kabbalah.'

"Does that answer your question, Jay," I ask."

"I'm fascinated, Danni; you don't cease to amaze me.

"Before we go on, Danni, I was wondering if we could get back, for a bit, to the discussion of the two souls." Jay remarks. "As I said, I'm intrigued by the subject and would like to know more about the Chassidic view on the matter."

"Sure thing, Jay, I'd be glad to," I respond, "although it's somewhat of a digression from the order I'm following. I guess a short detour can't really hurt. You ready?

---

[56] Recently released documents (letters written by Rashab himself about his visits to Freud) reveal that the Rebbe Rashab visited Freud in his capacity as a neurologist for electroshock therapy to the Rebbe's arm, not for psychoanalysis.* Any conversation was an incidental chat, held on the side. This explains why he's not mentioned in Freud's diaries. Any conversation they had while he was being treated would have been considered ordinary chatter between two brilliant people, not therapy. An account of the encounters between Freud and the Rebbe, the sixth Lubavitcher Rebbe, Rabbi YY Schneerson, is said to assert that his father, Rashab, discussed the nature of Chassidic philosophy with Freud.

*Wikipedia states that, according to Letters from the Rashab to his cousin Rabbi Isaiah Berlin of Riga, dated 6-Tevet through 22-Iyar 5663—January 5-May 19, 1903; in his early 40s, he suffered a loss of sensation in his left hand and, in 1903, he spent two months in Vienna, where Sigmund Freud treated him with electrotherapy and Wilhelm Stekel treated him with the talking cure. The treatment had some success, restoring some feeling to the hand; but he was unable to stay in Vienna longer than 2 months. Returning home, he attempted to continue his treatment with a small machine that he had bought in Vienna, he experienced no further improvement and, eventually, gave up.

REHABBING LIVES: HOW ONE WOMAN CATALYZES ADDICTION
TREATMENT WITH CHASSIDIC PHILOSOPHY. BY MIRIAM KARP

Excerpted with permission from Chabad.org, November 9, 2015

Donna Miller's daily planner reads a bit different than most. Meetings with
lawyers and probation officers. Intake of young man addicted to cocaine.
Therapy session with family torn apart by Dad's gambling. Just another day
in the life of the director of the Chabad Residential Treatment Center of
Los Angeles.

But Donna Miller doesn't see herself as a superwoman. She says she's just blessed
to have a meaningful job. A series of "circumstances" led to her involvement
with rehab and Chabad.

"I was studying to be a family therapist and wanted to integrate Jewish values into
my work. My guidance counselor suggested I intern at Chabad," Donna recalls.
"I did my intern hours, completed my license and then stayed for eight years,
eventually developing a family program for our women's treatment center."

Donna discovered that she loved the field of addiction, and after some time
she came back to Chabad as a supervisor for interns, where she started
strengthening the existing programs. A rabbi from Israel who was working
there, Rabbi Meir Kohen, saw her effectiveness and told her straight out: "You
need to become the director here."

Donna really wasn't looking for that level of responsibility, but, she says with a
laugh, "I took it, and that was over 15 years ago. It was quite challenging, and
one of my primary focuses was on developing more Jewish programming. The
center was always kosher, with holiday celebrations and a warm atmosphere,
but I built our shul (synagogue) and added more *Torah* classes, which are not
mandated but offered. We now have a full-time and several part-time rabbis
teaching classes and mentoring.

"Rather than solely focusing on discipline and a reward-and-punishment
system, we try to promote a higher level of moral reasoning. We try to help our
clients reclaim their true selves and develop a desire for a meaningful life."

Moral education? That sounds like a fit with Chabad.

Addiction is an insidious and difficult disease to successfully treat. How does

Donna find the inspiration and strength to fill her day and life with the kind of people many view as hopeless, bottomed out, deeply entangled in a web of negatives? How does she maintain the ability to see a person with a soul, a person worth redeeming in the midst of all the scars, trauma, fears and issues?

Donna credits Chassidic philosophy as being the driving force behind her work. "My joy and inspiration comes from the Rebbe and Chassidut, even more than from psychology. The Rebbe's teachings on building from strengths, phrasing things in the most positive way possible, and finding true purpose and meaning all influence my work as a therapist and the development of the program here," Donna states.

While Donna had a strong Jewish background, she became acquainted with Chabad through her involvement at the center. "An intern schlepped me to a women's retreat. When I saw the level of the women, I was very impressed and moved," she says.

Studies show that a connection to one's religion and spiritual traditions are important components of recovery, so discussions about G-d and spirituality are frequent at the center.

Donna's program is solidly built on the 12 Steps, which she has chunked into three primary steps, based on the Baal Shem Tov's teachings.

She cites her bubby, Ray Korn, and her parents as inspiring examples of loving-kindness and steadfast belief in the ability to make things better. And she helps her clients reconnect with the riches of their individual inheritance. "We all come from such rich traditions and histories. Even when things have gone incredibly wrong, I like to help our clients pull from the strengths of their backgrounds, and reconnect to their roots and the people who love them. I like to help the families learn and grow from our clients."

Donna is grateful for the vision and support of Rabbi Cunin, and for his steadfast encouragement. "There have been times when I said, 'I can't do it anymore!' But he wouldn't let me go there. He'd just calm me down and tell me, 'Look at what you're doing and accomplishing.' I am very grateful for the opportunity to be part of the 'Rebbe's army,' for being entrusted to work with our 'gems.'"

17

THE HUMAN PSYCHE

The 'yetzer hara,' evil inclination is an expert in his trade, an extraordinary specialist, particularly when he injects a most effective "bribe" – the person's natural self-love.

One of the accuser's tricks is to delude a person into thinking that he or she is prevented from performing a mitzvah, bolstering this delusion by various arguments and "proofs," giving no respite.

Because a person tends to be partial to oneself, and it is very difficult to be objective in a matter concerning one's own self, a person must always be aware that what seems to him or her a case of victim of circumstances, is not necessarily so in actual fact.

Therefore, in order to clarify one's true position, he or she must turn to a person who is beyond such bribery and corruption...one who is permeated by the spirit of the *Torah*, and truth brooks no compromise.

For only such a person can evaluate the situation and determine whether it is indeed a case of unavoidable constraint, or delusions stemming from the 'yetzer hara'...[57]

"While humans are exponentially superior to all other forms of creation, with which they share the earthly planet, they are not without fault. A comprehensive view reveals that the human is desperately lacking in his or her natural and unrefined state, one's Divine essence and spiritual potential, notwithstanding.

R' Schneur Zalman portrays humankind as comprising two souls.

"In *Tanya*, R' Schneur Zalman portrays humankind, the crown jewel of creation, as comprising two souls—the 'Nefesh Elokis' (G-dly soul) and the

---

[57] Excerpt from a letter written by the Lubavitcher Rebbe, Rabbi Menachem Mendel Schneerson, in the Days of Teshuva 5732.

'Nefesh Bahamis' (animal soul). Hence, the Talmudic statement: The Holy One, blessed be He, created two impulses, one good and the other evil.'[58] These two forces wage constant battle with each other.

"The two rival forces are diametrical in every sense of the imagination. The animal spirit is passionate and hedonistic; it continuously gravitates towards physical pleasure and gratification. Indeed, its very essence and temperament is one of wanting, desiring, and coveting. It can be compared to a machine that constantly craves. This life force epitomizes the ultimate of selfishness.

"On the other hand, the Divine soul is of a G-d-like quality. It is the inexplicable conscience within a human, distinguishing him or her from beast. This spirit impels one towards goodness and sanctity. It is the epitome of selflessness and virtue.

> At any given time, a person has the capacity to live on either the spiritual or the animal plane.

"Much the way the human mind is perpetually engaged in thought, human existence is invariably expressed through one of these two souls. Thus, at any given time, a person has the capacity and choice to live on either the spiritual or the animal plane.

"'Two nations are in your womb; two governments will separate from inside you and the upper hand will go from one government to the other.'[59] These are the words spoken to our matriarch Rebecca in response to her unusual maternity sensations. The Rabbis homiletically interpret this as a reference to the two rivaling forces within humans that vie for ascendancy in every thought and feeling.

"This rivalry affects every choice we make and every action we take in the course of our lives. At times, one gains the upper hand; at times, the

---

[58] *Talmud* Berochos, 61a.
[59] Genesis 25:23.

other rules our lives. True to the principle of free choice, the Almighty does not intervene in this battle. For, by conquering the animal soul through free choice, we rise to virtue and holiness and fulfill our purpose in this corporeal world.

"However, there is a fundamental difference between the animal and Divine souls that is of paramount importance. In contrast to the Divine spirit, requiring stimulation in order to function as a viable force within the human arena, the animal spirit needs no such prelude or introduction.

"Intellective by nature, the Divine spirit, inevitably is stimulated and nurtured through a meticulous process of development and cultivation. This is not the case regarding the animal spirit. Unlike its counterpart, the impulse and ambition of the animal spirit is spontaneous and automatic—its aggressive and emotional temperament is felt naturally, regardless of whether or not one makes any overtures towards it.

"To use a trivial analogy, the flowers and vegetation of a beautiful garden are the result of careful effort in cultivating and maintaining a piece of land. Remarkably though, the weeds that grow on the same piece of land require no effort whatsoever—they need no cultivation or care, no water or pruning. These organisms appear, whether they are planted or not, or whether they are wanted or not. In fact, if one desires a weed-free garden, one must take deliberate measures to rid the garden of the infiltration of such undesirables.

"The same is true regarding the Divine and animal souls. The Divine spirit, like a rose, requires meticulous care and cultivation. The animal soul, on the other hand, needs no cultivation. The impulse and ambition of this wild spirit are entirely spontaneous.

"The process of cultivating the Divine spirit is a diligent one. In addition to the aforementioned discrepancy regarding the modus operandi of Divine and animal souls—one is automatic, while the other requires cultivation—there is another distinction: The two do not even enter the person simultaneously.

"The *Midrash* states that only on the day of Bar or Bat Mitzvah (age 12 for a female and age 13 for a male) does the G-dly soul completely unite with the person. Hence, it is only from this point on that a person is truly able to wage war with his or her animal soul and set out to conquer the small city—the body. Accordingly, the animal spirit actually has first claim over the body, as it enters the body first. The latter only makes the process of becoming attuned with the Divine spirit that much more complex.

> ## The animal spirit actually has first claim over the body.

"The Rebbe Rashab discusses this idea in his acclaimed work, *Kuntres Uma'ayon*:

The animal and Divine souls are antagonistic entities, but the animal soul inhabits the body at birth while the Divine soul inhabits the body at thirteen. Hence, the claims of the Yetzer Hara precede those of the Yetzer Tov. In fact, the evil inclination takes control of the person before the Divine soul even has an opportunity to settle-in.

Adding to this is the fact that our bodies are naturally aligned with the animal soul as opposed to the Divine spirit. Bodily gratifications like food, drink, and so forth are immediate to the body. These habits are deeply ingrained within the human. It is, thus, a small wonder that the animal soul is more conspicuous than her Divine counterpart. Her claim is earlier; she dominates in all the body's affairs and is a veteran in persuading a human to pursue base physical matters.

The Divine soul is a mere stripling compared to her opponent. Her purpose is spiritual, while the body is attracted and accustomed to physical and worldly coarseness. In fact, the body regards spiritual substance rather contemptuously. [60]

"It is rather clear from the above discussion that the Divine soul is considerably disadvantaged in her battle with the animal soul. Thus, it is only natural that, in absence of higher spiritual definition and purpose, one finds oneself in the grasp of the animal order.

---

[60] Kehot Publishing Society, 13:2.

"This unique peek into the psyche of the human essential character, points out 'R Osher Chaimson, goes a long way in helping us understand ourselves and learn how to gain control over our unbecoming cravings, desires, and emotions.

"This model lays the foundation for 'R Schneur Zalman's foremost breakthrough in *Tanya*, how one can foster positive and righteous thoughts that, in turn; foster positive emotions and actions—how to gain self control."

"Very interesting, Danni, it sounds much like a saying that I once heard:

'Your Thinking Controls Your Thoughts.
Your Thoughts Control Your Emotions.
Your Emotions Control Your Actions.
Your Actions Control Your Results.'"

"This sounds right on the mark, Jay," I note.

SECOND THOUGHTS

Based on Once Upon A Chassid by Yanky Tauber

The 'wise-guy' nestled in the left chamber of the heart of man, wrote Rabbi Yosef Yitzchak of Lubavitch to a Chassid, comes in many guises. At times he may even appear in a silk caftan and shtreiml (Chassidic garb)... Rabbi Yosef Yitzchk illustrates this point with the following story:

Rabbi Menachem Nachum, Rebbe of Chernobyl, was poor and hard pressed to feed his household. One day a Chassid brought an unusually large gift of 300 rubles.

The Rebbe's family and the head-secretary, who managed the Rebbe's affairs, were highly relieved. They would finally enjoy a respite from the crushing debt incurred from food and other necessary household items.

Sometime after the gift-bearing Chassid left, Rabbi Nachum opened his door and requested that a certain Chassid, who had been received earlier, be summoned back. After the Chassid left, the Rebbe continued to receive his visitors late into the night.

When the last guest departed, the head secretary entered the room to obtain funds for needed expenditures. Knowing of the 300-ruble gift, he was pleased with the ability to settle a good part of the debts. He had already made a detailed list of how much to allocate to each creditor.

R' Nachum opened the drawer in which the money, brought by Chassidim to cover the Rebbe's expenses, was kept. The Rebbe's secretary saw a drawer filled with copper coins and a scant smattering of silver coins mixed in. Of the ruble-notes, there was not a trace.

The Rebbe indicated that the secretary collect the contents of the drawer. The secretary counted the silver and copper, among which were also interspersed three golden coins. They totaled close to 100 rubles.

The secretary stood there, unable to say a word. He was hesitant to raise the matter of 300 rubles, but the fact that he would be unable to even partially settle the Rebbe's debts pained his heart.

Noticing his distress, the Rebbe said to him: "Why are you so upset? He who provides bread for all flesh has, in His great kindness, sent us an undeserved gift. From far and wide, many of our brethren, may they live, have labored and toiled to earn and bring such a sum."

The secretary was truly a man worthy of his position with the Rebbe of Chernobyl. Nevertheless, he could no longer contain himself. The heavy debts and the terrible poverty, which prevailed in the Rebbe's home, so deeply distressed him. As if of their own accord, the words tore themselves from an anguished heart: "But where are the 300 rubles that were brought? Together with what we have here, we would be able to pay off part of what is owed..."

"True," said the Rebbe, I was brought 300 rubles. At the moment I received them I wondered: why do I deserve such a large amount?

Then I was filled with pleasure at the thought that I had found favor in the eyes of the Almighty so that He had chosen to provide sustenance for myself and for my household in such a generous and honorable manner.

But when I thought further, I was greatly distressed: perhaps I was receiving this money in place of some spiritual gift?

"Later in the day, one of the Chassidim who came to see me poured out his heart. For the past year he has been unable to pay the teacher of his children, a very poor but G-d-fearing man who continued to teach the children in the hope that he will someday be paid. This Chassid already owes eight months' rent for the mill and inn which he leases, and the landowner is sure to evict him soon. And to top it all off, he has arranged a match for his eldest daughter and has nothing with which to marry her off.

"When I heard this, it occurred to me that perhaps the Almighty has granted me the privilege of being an administrator of charity. Perhaps this large amount was entrusted to me so that I may merit such great Mitzvos as educating children, saving the livelihood of an entire family, and helping marry off a bride. I asked the Chassid how much his debts and marriage needs amounted to, and behold, it matched the sum, exactly 300 rubles!

"However, as soon as I decided to give the 300 rubles to this Chassid, another thought entered my mind: is it proper to give the entire sum to a single individual? Why, with such an amount one could support, at the very least, six entire families!

"I found myself in a dilemma, since both options – to give the entire amount to the one Chassid or to divide it between several needy families – seemed logical and virtuous. I couldn't decide between them, so I meditated for a long while in order to reach a decision in the matter.

"Upon contemplation, I came to recognize that these two opinions were coming from the two 'judges' within me, the 'good inclination' and the 'evil inclination' and that the argument to divide the sum among several families was definitely not coming from my 'good inclination.'

Was this indeed my good inclination speaking, why didn't it speak up immediately? As soon as I received the money, it should have immediately said, 'Nachum, 300 rubles were brought to you. Take the money and divide it into six parts. Distribute five parts to needy families and take the sixth for yourself.' But no, this voice spoke within me only after I had decided to give the entire sum.

"This gave him away. When at first I had assumed that the entire sum was meant for me, he was silent. No wonder: he was perfectly satisfied with my decision. Only after the Almighty had privileged me to realize why I had been given this money, did he wake up. Obviously, he did not say, 'keep the money!' Oh no, he is far too clever at this craft for that – he knew that I would recognize the source of such a desire and reject it immediately.

Thus, along he comes, this master of cunning, with an utterly pious and logical suggestion – anything to prevent me from acting on the role which Divine Providence so clearly designated for me to play in delivering a family from distress. "So, I called the Chassid back and gave him the 300 rubles."

18

Soul Within Soul

"Let us return to our previous discussion about the unique quality of Chabad Chassidus. During one of our early morning sessions, Rabbi Osher called particular attention to a prominent discourse presented by the seventh leader of Chabad, Rabbi Menachem Mendel, regarding the significance of the Chassidic dimension of *Torah* (later published as *On the Essence of Chassidus*[61]). The discourse comprises an in-depth analysis as to the nature of the Chassidic school of thought, especially Chabad Chassidus, and how it differs from the levels of *Torah* that preceded it.

"I ought to advise you, Jay, that this discussion requires a bit of concentration, because it references some Kabbalistic teachings, though quite basic. I assure you that, with a bit of attentiveness, you will have no problem comprehending the lesson, as long as you don't become sidetracked by some of the novel terminology.

"The Rebbe begins by sharing four reasons explaining the distinction and need of Chassidus, based on earlier sources and manuscripts.

"The first and most basic reason is that during the time of the Baal Shem Tov, the Jewish world, as we already know, was in a state of faint. They were physically crushed and impoverished by massacres (in particular, those of the Cossack leader Chmelnitzki in 1648-1649). They also were spiritually bereft and despondent, engendered, in good measure, by the false messiahs.

"This unfortunate combination caused religious observance to seriously wane. It was especially true in Eastern Europe, where Chassidism began. The Baal Shem Tov sought to awaken the people of Israel from their

---

[61] Published in 1978; Kehot Publishing Society.

trance-like condition through the use of the *Torah*'s most potent esoteric dimension—Kabbalah/Chassidus.

"The second reason is based on the Talmudic dictum that 'a Chassid— literally pious one—is someone who goes beyond the letter of the law.'[62] In this dictum, Chassidus sees the idea of serving G-d with true selflessness.

> The unique objective of Chassidus is to transform the core character of one's natural personality.

"While spiritual fulfillment is commended in Judaism, Chassidus teaches that, in order to achieve higher levels of service, one must reach beyond the call of duty—the minimal requirements for G-dly service and the quest for personal gains.

"In this regard, the purpose of Chassidus is to help the individual achieve the stated sublime goal of piety—'Chassid'—service out of love of the Creator, as opposed to just the minimal legal requirement.

"Third, the unique objective of Chassidus is to transform the core character and emotional attributes of one's natural personality. This transformation includes, not only one's negative and unpleasant qualities but one's instinctively good and positive traits as well.

"Chassidus teaches that one should not merely strive to improve one's character by embracing new habits and manners. Rather, a person should completely change the quality, depth, and maturity of his or her nature.

"This is to say that all our traits should become intentionally holy,

---

[62] Long before the 18th century, when Rabbi Israel Baal Shem Tov founded the Chassidic movement; the term chassid was used in the *Talmud* to refer to a humble and altruistic person, who went beyond the letter of the law in observance of *Torah*. The word chassid is derived from the word chessed, kindness. The chassid is both kind to his fellow and, according to the *Zohar*, seeks to do kindness to G-d. 'He is like a son who exerts himself for his father and mother, whom he loves more than himself. He would sacrifice his life for their sake, to redeem them would they be held in captivity.' Similarly, the chassid is motivated solely by the desire to serve G-d and redeem and reveal His presence that is held 'captive' in this world (*Tanya*, chapter 10, citing Ra'aya Meemna, Tetze).

rather than routine and instinctive by nature. The practices of Chassidic philosophy slowly accomplishes this change.

"Finally, the fourth essential purpose given for the revelation of Kabbalah/Chassidus is to afford all people an opportunity to grasp Divinity, even those who do not possess particularly lofty souls, or who have not yet refined themselves.

"Chassidus maintains that, through its teachings, the esoteric lessons of Kabbalah can be made understandable to all. Hence, by contemplating the ideas taught in Chassidus, everyone can gain insight into the Divine Creator. This helps refine a person. Likewise, it adds depth and vigor to one's ritual observance.

"Having established the four classic reasons for the revelation of Chassidus, the Rebbe proceeds to assert that they fall somewhat short. They all fail to capture the true essence of Chassidus, but rather are components or manifestations of the essence.

"Then the Rebbe offers a fifth explanation, advancing the idea that a soul has two qualities: It both transcends the body and also descends into the body, permeating it from its highest faculty—the head—down to the limbs with the simplest function—the feet. In this way, the fifth explanation frames the esoteric teachings as the soul of *Torah* in its essential state, as it transcends the body—four levels of manifestation.

"The Rebbe proceeds to draw a three-way parallel among the four levels of *Torah*-Pardes, the four spiritual worlds, and the four lower levels of soul. Each of the four levels of *Torah* corresponds to one of the four descending worlds and on a micro level, to one of the four categories of soul.

"There are generally four metaphysical worlds described in Kabbalah: Atzilus (Emanation), Beriah (Creation), Yetzirah (Formation), Assiyah (Action), Atzilus being the highest and Assiyah, the lowest.

"Each world comprises ten Supernal Attributes, three intellectual and seven emotional. The intellectual attributes of each world—Chochmah, Binah, and Da'as (wisdom, understanding, and knowledge)—manifest themselves through the *Torah* as it applies to the given world. The *Torah* of a particular world serves as its creative force. Each of the levels of Pardes dominates in one of the four worlds respectively.

"The four levels of *Torah*-Pardes, generally, are known to be derived from G-d's essence, nevertheless, they are affected by Tizmtzum— contractions and concealment—as they traverse through the chain of descent of the spiritual 'worlds.'

"According to the mystical teachings, G-d creates each of the worlds by gradually reducing the extent of His Divine manifestation by means of *Torah* revelation. This process produces a descending series of spiritual realms, or 'worlds' in the terminology of Kabbalah, that are intermediate realities, or levels of Divine consciousness, between G-d's essence and our physical world.

"The *Torah* of each world serves as the 'blueprint' of that world, inasmuch as each world is designed according to the Divine intellect manifest within it. While G-d is hidden within the nature of each world, He is revealed within the *Torah* of a given world.

"Although the *Torah* remains essentially unchanged, as it descends from one world to the next, it is projected divergently onto the screens of these worlds and, hence, perceived differently. In the basic scheme of creation, no world experiences a revelation of the *Torah*—consciousness of G-d— not endemic to that world. Such a revelation would be supernatural and miraculous in the context of that world. Therefore, each world is 'locked,' so to speak, in the Divinely-ordained parameters of its 'natural' or 'native' G-d-consciousness.

"The nature of each of the four descending worlds, accordingly, is determined by its respective *Torah* revelation, that is, one of the four levels of Pardes.

"Each of the four worlds is limited and fixed by its own defining qualities based on its connection with one of the levels of Pardes. Even the loftiest and abstract world of Atzilus is associated with the highest level of Pardes, namely, 'Sod'.

"Similarly, this phenomenon is reflected in the person's soul, a microcosm of the soul of the universe. Humans, too, have four basic levels of soul corresponding to the four descending levels of Pardes, as well as the four worlds.

"In the end, the Rebbe compares the mystical teachings of Chassidus—the most 'inner' explanation of *Torah* and its true infinite essence—to an even higher level of one's soul: A fifth level known as Y'chida—complete 'singular unity' with G-d.

"The implication is that, while the four levels of Pardes, as stated, traverse and are affected by the four metaphysical worlds, Chassidus remains unrestricted and unaffected by Tizmtzum. This is why it is not listed among the four levels, similar to the way a person's soul is not listed in relation to his bodily organs, such as his head or foot. The fourth level, the Kabbalistic interpretation, is called 'the soul of the *Torah*,' because it contains the metaphysical explanation of *Torah*. Similarly, Chassidus is called the 'soul of the soul;' this is why it's so unique and necessary.

> Chassidus is called the 'soul of the soul.

"This idea is similar, though not identical, to the way Chassidus describes the function of the Tabernacle (and later the Temple) in our world. The Divine consciousness that existed inside the Holy of Holies of the Tabernacle was not acclimated to one of the cascading worlds of the creation process.

"The level of Divine consciousness present in the Holy of Holies was above the world of Atzilus. Because the revelation bypassed the worlds, the Ark and the tablets contained miraculous qualities. For example, they miraculously transcended time and space. The Ark, simultaneously, occupied and did not occupy space, and the inside of the letter Samech and final Mem of the tablets were suspended in midair."

"What does that mean, Danni," asks Jay.

"To answer your question, Jay, the Divine Presence rested in the Holy of Holies; the inner sanctum of the Temple in Jerusalem, above the Ark housing the tablets, upon which the Ten Commandments were engraved. The Mishnah teaches that the place of the Ark was dimensionless space. When you measured it, it took up 2.5 cubits; when you measured around it, it took up no space at all.[63] So, it was in two superimposed states, just like the duality of the quantum.

"Regarding the Samech and final Mem," I explain, "the engraving of the Tablets was miraculous. Although the letters were engraved completely through and through, the centers of the letters Final Mem and Samech, like the 'zero,' did not fall out, but remained suspended in midair.

"To conclude, the Rebbe illustrates how Chassidus unites the four levels of Pardes by revealing the essential common essence running through them, because essence permeates all manifestations.

"As the soul of Chassidus permeates the four levels, they become illuminated with the 'light of Chassidus.' They each become alive, soulful, and imbued with meaning.

"Because Chassidus stems from unrestricted essence, it contains the capacity to incorporate, in its explanation, other forms of historical Jewish thought. It can unite the different disciplines, Kabbalah, Rabbinic teachings, and Jewish philosophy—Chakira—by upping the level of the discussion to a higher place in the sublime metaphysical structure, a level where complementary or initially contradictory concepts of *Torah* can become synthesized into one. Thus, diverse and conflicting ideas can be transformed to harmonious partners.

"Chabad views *Tanya* as the defining Chassidic text and a subsequent

---

[63] Yoma, 21 a.

stage of Jewish mystical evolution. This intellectual 'exposé' of Jewish wisdom synthesizes Chassidic mysticism and Jewish soulfulness with other historical components of written and Rabbinic literature, embodied in the *Torah*, the *Talmud*, Medieval philosophy, Musar (ethical) literature, and Lurianic Kabbalah.

"The following simplified analogy summarizes the idea: The *Torah* is G-d's knowledge, meaning it is infinite. Therefore, there are different levels of the *Torah*, each deeper than the other. The hidden mystical aspect of the *Torah* is called Kabbalah, which often is compared to wine: Just as wine is hidden in the grape, and by squeezing the grape, wine is obtained; a similar analogy can be made with the *Torah* and Kabbalah.

Chassidus unifies all the different levels of Torah.

"However, the deepest and highest level of the *Torah* is Chassidus, which is compared to oil. Oil floats on top of all liquids, indicating its superior quality. At the same time, oil makes everything oily. Another characteristic of oil is that all substances contain oil. If any substance is pressed enough, oil will be obtained; therefore, oil is contained in the essence of everything.

"Chassidus is also the essence of the *Torah* and within it is contained all the other levels. In Chassidus, not only are the mystical and Kabalistic dimensions discussed, but all the other levels are an integral part. Chassidus unifies all the different levels of *Torah* for the purpose of elevating the world and the person to make the world and the person G-dly. As a result, the world becomes a dwelling place for G-d and causes the coming of Moshiach (Messiah), the ultimate purpose of creation.

ORDINARY BREAD:

"Bread from earth," which is the product of hard physical labor, is a metaphor for the "Nigleh"—revealed interpretations of the *Torah*, found in the *Talmud*, which require arduous analysis, questioning, etc.

Manna: "Bread from heaven'—on the other hand, represents the mystical teachings of the *Torah*, which are of such a "Heavenly" nature that there is no disagreement, argument, etc.

Logically speaking, a person might think that it is necessary to have a firm grounding in the classic texts, and achieve a certain degree of spiritual greatness before one can progress to the study of mysticism. However, the *Torah* teaches here that even the wicked individuals who complained to Moses ate manna.

From this we can learn that it is appropriate for people from all walks of life to study the mystical teachings of the *Torah*—particularly as they are formulated clearly and methodically in the teachings of Chabad.

(Lubavitcher Rebbe R' M. Mendel Schneerson, *Likutei Sichos* vol. 4, pp. 1038-9)

19

TANYA

"The renowned book *Tanya*, authored by Rabbi Schneur Zalman of Liadi, is the foremost work on Chabad's mystical theology, as it defines its general principles and method. The subsequent extensive library of the Chabad School, authored by successive leaders, builds upon the approach of *Tanya*.

"*Tanya* was printed in the year 1797, after hundreds of manuscripts had circulated throughout the cities and towns of the Russian empire. The common method of handwritten reproduction resulted in a disproportionate number of errors, ergo, the need for its formal printing.

"Named for the first word of the volume, *Tanya*, also known as Likutei Amarim—Collected Discourses—serves as the basis of Chabad Chassidic mysticism. It was written for those craving Divine knowledge.

"Unlike the renowned *Moreh Nevuchim*-Guide for the Perplexed—authored by Maimonides 6 centuries earlier for people who are confused or entangled in the web of philosophy and skepticism, *Tanya* is intended for people of unshakeable faith. It is geared towards sincere people searching for deeper ways to connect with their Heavenly Maker.

> Tanya teaches how to serve G-d in one's daily life.

"While its genre is Jewish spirituality, psychology, and theology, the work is a revised version of the advice and counsel, given by its author, to questions posed by followers during personal counseling sessions.

"*Tanya* teaches how to serve G-d in one's daily life, putting novel interpretations of Jewish mysticism into practical articulation and definition. It emphasizes the need to use reason in striving to know G-d and His purpose for creation. A diverse range of Chassidic schools venerate the work, even as its meditative advice may be embraced to a lesser extent.

"*Tanya* is noted for the way it fuses the revealed dimension of *Torah*—based primarily on the *Talmud*—with the hidden aspect of *Torah*. It draws on the *Zohar*, teachings of the Holy Ari, Rabbi Moses Cordovero,[64] and other Kabbalistic works. Mostly, however, it is based on the teachings of the Baal Shem Tov and the Maggid of Mezritch.

"*Tanya* focuses on the required emotions of love and fear of the Supernal Creator and the Baal Shem Tov's primary teachings, as their prerequisite. Of particular importance, is the principle of 'constant re-creation and the idea of omnipotent Divine Providence.'

"We will elaborate on those ideas later in the discussion, Jay, but, for now, a brief depiction will suffice. The first principle maintains that the Almighty constantly re-creates and sustains the existence of every object and every living creature. The second key belief is that the Almighty exercises complete control and oversight over every detail of creation.

"In Chabad, the *Tanya* is said to be the 'Written *Torah*' of Chassidic philosophy, with the many subsequent Chabad writings analogous to 'Oral *Torah*' explanation. This notion is buttressed by the fact that *Tanya* is the first work of Chassidic philosophy recorded by its own author. In contrast, the preceding works of the Ba'al Shem Tov and the Maggid of Mezritch were transcribed by their disciples.

---

[64] Moses Cordovero—or Ramak (an acronym taken from the first letters of his title and name, Rabbi Moses Cordovero), as he is commonly known—was born in 1522 to a distinguished family of Spanish descent, apparently originally from the town of Cordova. Although it is not certain that Ramak himself was born in Safed, he spent most of his life in that holy city, the home of Kabbalah. At the young age of 48, Rabbi Moses Cordovero passed away in Safed on 23rd of Tammuz 1570. Among the great luminaries of Kabbalah, Rabbi Moses Cordovero holds a particularly important place as one of the most prolific and systematic exponents of the teachings of the *Zohar*, as well as the writings of almost all the early Kabbalists.

At age 20, Ramak became a student of his brother-in-law, Rabbi Shlomo HaLevi Alkabetz (author of the Lecha Dodi hymn), in the esoteric aspect of *Torah*—the Kabbalah. Despite Ramak's formidable achievements in *Talmud*, he states that, until he began learning Kabbalah; he was, as if, asleep and pursuing idle thoughts (Pardes Rimonim, Intro.) Ramak became one of the leading Kabbalists in Safed. He acted as spokesman for the group of Kabbalists, headed by Rabbi Alkabetz; and he wrote several treatises, explaining the fallacies of philosophy. In addition, he exhorted *Torah* students everywhere to study Kabbalah.

"The implication is that the teachings of Chabad Chassidus are all an exposition of *Tanya*, just as Judaism teaches that the entire purpose of the Oral *Torah* is to elucidate the Written *Torah*.

"Another interesting parallel is that Likutei Amarim, the first and foremost section of *Tanya,* comprises 53 chapters, ostensibly, corresponding to the 53 portions comprising the Written *Torah.*"

Jay sits there gazing at me with his eyebrows knitted for a long moment.

"It seems like things have come full circle," he notes. "If I understood you correctly, Chassidus was conceived out of the need to reach out and to include the simple, unlettered folk—the majority of Jews who found themselves disenfranchised from Jewish life as a result of its exclusive, erudite, and scholarly nature. Yet, it appears Rabbi Schneur Zalman turned all that on its head.

"Wasn't it the Baal Shem Tov's intention to underscore the simplicity of Judaism through the innovation of the individual's ability to serve G-d through simple faith, fervent prayer, and the simple joy of a Mitzvah? From what you describe, the book of *Tanya* and subsequent Chassidic teachings are profound works, depicting a complex theological system. Isn't that somewhat of a contradiction? Does this not once again alienate the simple unlearned folk or, for that matter, the multitude of Jews who are not Jewishly literate?"

"Your question, Jay, is obviously an important one," I concur. "In fact, R' Osher spent quite some time addressing this conundrum. However, when one develops an understanding of Chassidus, particularly regarding why it has only recently come to fruition, the answer becomes apparent. For now, let me just share a thought or two that may somewhat clarify the matter.

"R' Schneur Zalman did not come to rescind or diminish the Baal Shem Tov's teachings and innovations, in any way. He merely added another dimension. Chabad is not a breakaway from the philosophy of the founders of Chassidism; rather, it is an extrapolation, remaining completely in sync with its source. Accordingly, the trail the Baal Shem Tov blazed remains viable and intact—his mantra that 'G-d seeks the heart,' remains as true today as it was then, especially for the simple and unlearned folk. R' Schneur Zalman presented a profound cognitive structure for those who are capable of more.

"This said, I must add a vital observation: In our modern and advanced age, the idea of simple-minded people of yesteryear no longer exists; it is a phenomenon of the past. Hence, we are all capable of more."

> Chabad is not a breakaway from the philosophy of the founders of Chassidism, but, rather an extrapolation.

"How do you mean?" Jay inquires.

"I think that we should leave this for a future discussion," I suggest. "R' Osher, after all, devoted an entire lesson to this issue. Let me just throw out something for you to ponder. You certainly are aware that if we were to go back a mere 2 hundred years, we would find that, generally, people did not think critically for themselves. People, for the most part, followed traditional paths and authoritative figures.

"Critical thinking about life's source and purpose began with the emergence of the enlightenment. The timing of Chassidic philosophy and, especially, of the Chabad school, vis-à-vis the onset of the enlightenment, provides a clue as to the need for the discipline of Chassidus at that time in history."

"Do you mean to say," asks Jay, "that, somehow, this potent body of knowledge was hidden away for thousands of years, preserved for that exact time and place?

"That's a fascinating concept, Danni."

"Indeed, it is. We'll come back to this subject," I reply.

20

A Time to Rethink

At this point, the Captain's voice over the loudspeaker interrupts our conversation: "Ladies and gentlemen, we have begun our initial descent into Warsaw's Chopin International Airport..." Time passed quickly; we agreed to end the conversation for now, but to continue, perhaps sometime during the mission or, at the latest, on the trip home. We turn our attention toward getting ready for landing and the momentous journey ahead. I take out the travel portfolio issued by the mission organizers and check the schedule to get an idea of the immediate agenda. The program reads:

Monday, April 27:

- Arrive in Warsaw and meet local staff
- Check-in to hotel
- Overnight—Warsaw, Poland

Tuesday, April 28:

- Orientation tour of Warsaw (2 hours)
- Ceremony at the Treblinka Memorial

Then, I reach for the pamphlet on Treblinka and begin to read the detailed bone-chilling description of its infamous history:

> Before its liberation by the Allies, the retreating German army liquidated the camp and destroyed whatever evidence remained of the atrocities committed within its gates. For many decades, the only evidence of the horrors at Treblinka came from testimonies of Nazi SS-men stationed there, as well as, a few Jewish survivors who were willing to share their stories. Then, in January 2012, British forensic archaeologist, Caroline Sturdy Colls, uncovered previously unknown mass graves in the Treblinka camp. Our current understanding is that the Nazi's murdered more than 850,000 people there, the vast majority of whom were Jews.

While Dachau and Buchenwald were horrible places where many people died, they were Concentration Camps, not Extermination Centers, designed for the express purpose of annihilating the Jews of Europe. The little-known camp of Treblinka, hidden in the remote forests of northeastern Poland, was one of six extermination centers.

An information pamphlet available at the entrance to the former camp at Treblinka says, 'Within a short time of its opening, over 800,000 victims of Jews from Poland, Austria, Belgium, Czechoslovakia, France, Greece, Yugoslavia, Germany, and the Soviet Union were callously murdered.'

From Warsaw, the route to Treblinka starts with crossing the river Vistula, then turning onto Highway 18 northeast towards Bialystok. Highway 18 is a two-lane concrete road that goes through mile after mile of dense forest. During the war, Polish and Jewish Partisans hid in these woods along with escaped Russian Prisoners of War and fought the Nazis. They blew up bridges and train tracks to disrupt German logistics and placed land mines to kill columns of German soldiers. Twenty two kilometers from Treblinka, the route turns southeast off of Highway 18. The farther you travel down this road, the farther you seem to go back in time. When you finally arrive at the entrance to the site of the former extermination camp, you are on an old logging road that goes through another dense forest.

At this time, the Captain announces our final approach. We make our final preparations for landing and I continue reading:

The extermination camp in Treblinka was built in the middle of 1942 near the already existing labor camp. It was surrounded by a fence and rows of barbed wire along which there were watchtowers with machine guns every ten meters. The main part of the camp constituted two buildings in which there were thirteen gas chambers altogether. Two thousand people could be put to death at a time in them. Death by suffocation with fumes came after 10-15 minutes. The bodies of the victims were cremated outdoors on big grates. The ashes were mixed with sand and buried in one spot.

Killing took place with great speed. The whole process, from arriving at the camp railroad and ending with removing the corpses from the gas chambers, lasted about 2 hours. Treblinka was known among the Nazis as an example of good organization of a death camp. It was a real extermination center.

By November of 1943, the camp was no longer in existence. The Germans had been losing the war on the Russian front and were in retreat. Treblinka was completely dismantled and destroyed when the whole camp was liquidated. Among the few survivors were those who escaped during the uprising and joined the partisans in the forests.

Since the Allies discovery of Treblinka and its liquidation before the war's end, Holocaust deniers have claimed that no proof of the exterminations was found. The evidence uncovered by Caroline Colls ends the myth that the Treblinka camp was nothing more than a transit camp that moved Jews from Poland to the other concentration camps across Europe.

By now, we already touched down, taxied to the gate, and began to deplane. The local time is 9:00 p.m. We gather our luggage and move quickly through customs. By 11:00 p.m., our group of 43 is settling in comfortably at the hotel, where I share a room with Jay. Both of us, understandably, are exhausted and went straight to bed, without engaging in much conversation. Breakfast is 8:00 a.m. I'm out of bed and showered by 7:00, leaving me enough time for my prayers. Jay sleeps a little longer, but is up by 7:30. At 9:00, we board the bus for an orientation tour of the city.

We have a nice time learning about the history of Poland's capital, visiting the Old Town, the Ghetto Memorial, the Monument of The Warsaw Uprising, and Tomb of the Unknown Soldier. Riding along the Royal Route, we take in its beautiful palaces, aristocratic residences, famous statues, and historic churches. By noon, we're headed for lunch. To my surprise, the restaurant is a Glatt Kosher establishment, a place called Galil, housed in one of the old townhouses on Ulica Zielna and bordering the area of the former Warsaw Ghetto. This is a true delight considering that, otherwise, it would be one of those frozen airline meals for me.

Galil offers a fusion of Israeli, Arabic, Mediterranean, and Polish influences. I enjoyed my choice of date syrup-glazed chicken breast, served with Lyonnais potatoes and a fattoush salad. At 1:00 p.m., we set out for the Treblinka Extermination Camp.

At Treblinka, there is a large memorial stone at the entrance to the cobblestone path up to the virtual cemetery. A map on the stone shows the gravel pit in the center, with the labor camp to the left and the extermination camp to the right. Six memorial stones, set close together, are located just beyond the stone with the map. Each of the six is inscribed with a different language, including Hebrew, English, and Polish. The inscription says that the camp was in operation from July 1942 to August 1943, during which 800 thousand Jews were killed there.

A storehouse at the camp was disguised as a train station. Nearby, is the end of the railroad line with a stone platform to the left. When the camp was in operation, there was a real train platform in this spot and behind it, the storehouse disguised as a train depot that contained clothing and other items the victims had brought with them. A line of stones represents the 10 different countries, including Greece, Czechoslovakia, Poland, Bulgaria, and others from which Jews were transported by train to be exterminated in this remote, G-d-forsaken spot in the forest.

Just south of the recreated stone train platform are "burial pits," for those who died during transportation. East of the burial pits, according to a map in the camp pamphlet, was an "execution site," disguised as a hospital. Farther east, half way up the gentle slope to where a symbolic graveyard now stands, there were three old gas chambers, and a short distance to the north, 10 new gas chambers were built. The first gas chambers used carbon monoxide. Some of the later gas chambers were disguised to look like showers; these used the insecticide Zyklon B for gassing. A short distance farther up the slope to the east of the gas chambers were "cremation pyres."

We meet up with other missions from around the world for a memorial service. By now, several hundred people gathered at the symbolic crematoria pit, including Rabbis and holocaust survivors. We hear speeches that decry the horror of the Holocaust. "It's hard to grasp what happened here just 70 years ago," said one speaker, "I stand here today emotional, moved to tears by the great pain of my brothers, my people, whose ashes are scattered here around us. I'm proud to be part of the continued existence of the Jews despite everything," he declared.

"Is there a single Jewish heart that does not tremble from the intensity of the pain and the greatness of the achievement," wondered another. "Maybe, what we need to do in this place is simply to be silent. To be silent, and to listen to the silence and hear the screams of the hundreds of thousands of children, mothers, fathers, grandfathers, and grandmothers. I can hear their screams..."

In a tone of defiance, the final speaker asserts, "We are gathered here in order never to forget our brothers and sisters who were killed here. 'Your people will rebuild the ancient ruins and will raise up the age-old foundations; you will be called Repairer of Broken Walls, Restorer of Streets with Dwellings.'"[65] Six candles, symbolizing 6 million Holocaust victims, are lit, followed by a moment of silence.

The entire experience was extremely emotional. After the service, people just stood there frozen in their places, not able to speak a word. During those solemn moments, something overtook me. Without thinking the matter through, I called out: "How many of you have put on Tefillin today?" I waited while everyone turned their attention towards me and, then, repeated the question: "How many of you, here, have put on Tefillin today? After a moment of odd silence, a hand went up, followed by a few more. In total, maybe, 10 or 12 hands went up.

"We're all here because we care," I found myself saying, "we care about Jews, and we care about Judaism. Yet, I ask you to consider this important question: What are you doing about it? What exactly are we trying to preserve here? What do you perceive the future of Judaism to

---

[65] Isaiah 58:12.

be: a country, a race? Is there any hope for Jewish continuity without its religious dimension?" The words kept coming. "Are the Nazis continuing their assault on us from within their graves, by virtue of our religious indifference and assimilation?"

"I urge each and everyone here today to do something for the sake of all the Jewish people, whose lives were ended in this hellhole. At this auspicious moment, I ask you to take upon yourselves one new Mitzvah, as a gift and vindication to the hundreds of thousands of souls whose bodies were destroyed in this horrific abyss where we stand right now." I felt like going on, but forced myself to stop. My words were met with initial silence and then, with warm applause, maybe, out of pity for me or, maybe, out of respect, I could not be sure.

Until this day, I'm puzzled by my uncharacteristic, involuntary eruption. But, I know that it came from some place deep within me, far beyond my conscious understanding. What I could be sure of is that I was no longer inconspicuous. For the rest of the trip I would be known to everyone for what I did in Treblinka. But that was not, necessarily, a bad thing, in fact, the incident lead to many intense conversations about G-d and religion over the remaining course of the trip and in some cases, well after.

Though, I have to be honest, I was apprehensive about facing Jay after the incident. Oh, how embarrassed he must have been at his friend making a jerk of himself. I was relieved to discover that was not the case. When I met up with Jay, he seemed cool, maybe, even a bit proud of me, or was that my imagination? Nevertheless, the next morning, as we arose, he asked me if I would be willing to help him put on the Tefillin, something he hasn't done since his Bar Mitzvah.

Witnessing firsthand the horrible history of the Holocaust was not an easy experience. During the compact week, we were subjected to sights that never fail to shock even the most hardened individual. From the Warsaw cemetery to the heart breaking remains of the former Warsaw Ghetto, to the various death camps, with our own eyes, we saw the unbelievable and listened to the unthinkable, trying to take in and cope with the appalling cruelty that unfolded in the heart of Europe in the first half of the 20th century.

Talking to some of the people in the group, the recurring lesson from it all seemed to be that the Jewish people cannot be defeated. The Nazis may have murdered our ancestors, but they could never murder our spirit. Despite the efforts to tear us down, now we contain a resurrected spirit and passion to live on. Fair enough, but there is more. This experience should wake one up, and make one think and rethink. The experience should shatter our existing paradigm of life. It should make us ponder the true purpose of life; to consider and reconsider the miraculous survival of the Jewish people, and what it means. The experience should make one think in such a way that leads the individual to commit to true Jewish continuity. This continuity can be based only on its heart, its religious essence.

> The experience should shatter our existing paradigm of life.

With all this going on, Jay and I did not really get much of an opportunity to continue our discussion during the mission to Poland. By early Friday morning, we were off to Israel. We spent Shabbos in Jerusalem, the city of hope and promise; the place where faith melds millennia of dreams and prayers ascend directly to heaven. Home to some of Israel's finest cultural institutions, museums, restaurants, and hotels, Jerusalem is a remarkable city, where the past and future converge to kindle the eternal Jewish spirit. It is a glorious symbol of our eternal heritage and the embodiment of the Jewish people's permanence and resolute commitment to survival.

The Kosel—Western-Wall complex—is packed each day with thousands of people from Israel and abroad, celebrating different Jewish life cycle events, taking part in daily prayer services or, simply, visiting the area for some inspiration or to become acquainted with this much talked about religious and historical symbol. Friday evening at the Western Wall, we experience the vibrancy and diversity of Jewish traditions and cultures, as all chant the special Friday evening prayers known as Kabbolas Shabbos—the joyous Jewish ritual of welcoming the Sabbath. Jews around the world have recited these prayers for centuries. The mixture of silent prayers, singing, and spontaneous dancing made this a truly moving experience.

Our Shabbos morning visit to the Great Synagogue was another wonderful moment. The size and majesty of the edifice felt awesome; the service, cantor, and choir were inspirational.

The food and accommodations at the King David Hotel were truly delightful, as well.

We spent the next few days touring the country, attending ceremonies, including an affirmation ceremony atop Masada. We visited the Israel Museum and the Beit She'an Archaeological Park. I don't need to say that our stay in Israel was filled with incredible inspiration and pride. But, nothing could give the visit more meaning than the underlying contrast with the trip's first segment—Poland. Coming as an epilogue to witnessing the horrors and destruction of that bastion of world Jewry during the Holocaust, it could not help but paint an awesome portrait of victory. It could not help but declare that "Am Yisrael Chai"—"The nation of Israel is alive!"—even as Hitler and his Nazi cohorts are rotting in hell; forever regarded as the most evil monsters the world had ever encountered. So much for their Herrenvolk aspirations.

21

IDENTITY THEFT

Wednesday morning, our group gathers at Ben Gurion Airport to check in for our return flight to the United States. Again, Jay and I get seats near each other. As we board the plane, Jay turns to me with a slight grin and says, "Looking forward to another interesting twelve hours. You plan on relating more of your study sessions with the Rabbi, I hope."

"Do I have a choice in the matter," I ask.

"No," responds Jay, "As long as you understand that."

"I'm only kidding, Jay." I assure him, "I enjoy sharing these ideas with you, as much as you appreciate hearing them; besides, this stuff is meant to share."

After takeoff, we begin to engage in some small talk, mostly reflecting on the stimulating events of the past 10 days. We both agree that it was a highly moving and life-changing experience that could benefit most people, especially unaffiliated and non-active Jews.

"You know, Danni," Jay remarks to my chagrin, "The most moving and memorable moment of the entire adventure for me, believe it or not, was your impromptu speech at the memorial event in Treblinka. I haven't stopped thinking about your words, 'We're all here because we care about Jews and about Judaism... yet, what are you doing about it? What exactly are we trying to preserve? What do you perceive the future of Judaism to be, a country, a race? Is there any hope for Jewish continuity without its religious dimension...?' Those are powerful questions that, in the past, I haven't given much thought and, for which I have no answers.

> Is there any hope for Jewish continuity without its religious dimension?

"I used to think that Israel, the Jewish State and homeland, is the complete answer, but I've come to realize that the emphasis on Israel puts the cart before the horse. Israel is not the reason for the Jewish people to exist. Rather, the Land of Israel is important because of the existence of the Jewish people. True, the Jewish people can only flourish to the maximum extent in the Land of Israel and fulfill their national destiny, but the Jewish people survived in exile for 2 millennia without a land. However, no Jewish community ever survived for any period of time, without *Torah*.

> No Jewish community ever survived, for any period of time, without Torah.

"Trips to Israel can be a powerful emotional experience, but the power of that experience, usually, is directly proportional to the degree to which being a Jew is a primary aspect of self-definition, which is less true of most young American Jews. Likely, they view a common culture, particular sense of humor, or taste for certain ethnic foods—qualities shared with many non-Jews—as central to their Jewish identity. Their Jewish identity is shallow, because it does not center on religious beliefs or practices.

"Birthright was started in 1994, with the goal of bringing young Jews to the homeland to find or develop roots within the state of Israel. Jewish young adults between 18 and 27 get the opportunity to go to Israel for 10 days completely free, just because they are Jewish. It since has become a prerequisite for any young Jew who wants to keep their parents happy, knowing their child is getting in touch with their heritage. They make sure their passport is in good standing and their bags are packed.

"The kids actually end up having a great time. They soon realize the trip is mostly partying in Israel and getting to meet other young Jews, whose parents were also convinced this is a 'spiritual trip.'

"In the end, if being Jewish is a slight matter, it does not really matter whether the Jewish people continue to exist. If the continued existence of the Jewish people is insignificant, of what importance is a state, primarily of Jewish citizens? Israel works most powerfully on those who, at minimum, have been entranced by the Jewish story; wondering how this people, of all the peoples of the world, preserved its national identity, removed from their land for over 2 thousand years. How did we survive? What did we find so important to preserve that we were willing to sacrifice so much to maintain our identity as Jews? Our forebears were willing to die for Judaism; yet, we're hardly willing to live for it.

How can I be charged with the task of preserving the Jewish future, when I don't know the first thing about our Jewish religion?

"I mean, here I am a proud Jew, who is even active in the Jewish community, yet I haven't a clue what Judaism really means to my very self, let alone anyone else. It is one thing, albeit unfortunate, to be assimilated, to have lost your Jewish identity and connection. But it's quite another thing to be a proud, active Jew and not know the true nature of what you're a part of. It's kind of like the proverbial messenger who forgot the message.

"I cannot help but ask myself, whether I'm truly fit to be in a leadership position. I have to admit that I'm one of those who resonate with a Judaism that is devoid of its religious dimension. So, as you well point out, I'm left to grapple with what I am ultimately left with? What is the value and meaning of a Judaism that is bereft of its vital religious essence? Sadly, I don't have an answer to the question.

"Ironically, I'm not, in the least bit, an anomaly. I am actually part of the norm when it comes to Jewish lay leadership these days. It's like, that's the way it's meant to be; no one questions or tries to change it. To be honest, it's crazy how normal it actually is. What future can Judaism hold, if its very leadership contains but a foggy notion of what it is they're trying to preserve?"

I listen to Jay, not knowing whether to feel bad or good for him. Obviously, he is having an epiphany and is unnerved. But, in reality, his eyes are being opened to the unwavering truth and despite the pain, it is no doubt a healthy thing. I can only tell him that I relate to the way he is feeling, because I've been there myself.

"Sorry, Danni, I didn't mean to get off like that, but I feel like I've been misled and I am misleading others. I don't even know the Hebrew Aleph-Bet, how am I a leader? How can I be charged with the task of preserving the Jewish future or, as the prevailing buzzword goes, 'Jewish Continuity,' when I don't know the first thing about our Jewish religion and heritage? Isn't that like the proverbial adage, 'The blind leading the blind?'"

"Well congratulations on your epiphany, Jay. Now what do you plan to do about it?"

"Do about it? About what? I'm merely making an observation, albeit an uncomfortable one," asserts Jay. "What do you expect me to do, change reality?"

"No," I say "Only to change yourself!"

"I need time to sort things out, Danni. I can't think about what I should do or not do at this very moment."

"Fair enough, Jay, I understand where you're coming from, I'll respect your wishes and drop the subject for now. I'm always available for you, if and when you decide to talk about it."

"Thank you, Danni, that's very kind of you. You're a good friend and a true blessing in my life," Jay offers. "I hope you really understand that I'm not trying to push you away or anything; it's just that I need time. I need some more time."

In truth, I did understand where Jay was coming from; yet, I was still somewhat perplexed. Something didn't feel quite right about the situation. Jay seemed a little overly emotional or stressed about his circumstance. Yes, he may have realized that his life's paradigm was shattered in some way, but it's not like he couldn't fix it. Many people realize half way through life that they're cruising down the wrong highway, only to make a U-turn and pick up on the right road.

Among the many great figures in Jewish history, R' Akiva's influence and stature is a source of inspiration throughout the ages. The *Talmud* compares him to Moses,[66] the ultimate compliment within Judaism. His story is one of the most inspirational Jewish stories:

The *Midrash* relates that during the first four decades of his life, Rabbi Akiva was a completely unlettered and ignorant Jew. Moreover, later in life, he freely admitted that when he was ignorant, he possessed a deep and abiding hatred toward the *Torah* scholars of his time.

While shepherding his flock in the hills of Judah, one day R' Akiva became thirsty and went to a brook to take a drink. As he was drawing water, something caught his eye. He saw drops of water falling on a huge stone; directly where the drops were falling was a deep hole in the stone. The shepherd was fascinated. He gazed at the drops and at the stone. "What mighty power there is in a drop of water," mused the shepherd.

"What are you gazing at," he heard someone ask. It was Rachel, his wife and master's daughter. "Look what the little drops of water did to the rock," R' Akiva exclaimed. "Do you think there is hope for me? Suppose I began to study *Torah*, could my heart be penetrated? I'm already 40 years old! Is it not too late to start?"

"It is never too late, Akiva," she assured him.

Upon gazing at the drops of water for a long while, the shepherd's mind was made up. Then and there, Akiva ben Joseph decided to go off and learn *Torah*. If dripping water could bore a hole into solid rock, then, even he—a 40 year old man—could learn *Torah* through diligent effort.[67]

I'm not sure if Jay was familiar with the story of Rabbi Akiva, but in our

---

[66] Menachos 29a.

[67] Avot d'Rav Natan 6:2.

modern day and age there are many stories of people from all walks of life, who, like R' Akiva, turned their lives around midway through. So why is Jay experiencing so much anxiety about his situation? Suddenly it dawned upon me. It was his marriage! How could I have forgotten about Arlene, his wife of many years? She is a convert, whose conversion would not be considered valid by Orthodox standards. Truly, it was not a simple issue, especially considering that the kids' status would also be in question. Now, it all started to make sense. No wonder his anxiety, no wonder he hasn't stopped thinking about it.

Since he hadn't mentioned the matter, I didn't feel that it was my place to bring it up. We both sat in silence for a long while. Jay was lost in thought and I didn't want to disturb him. It was Jay who finally broke the silence.

> We're born Jewish with a rich heritage and a Divine mission in life, and we're never taught a thing about it.

"You know Danni, it doesn't seem right! Why are we not given a fair chance? Why do our parents take the liberty of uprooting our Judaism from under us, even before it has the slightest chance to take hold? I mean, we're born Jewish with a rich heritage and a Divine mission in life, and we're never taught a thing about it. Why are we misled by the prevailing Jewish culture to believe that Judaism is not what it is and that it is what it's not? All I was ever taught about Judaism was that it is about social justice and kindness—'Tikun Olam.' Oh, of course, we had a Passover Seder in our home, went to Synagogue on Yom Kippur, and ate latkes on Chanukah. But that was the extent of our Judaism and even that was entirely pro forma.

"I'm not one to play the victim, but this doesn't seem fair. Where do people get the right to steal your true identity and play with your life like that? Talk about 'Identity theft!' I love my parents, and I'm sure they had my best interest in mind, but there is no greater identity theft imaginable!

"You want to know something, Danni? By traditional Jewish standards, my wife and kids would not be considered Jewish! Who had the right to misguide me into believing that Arlene was Jewish when we got married, when I had no idea that it could ever be questioned? Is this some kind of game? At the very least, they could have told me that the conversion had a limited warranty and that it was not valid in all locations. Where does this leave me now...?"

Jay was not just anxious about his situation, he was actually angry. I could only tell him that he was right, which is exactly what I did.

"I feel like I have two choices, Danni, and I don't like either of them. One is to despise the people who kept me ignorant and led me to believe that Arlene's conversion was valid. My other option is to despise those who consider it invalid. That's not right; no one should have to feel like that. This ignorance only leads to broken hearts, broken families, and broken Jewish communities."

"Believe me, Jay, when I tell you that I truly feel your pain," I assure him, "To say that what is happening is wrong, is a gross understatement, but, believe it or not there is a Chassidic outlook on this type of situation, as well. It is called Hashgacha Pratis—Divine Providence. When you are ready, I think we should make that our next discussion."

"Oh, Danni, I'm ready; I don't think I've ever been more ready. I really hope this will give me the boost I need, some perspective in sorting all this out."

"Most likely, it will," I tell Jay. "But let me be up front with you, this is a complex subject that will probably leave you with a few questions. Regardless, I think you'll be able to relate to the wisdom and discern the validity of the ideology."

22

Hashgacha Pratis

"Divine Providence is a central principle within Jewish theology. Still, like so many other key tenets that make up our rich ideology, this ethos takes on new and deeper significance in light of Chassidic philosophy.

"Before we get to the finer intricacies of Divine Providence, its inner complexities," I tell Jay, "I think it would be best to step back and take a birds-eye view of the subject. It couldn't hurt," I add with a smile, "to start this discussion with a tad of humor:

"The children were lined up for lunch in the cafeteria of a Catholic elementary school. At the head of the table was a large pile of apples. A note posted to the basket read, 'Take only ONE, G-d is watching.' Further along the lunch line, at the other end of the table was a large tray of chocolate chip cookies, to which a child had attached her own note that read, 'Take as many as you want, while G-d is watching the apples.'

"*Fiddler on the Roof,* the sentimental dollop of schmaltz that warmed Jewish hearts and souls for decades, does not owe its enormous popularity to theological profundity. Yet, philosophy, it appears, crops-up in the oddest places, even in, as strange a place as the mouth of Tevye the milkman, 'Would it spoil some vast eternal plan if I were a wealthy man?'

"Tevye's rhetorical question is intended as a little dig at the Almighty for His apparent indifference to the debilitating poverty that plagued him. The notion that, in some way, the universe would be disrupted should Tevye come into a few measly rubles is simply absurd. Or is it?

"What Tevye never could imagine is that he unwittingly stumbled upon one of the great enigmas of religious theology; the relationship between the Sublime creator of heaven and earth and the mundane order of the cosmos. The poor milkman would be in utter shock to learn that the answer to his innocent question is Yes! Indeed, it would spoil some vast eternal plan, if he were a wealthy man.

"The *Talmud* relates that a sage by the name of Rabbi Elazar Ben Pedas once fell ill, requiring the ancient medical treatment of bloodletting. Being completely destitute, R' Elazar could find nothing but a measly garlic peel to nurture himself back to health following the procedure.

"Upon eating the peel, R' Elazar fell into a faint where he had a vision of the Shechinah—Divine Presence. He inquired of the Shechinah how long he would be subjected to such grinding poverty: 'Elazar, my son,' came the Heavenly answer, 'Do you wish for me to destroy the entire universe and reconstruct it, all so that you may find yourself in more desirable monetary circumstances?'[68]

"Apparently, R' Elazar's impoverishment was so enmeshed in the Creator's vast eternal scheme that, for his situation to change, the very narrative of creation would have to be rewritten.

"Creation is not unlike the symbols of a language, in which letters and words are chosen and arranged to capture and reveal a particular thought or feeling. Every word in a sentence, including its relative position, contributes to the intent and clarity of its expression.

> Would it spoil some vast eternal plan if I were a wealthy man?

"Joseph Stein, the writer of *Fiddler on the Roof*, could well have created Tevye a wealthy man. That would leave him with but one small problem: he would no longer have a play.

"The idea of Divine Providence or Intervention is the belief in a Supernal existence that is in control of nature; one whose cognition and will constitute the mechanism of the universe, and who has a personal relationship with all of humankind.

---

[68] Taanis, 25a.

"Simply, Hashgacha Pratis means that nothing happens in this world outside the will and oversight of the Almighty. This Providence is both individual, extending to each and every person and, in general, over peoples and groups. The Biblical narratives, beginning with the

> Hashgacha Pratis means that nothing happens in this world outside the will and oversight of the Almighty.

guarding and guiding of the Patriarchs: Abraham, Isaac, Jacob and their families; Sarah in the house of Pharaoh or Abimelach; and Hagar in the desert, all speak of direct Divine Intervention.

"The story of Joseph's life—his dramatic rise and fall and his ultimate ascendance to the position of viceroy over Egypt—is, perhaps, the most manifest Biblical account of Divine Providence. Its entire gist is one of Higher Intervention.

"Joseph, himself, avows this ideology to his brothers: 'I am Joseph your brother whom you sold into Egypt. And now, do not be grieved and let it not be evil in your eyes that you sold me here, for it was to be a provider that G-d sent me ahead of you... to ensure your survival in the land and to sustain you for a momentous deliverance. And now, it was not you who sent me here but G-d.'[69]

"When Joseph revealed himself to his brothers, they were afraid of him. In order to calm them, he implored them to 'Come close to me please.' The preeminent commentator, Rashi,[70] describes his words as calling to them 'tenderly and pleadingly.' Yet, he seemed to be doing the opposite.

---

[69] Genesis 45:4-8.

[70] Shlomo Yitzchaki (1040-1105), generally known by the acronym Rashi (RAbbi SHlomo Itzhaki), was a medieval French rabbi and author of a comprehensive commentary on the *Talmud* and the *Tanach*. Acclaimed for his ability to present the basic meaning of the text in a concise and lucid fashion, Rashi appeals to both learned scholars and beginning students. His works remain a centerpiece of contemporary Jewish study. His commentary on the *Talmud*, which covers nearly all of the Babylonian *Talmud* (a total of 30 tractates), has been included in every edition of the *Talmud* since its first printing. His commentary on Tanach—especially on the Chumash ("Five Books of Moses")—is an indispensable aid to students of all levels. The latter commentary alone serves as the basis for more than 300 "supercommentaries" which analyze Rashi's choice of language and citations, penned by some of the greatest names in rabbinic literature.

Instead of dropping the subject, as one may have expected, he keeps harping on it: 'I am Joseph your brother whom you sold into Egypt...' Is this his idea of calming his brothers who feared his vengeance? Is this how he intended to show them that he felt no resentment for what they did to him? Why then, did he see fit to remind them of the painful incident of his sale?

"The answer lies in his comment, 'And now, it was not you who sent me here but G-d.' He is saying here, 'While it was you who physically sold me, it was a 'Higher Authority' who actually sent me here; it was Hashgacha Pratis! Therefore, do not be grieved and let it not be evil in your eyes; for I've come to fully accept that this matter did not depend on you or on me, but there was something far greater at work here. The entire chain of events left me clear that everything the Merciful One does is for the good, therefore, you have nothing to fear because there is no reason for reprisal. It was all the Almighty's will for good; I was but a messenger.'

"Indeed, regarding Joseph's faith the Sages teach that the verse, 'Happy is the man who has made G-d his trust,'[71] alludes to Joseph. The reason is because a person who trusts in G-d is happy, content with his lot both in this world and in the World to Come. He experiences neither agony nor doubts, and has no desire to avenge himself or harbor resentment. He does not get upset or angry, for he realizes that all that happens is by the will of the Almighty.[72]

"While Joseph's story is one of open Hashgacha, the entire Biblical history of the Israelites, including their enslavement in Egypt, is a continuous unfolding of Divine Guidance. The guidance affects the people as a whole, as well as individual members.

"The Biblical narrative is essentially about the ultimate purpose designated for the Israelites, the creation of an exemplary people. Even

---

[71] Psalms 40:5.
[72] Genesis Rabba. 89:3.

the sufferings undergone by the people belong to the mysteries of Divine Providence.

"This reminds me of a charming little anecdote, Jay: Young Moish Goldberg was walking home from school holding his *Tanach* (Hebrew Bible). Recalling the day's lesson, he exclaimed loudly 'Baruch Hashem' (praise G-d). A university student, who recently completed a religious studies course, soon caught up with him. The student asked the youngster why he was so excited.

"'Today in class, my teacher taught us that G-d opened up the waves of the Sea of Reeds and led the whole nation of Israel right through the middle. Isn't G-d great?'

"The university student chuckled and began to open Moish's eyes to the 'realities' of the miracles of the Bible. 'That can all be easily explained. Modern scholarship proves that the Red Sea in that area was only ten inches deep at that time. So you see, it would have been no problem for the Israelites to wade across.'

"Little Moish was stumped. The university student, content that he enlightened a poor, naive, young person to the finer points of scientific insight, turned to go. Scarcely had he taken two steps when little Moish exclaimed, Baruch Hashem! Confused, the student asked for an explanation.

"'Wow!' exclaimed little Moish happily, 'G-d is actually greater than I had figured! Not only did He lead the whole nation of Israel through the Sea of Reeds, He topped it off by drowning the whole Egyptian army in a measly ten inches of water!'

"The entire *Tanach* is permeated with the spirit of predetermination. Psalms and Proverbs promote G-d's concern with the individual. He hears the cry of the wretched, desires the well-being of the righteous, and directs the individual, even against his or her will, to the destiny that He determines for him or her. Likewise, Ecclesiastes and Job are replete with the theme of Divine oversight and guidance.

"Individual Providence is a prevailing premise in Talmudic literature, as well: 'No person on earth so much as stubs a finger, unless it is decreed in heaven.'[73] Similarly, it is specified in Talmudic literature: 'The Holy One sits and pairs couples—the daughter of so-and-so to so-and-so.'[74]

"Nor is the Talmudic doctrine of Divine Providence limited to humans. In fact, it concerns all creatures, as the *Talmud* states, 'For the gazelle that is wont to cast its seed while birthing from the top of the mountain, the Holy One prepares an eagle that catches it in its wings and places it before her. Were it to come a moment earlier or a moment later [the offspring] would die at once.'[75] A parallel dictum asserts, 'The Holy One sits and nourishes both the horns of the wild ox and the ova of lice.'[76] We also have the more renowned Talmudic stories that stress this very point:

Rabbi Akiva was accustomed to saying, 'Kol Mah D'ovied Rachmono, l'tav Ovied,'— 'Everything that the Merciful-One does is for the good.' Once, while he was traveling, he was in dire need of lodging. He came to a village and knocked on the door of a home, but was refused hospitality. Yet, instead of being discouraged, R' Akiva declared: 'Everything that the Merciful-One does is for the good.'

> Everything that the Merciful-One does is for the good.

He knocked on another door but the response was much the same and so too was his reaction: 'Everything that the Merciful-One does is for the good.' His demeanor did not change even as he knocked on every door in town and was refused entry. Lacking a more favorable alternative, he encamped in a field on the outskirts of the town.

R' Akiva was accustomed to travel with some paraphernalia, including a donkey to carry his belongings, a rooster to awaken him early, and a lamp so that he might study at night. Much to his regret, a lion appeared before long and killed his donkey. 'Everything that the Merciful-One does is for the good,' declared R' Akiva. So he repeated

---

[73] Chulin 7b.
[74] Leviticus Rabba 8:1, Genesis Rabba 68:4.
[75] Babba Basra 16a.
[76] Shabbos 107b.

even as a fox devoured his rooster and his torch was extinguished by the wind.

The following morning Rabbi Akiva learned of the dreadful calamity that befell the people of the village. During the night a Roman legion converged on the town taking all its residents captive. Had he been welcomed in any of the homes, he would have met their same fate. Had his donkey or rooster remained alive they would have promptly given him up to the legionnaires. And had his fire remained burning it would have led them directly to him.[77]

"A similar Talmudic story tells about a pious man, named Nachum Ish Gamzu:

R' Nachum was once sent as an emissary on behalf of the Jewish people to the Roman emperor with the mission to try and avert a harsh edict that was decreed upon them. As a good will gesture the Jews sent along a chest filled with precious gems, hoping that it would help appease his Majesty.

On the way R' Nachum spent a night at a roadside inn. The deceitful innkeeper snuck into his room under the cover of night, removed the gems and replaced them with sand. The following morning R' Nachum awoke and continued on his way with the chest securely at his side.

Once in Rome, he proudly presented the chest to the emperor on behalf of the Jewish people. When the emperor opened the chest he was anything but impressed, alas, the poor messenger was quickly treated to a cell in the royal dungeon. But Nachum Ish Gamzu—having earned his name on account of his favorite remark, 'Gam Zu L'tovah'—'this too is for good,' did not fret. In keeping with his tradition, he confidently declared: 'This too is for good!'

One of the king's advisors—who the *Talmud* describes as Elijah the Prophet in disguise—spoke up on behalf of the messenger. 'Do you think the Jews have lost their minds?,' he argued. 'Why on earth would they want to mock you? Do they not seek your favor and goodwill? This is certainly not ordinary sand. Tradition has it,' said the minister,

'That when their ancestor Abraham went to war against the four strong kings, he used special sand that when scattered into the air, functioned like weapons. This supernatural sand led to the defeat of the enemy, perhaps this is the same sand.'

The emperor, embroiled at the time in a battle against an enemy of his own, was willing to try anything. He had the sand rushed to the battlefront. Remarkably, the miracle was repeated and the tide of the war turned in his favor. Quite pleased with the thoughtful gift, the emperor had R' Nachum released at once. After thanking him profusely, he refilled the chest with precious gems and sent him on his way with the assurance that the decree against his people was annulled.[78]

"The above Talmudic anecdotes incontrovertibly affirm the deep-rooted Jewish belief that everything that happens, even that which appears to be negative, is from the hand of G-d and is for good. The *Torah's* perspective on all life's events is 'Everything that the Merciful-One does is for the good,' and 'This too is for good.'

This too is for good!

"The Kabbalistic view of Providence is in full sync with what is implied from the Bible and the *Talmud*. Kabbalah associates Providence with the existence of an orderly and continuous system of governance of the cosmos, carried out by the Divine energies that involve the Sefiros and their revelations.

"However, where the rules of Divine Providence become more complicated is in the writings of the medieval philosophers, including R' Saadiah Gaon,[79] Maimonides,[80] and Nachmanides.[81] The Jewish

---

[78] Ta'anis 21a.

[79] Rabbi Sa'adiah ben Yosef Gaon (882-942)was a prominent rabbi, Jewish philosopher, and exegete of the Geonic period. The first important rabbinic figure to write extensively in Arabic, he is considered the founder of Judeo-Arabic literature. Known for his works on Hebrew linguistics, Halakha, and Jewish philosophy; he was one of the more sophisticated practitioners of the philosophical school known as the "Jewish Kalam" (Stroumsa, 2003). In this capacity, his philosophical work Emunos Ve-De'os represents the first systematic attempt to integrate Jewish theology with components of Greek philosophy. Saadia also was active in opposition to Karaism, in defense of rabbinic Judaism.

[80] See footnote 45.

[81] Rabbi Moses ben Nachman Gerondi, (called Gerondi after his native town Gerona, Spain, where he

medieval commentators seem to approach the issue with a new degree of sophistication and complexity, leaving room for a non-absolute form of Providence.

"R' Abraham Ben David,[82] for example, devotes an entire chapter in his book *Emunah Ramah* to the problems surrounding the principle of Divine Providence. Maimonides, in his acclaimed *Guide to the Perplexed*, presents no less than five main views on the subject—Epicurus, Aristotle, the Ash'rites, the Mu'tazilites and, last, the *Torah*—and has a rather complicated perspective on the issue. His discussion appears to limit the scope of Divine Providence in various ways.

"It's quite possible that the approach of the Jewish philosophers of the Middle Ages, toward Divine Governance, was meant as an exercise of the individual's independent grasp of first principles.

"Perhaps, they sought to prove that monotheism and Divine Providence can withstand the test of logic and philosophy; that it's more than just a dogmatic belief system that can't hold up to reason. Therefore, they took an intellectual approach and reckoned with the leading science of the time, Greek philosophy. However, they were not necessarily suggesting that they were presenting the ultimate *Torah* view on the matter.

"The above notwithstanding, the various other *Torah* disciplines do in fact approach the subject axiomatically, each in accordance with its respective tradition.

---

was born) known by the abbreviation "Ramban" and, in broader circles, as Nachmanides, was born in the year 4954 (1195) into a noble family that included many prominent Talmudists.

Nachmanides studied medicine that he practiced as a means of livelihood. He studied philosophy, as well. His writings on Jewish law began at that tender age of 16, having already developed a reputation as a learned scholar, who mastered the entire *Talmud* and its commentaries. Included in his early writings is a book called Milchamos Hashem, defending the work of the great codifier and Talmudist, Rabbi Isaac Alfasi that came under attack by Zerachiah Halevi, author of Sefer Hamaor.

[82] Abraham ben David (c. 1125–27 November 1198), also known by the abbreviation Raabad (for Rabbeinu Abraham ben David), Raavad, or Raabad III, was a Provençal rabbi, a great commentator on the *Talmud*, *Sefer Halachot* of Rabbi Yitzhak Alfasi, and *Mishne Torah* of Maimonides. He is regarded as a father of Kabbalah and one of the key and important links in the chain of Jewish mystics. He was born in Provence, France and died at Posquières.

"What's important to take away from all this is the significant role of Divine Providence even according to classic *Torah* teachings. Chassidus, however, takes it to a new level. It assigns Hashgacha Pratis its most expansive application.

23

PROVIDENCE ACCORDING TO CHASSIDUS

"Chassidus belongs to a class of *Torah* whose teachings derive from higher metaphysical axioms handed down by tradition. These mystical principles were eventually recorded in a book called Zohar, as well as in a number of similar works.[83] Together, these manuscripts comprise the basis of the esoteric stratum of *Torah*, known as Kabbalah and, by extension, Chassidus.

"Rather than the product of deduction, logic, debate and hermeneutic principles, such as those applied in the Talmud—as a means of deriving the law from the written *Torah*, i.e. the five books of Moses—these metaphysical axioms, originating at Sinai, were handed down, together with the rest of the oral *Torah*, from one generation to the next. In fact, the word Kabbalah stems from the word 'Kabbel' (receive).

> Every detailed happening in the universe is part of a Divine plan.

"Chassidus ascribes Hashgacha Pratis its broadest application. The Baal Shem Tov taught that every detailed happening in the universe is part of a Divine plan. Moreover, every particular aspect of a given circumstance happens for an immediate and good purpose. Because G-d, by definition, is good and everything that He does is good, there is nothing in this world that can be inherently bad.

"The Shomer Emunim[84] in the name of the Ba'al Shem Tov, explains that the two aforementioned Talmudic dictums—'This too is for the good' and 'Everything that the Merciful One does...'—represent two distinctive

---

[83] See chapter 9—The Orchard. Also see footnote 24-28.

[84] The book Shomer Emunim, first published in Amsterdam, in 1736, was written by Rabbi Joseph Ergas (1685 1730), of Livorno, Italy, one of the foremost Talmudists and Kabbalists of his day. Because of its clear, succinct, and logical style; his work was highly influential amongst students of Kabbalah, most notably, among the Chassidic masters.

levels of Providence: 'Everything that the Merciful One does...' implies a temporarily disguised goodness, meaning that while only love and goodness come from above, as the good travels downward to our lowly world, the impure forces caused by sin intervene, disguising the good as bad.

"However, if a person remains strong in his or her faith that the Holy One will not allow anything bad, then the disguise, ultimately, will be removed and the good will come forth. In the words of the late Lubavitcher Rebbe, Rabbi Menachem Mendel Schneerson:

> How could G-d, who is the very essence of good, issue a curse (Deuteronomy 11:26)? Are we not taught, "No evil thing is issued from Above" (Bereishis Rabbah 51:3)?

> In truth, however, G-d does not issue curses at all, only blessings are "issued from Above." The problem lies "below," in our ability to receive G-d's blessings. If a person is not a fitting receptacle for the goodness which G-d bestows upon him, he will simply be unable to accommodate G-d's blessings. The result will be that after its downward path through the spiritual worlds, the blessing is received in a way that appears, to our human eyes, as a curse (See Shaloh, Re'eh 374b)... This also explains why, in the Messianic Era, we will not only 'forgive' G-d for the sufferings of exile, but we will 'thank' Him (see Isaiah 12:1), for then it will be evident how even G-d's 'curses' were in fact blessings in disguise.[85]

"In the case of 'Everything that the Merciful One does...,' the good is there, but it has yet to be demonstrated. Through unwavering faith, the strict judgment is sweetened and turned into mercy. The good and salvation then are revealed. However, in the event that one lacks proper faith and does not remain strong... the converse is true; for example, the judgment persists and the good and salvation remain hidden.

"This is the lesson demonstrated in the story of Rabbi Akiva. It is why he said, 'Everything the Merciful One does is for the good.' It may look bad now, but with faith it will turn to good. Despite the calamities that befell

---

[85] Based on Likutei Sichos vol. 19 p. 133ff, vol. 4, p. 1091.

him that night, because of his faith, he was saved from being taken into captivity and sold as a slave.

"This level of Providence is also the subject of the Talmudic declaration: 'One must bless the Lord for the evil in one's life even as he or she blesses Him for the good.' Hence, according to Jewish law, when we hear good tidings, we are meant to bless G-d who 'is good and does good;' and, when we hear bad news of death and destruction, heaven forbid, we similarly praise G-d, 'blessed are you 'O Lord the true judge.'[86]

"The second category, 'this too is for the good,' is deeper. It represents the belief that all one's suffering, in reality, is a true benefit and was never bad at all. This was the level of Nachum Ish GamZu; nothing bad ever happened to him. When the precious gems were stolen and replaced with dirt, the dirt itself must be good! One doesn't have to wait to have the good. The bad incident doesn't have to turn into a happy ending; it's good now!

"The notion that the bad in our lives is as good as the good in our lives, is difficult to adopt, it seems rather elusive. Perhaps the following Chassidic tale can offer some perspective on the matter:

"A man once came to R' DovBer, the prominent Maggid of Mezritch, with a question: 'The Talmud asserts, that a person should bless the Lord for the bad, just as he or she blesses Him for the good. Is this really possible?' asked the man.

"'Had we been instructed to accept whatever Heaven doles out for us, I could understand. I can relate to the idea that ultimately, everything is for the good. We are, therefore, enjoined to bless the Creator even for the pain and adversity in our lives. But how can a human possibly regard the bad in their life, exactly the way they regard the good? How can a person be as grateful for his or her hardship and misfortune as he or she is for the joy and blessings in their lives?'

"R' DovBer replied, 'for an answer to this quandary you'd best pay a visit

---

[86] Berachot, 59b.

to my disciple, R' Zusha of Anipoli. There you will find the answer to the enigma.'

"R' Zusha received his guest warmly, inviting him to make himself comfortable. Upon observing his host for a while and the conditions in the house, the guest concluded that the man clearly fits the description. He exhibits the perplexing traits cited in the Talmudic dictum that so baffled him.

"It was evident that R' Zusha suffered a great deal of hardship: A frightful pauper, there was hardly enough food in the house, and his family suffered all sorts of illnesses. Still, R' Zusha was always relaxed and in good spirits, always expressing his gratitude to the Almighty for all the unearned, unconditional kindness that He continues to bestow upon him.

"But what was his secret? How does he do it?

"The visitor decided that it was time to present his concern, 'I wish to ask you a question,' he said to his host. 'In fact, this is the reason of my visit—our Rebbe advised me to come here for the answer.'

"'Nu, so tell me, what's your question?' prodded a curious R' Zusha.

"The visitor repeated his discussion with the Maggid. 'You raise a good question,' said R' Zusha after a bit of thinking. 'But why did our Rebbe send you to me? How would I know? He should have sent you to someone who really experienced suffering.' R' Zusha insisted that he hadn't experienced any suffering in his life, so he knew not how to answer the man.

"Getting back to our earlier point, the Baal Shem Tov, as mentioned, extended the principles of Hashgacha Pratis to the fullest extent, to include every detailed occurrence of every one of G-d's creations, including plants and inanimate matter.

"Each moment in time, the Master of the universe causes every given circumstance to occur with immediate intent. 'A leaf on the ground, nudged by a breath of wind,' asserts the Baal Shem Tov, 'is not by accident, but has a specific Divinely designed plan.'

A leaf on the ground, being nudged by a breath of wind, has a specific Divine cause.

"With all due respect Danni," Jay interjects. "I'm having trouble relating to the Chassidic perspective of Divine Intervention in the world. I'm not quite sure why, but it just doesn't seem plausible to me that the Holy, Exalted Almighty would care to involve Himself in every detail and nuance of our lowly world, or that there is even a need for it."

"I agree with you, Jay," I acknowledge. "At first glance, it does seem somewhat extreme. However, when considering the greater context of the first principles of creation according to Chassidic logic, it tends to be far more reasonable.

"Shall we continue?

24

CREATION EX NIHILO

"Based on the verse in Psalms: 'Forever, O Lord, Your word stands in the heavens'[87]—referring to the Supernal utterances by which the universe was created—the Baal Shem Tov derives as a first principle, that the cosmos is not the product of a Creator that made it and left it to run on its own, the way a pot or a chair continues to exist even after its creator departs.

"It is immutable that physical matter depends on being continuously re-created at every instant, and should the re-creation process stop for even a moment, it would disappear. This is true of a microcosmic particle as it is of the entire universe. Because the universe is a creation from nothingness—ex nihilo—it inevitably demands continuous creation.

"In this light, the Baal Shem Tov's grand view of Hashgacha Pratis—to encompass every detail of every occurrence, every minute of creation, regarding inanimate objects, plants, animals and, of course, humans—is not all that difficult to understand. Considering that G-d is continuously breathing the universe into existence, creation ex nihilo, why should ascribing immediate Divine purpose to His actions make it any less logical? To the contrary, denying it higher reason would seem to defy logic.

"So, Jay, you need to apply the concept of Hashgacha Pratis to your situation. Blaming others is a waste of time and energy. Like Joseph, G-d put you in the situation that you find yourself and is causing you to feel uncomfortable because He wants you to change, to grow."

"Hold on a minute," cries Jay, "before we get to me, I have a million questions on the Hashgacha Pratis doctrine, I don't know where to

---

[87] Psalms 1:19.

begin. Let's see... to start with, there is an apparent conflict between Providence and free will. How could there be Divine knowledge and guidance and at the same time allow the individual free choice to do what he or she wants?

"Another question that lingers in my mind is why would an infinite and exalted G-d care to be involved in the day-to-day, minute-to-minute operation of our universe and its trivial details? Doesn't He believe in delegation? And what would be so terrible if He allowed for some randomness regarding the lower creations, such as insects, foliage and the like? Is it not demeaning to cast Him in such a petty light; isn't it beneath Him to worry about the details surrounding these inconsequential beings?"

"See, I told you, Jay, that this topic will leave you with some questions," I remark humorously. "Imagine what the reaction was like when Rabbi Chaimson first shared this idea. I remember spending quite a few lessons on this subject. I'm not sure that your questions will be answered satisfactorily, but I think I can shed some light.

"Concerning your first query about Divine Providence versus freedom of choice, we might turn to a Talmudic dictum that makes the following observation: 'Everything is in the hand of Heaven except for the fear of Heaven.'[88] Herein lies an important insight. What is being suggested is that a person essentially has only one choice to make. He or she either chooses to have trust and fear of Heaven, or not. The rest is left to Providence.

"'Everything is in the hand of Heaven except for the fear of Heaven,' implies that free choice is a lot narrower a concept than most tend to believe. In fact, the only choices that are actually left to the individual are matters concerning Divinely ordained right and wrong, which flow from the one key question; whether we accept the Heavenly yoke or not.

"There is reward and punishment for the choices we make in moral

[88] Berachos 33b.

and religious matters. Everything else in our lives outside of moral or religious matters is left to the guidance of the Heavenly Hand.

"This caveat, Jay, greatly reduces the conundrum of Providence versus free choice, because the vast majority of a person's actions are not of a moral religious nature."

"But what about the narrow area where we do have free choice?" Jay persists. "How do you reconcile it with Divine Omniscience? An all-knowing G-d must know what I'm going to do before I decide to do it; where then is the free choice?

"The question becomes even stronger regarding Hashgacha Pratis—that every movement one makes is by Divine control and guidance. How does that fit with our freedom to choose?"

"To be honest with you, Jay, Chassidus deals extensively with this subject, but it's not something for our current conversation. It requires its own time and space. I'll just say that Chassidus approaches this subject by pondering a greater question:

"What is the meaning of knowledge in relation to the Almighty? Isn't it immutable that for there to be a knower there must be a known, an existence that is knowable? The very concept of 'knowledge' implies something outside of the knower, there must exist some object or event. But is there anything outside of Him to be known?

"In resolving this quandary, our question regarding free choice is resolved as well, because the conclusion is that G-d's knowledge is not like our knowledge, as is discussed in *Tanya*:

> His Thoughts and His Mind, which knows all created beings, encompasses each and every created thing... For example, in the case of the orb of this earth, His knowledge encompasses the entire diameter of the globe of the earth, together with all that is in it and its deepest interior to its lowest depths, all in actual reality.
>
> ...But His blessed knowledge which is united with His essence and

being— for "He is the Knowledge, the Knower, and the Known, and knowing Himself, as it were, He knows all created things, but not with a knowledge that is external to Himself, like the knowledge of a human being, for all of them [the created things] are derived from His blessed Reality, and this thing is not within the power of human beings to comprehend clearly," and so forth.[89]

"But, like I said, we ought to leave this for a different time."

"Okay Danni," says Jay, I'll let you off the hook on this one, but what about the other questions: Why would an exalted G-d desire to be in control of the administration of every petty detail of this lowly universe? And how is randomness in the lowest spheres of this world, such as the mineral and vegetative domains, a threat to His absolute perfection?"

"Those are extremely insightful and important questions," I tell Danni, "However, in order to resolve them, we need to view the Chassidic interpretation of Divine Providence within the wider Chassidic context of Divine Unity."

---

[89] Tanya, Likutei Amarim, Chapter 48

25

DIVINE UNITY

"Belief in the 'unity' of the Primordial Being is at the core of Chassidus. The belief in Divine unity, by no means, is a novelty of Chassidus. However, according to medieval Jewish philosophers such as Maimonides, Divine unity means that G-d's existence is simple; a unity that transcends all parts and that He is the only Creator. He doesn't share His control over the universe with any other force, nor does He have any helpers. Therefore, one's prayers should be directed to Him alone. According to this view, the world exists. Although it only exists because G-d continues to create it, but once created, the world in fact is real. This is in contrast to the teachings of Chassidus.

"Chassidus sees Divine unity in a complete different light. It maintains that not only is the Primal Being the one and only Deity, He is actually the only 'Existence.' As Moses tells the Israelites, 'Know today, and implant within your heart that G-d is Lord in the heavens above and the earth below; there is nothing else—"Ein Od Milvado"—nothing beside Him exists.'[90] It is through effortless Divine concentration to sustain physical matter every split second, that it remains in existence.

"Rabbi Osher tells the story of a certain mystic who said to his friend, the philosopher, 'I think I've finally figured out what lies at the heart of our divergent outlooks. You see, while I am forever thinking about myself, you are constantly thinking about G-d.'

"At first, though genuinely surprised, the philosopher could not help but feel a bit elated by the seemingly generous compliment. On second thought, however, it dawned on him that his good friend was not quite so complimentary after all.

---

[90] Deuteronomy 4:39.

"It occurred to him that, in the mind of his mystic friend, G-d's primordial existence was undeniable—the essence and core of all reality.

"The Divine truth a given, the mystic forever pondered the nature of his own being. 'Do 'I' really exist? What possible significance can the life of a finite and transitory mortal have within the all-pervading reality of G-d?'

"'As for me,' the philosopher continued to muse, 'consummate logician that I am, my existence is obvious—not subject to second thought. So, I am preoccupied pondering the reality of G-d: Does G-d truly exist? What is the nature of His existence, and where does He fit into the human reality? This then is the meaning of the mystic's contention that I was 'constantly thinking about G-d. Not quite the tribute I've anticipated.'"

"But Danni, what you say raises many questions. How can Chassidus assert that the world doesn't exist if the *Torah* says that G-d created the world? How can one reconcile the belief that only the Almighty exists when one tangibly observes the multiplicity in the world? Doesn't the *Torah*, itself, recognize the world's existence by requiring that we perform Mitzvos with physical objects according to certain physical specifications?"

"Great point Jay," says Danni. "Let me advise you that this is a complex matter, it is part of what Chassidus is all about.

"I might further note, Jay, that, at some point, the search to understand these deep concepts inevitably will reach beyond the scope of our limited discussions. These and many other questions on the matter are discussed in the vast corpus of Chassidic literature. One who truly seeks to understand will not be satisfied with a glib summary of this incredibly profound ethos. The serious student will fulfill his or her duty to continue learning and explore the vast depth of this subject and its deeper lessons.

"Having said that, let me try to go a step further in explaining this axiom. You ask how Chassidus can maintain that the world doesn't exist when the *Torah*, itself, states that G-d created the world and requires us to keep Mitzvos with physical objects. Moreover, we can tangibly observe the vast multiplicity within the world with our very eyes. Let me ask you a question, Jay, how would you define a person's thoughts? In particular, would you consider them to be in the realm of existence?"

"Well," says Jay, "the thoughts of an individual's mind belongs to the individual. I guess it depends on what you mean by existence. It exists within the individual as part of the individual, but cannot be considered an existence outside of him or her. So, I would have to say that it exists and, yet, does not exist simultaneously."

"That's correct, Jay," I concur, "a person's thoughts cannot really be considered an entity or a reality, because they only exist within the person. Even then, they have no independence of their own. They are totally reliant on the thinker's regeneration of them, kind of like creation ex nihilo. The moment the thinker discontinues nurturing the thought, it dissipates instantaneously. So, a thought essentially has no existence of its own, and yet, one cannot say it is completely nothing.

"Picture the Mona Lisa: A lady with her hands folded, a smile on her face, mountains in the background, and a winding road. By concentrating, we can create a picture of the Mona Lisa. But, for its existence, that mind-picture depends on our concentration. If we break our concentration, the picture disappears. If we sit intently concentrating on the Mona Lisa and the doorbell rings, our concentration breaks and the Mona Lisa is gone. According to Chassidus, this is the model of creation. Creation is dependent on G-d and within Him, like a thought is in the mind of a person.[91]

> Creation is dependent on G-d and within Him, like a thought is in the mind of a person.

"Now let's take another look at Hashgacha Pratis. It would be erroneous

---

[91] This analogy is found in the Ladder Up by Robert Kremnizer.

to perceive the universe as an independent entity, over which the Almighty maintains full control and governance by virtue of Providence, and that the only question remaining is to determine how extensive or particular is His imposed Providence. If that were the case then one, indeed, could question why an exalted G-d would want to be involved in every intricate detail, and why He cannot allow for some randomness regarding the unimportant incidentals. But, as stated, that's not the way it actually works.

"According to our model, the world and all its creations are like thoughts compared to reality, in this case, G-d's thoughts as it were; thus, only what is in the mind of the thinker exists, otherwise there is nothing. Consequently, for something as minute as a blade of grass to exist, it must be part of the Creator's thoughts, and for it to blow in the wind, it must also be in the Creator's thoughts. Jay, now do you understand why Hashgacha Pratis must encompass every detail? Hashgacha Pratis is synonymous with the very thoughts that keep the world in existence and operational. That is why Hashgacha Pratis must apply to every minute facet of life.

"Now, let us get back to you Jay," I assert, "you mustn't be angry with anyone about your situation, nor should you be upset with yourself. All that happened came about because the heavenly Ruler wanted it that way. Now, what's important is what you learn from your mistakes, and what you do as a result."

"One minute, Danni," says Jay resolutely, "you mean to tell me that this Hashgacha Pratis idea applies to a person's wrong choices as well? How could that be?"

"How could it not be?" I respond.

"This reminds me of joke, Danni," says Jay: "A rabbi was asked why Jews always answer a question with another question. 'Why not?' he asked.

"But seriously, if that's the case," Jay argues vigorously, "No one can ever do anything wrong, because Divine Providence always guides one's actions. I thought you said that G-d leaves matters of right and wrong to a person's free will; that G-d chooses not to assert His guidance in such matters."

"First, Jay, let me ask you, would you say that in your situation, you really had a choice? I mean given your level of education and knowledge at the time, can you really consider your decision of who you married a matter of choosing to go against Judaism's rules? The answer is of course not. Then, the point is moot regarding your situation; it was definitely the hand of the Almighty at work.

"Regarding anyone else's involvement, that's between them and G-d. As far as you're concerned, they have no power over you. Because everything is by Divine Providence, no one can harm another without G-d's allowance or, more accurately, ordination."

"Wow, what a wonderful way of looking at life," says Jay. "It eliminates so much of the cause for blame, animosity, hate, and revenge in life; it really makes a lot of sense. But, is it not like fatalism, Danni? Is one supposed to just accept that everything is from G-d and just do nothing; not get upset or involved? That seems like callousness and indifference; it just doesn't seem right?"

"No, that wouldn't be right" I interject, "no one said not to get involved or not do anything, Jay. What was said is that one should not get 'angry,' because the only one to be angry with is the Almighty Himself, for in the end, He calls the shots. Does it really make sense to be angry with G-d? To the contrary, as a victim of injustice, one should do everything to stop other people from being harmed in the same way. But, that is not accomplished through blame and dwelling on the past. Instead, you fix the problem through positive action.

"Notice how we've come full circle, Jay. This is precisely the philosophy of Chabad. Chabad is not out there pointing fingers at anyone blaming them for the disconcerting circumstances regarding Judaism, for what good would that do? Rather, they concentrate on bringing about change through unconditional love, education, and a wide spectrum of creative outreach activities. You ought to use that as your model."

"You have it all figured out Danni, don't you" says Jay, "I have to admit that the philosophy is actually brilliant. But, you still haven't answered the essential question, how can there be Divine Providence regarding one's wrongdoing?"

"Let me remind you about what I said before, Jay; there is only so far that one can get in a limited conversation concerning these complex subjects. I think we've just about reached that point, regarding this particular topic. I will try one last time to answer your question, because you've just about exhausted me on this issue.

"I'm not sure that Divine Providence is the correct term concerning our misdeeds, because G-d gives us free choice in matters of right and wrong, as they pertain to *Torah* values. On the other hand, even these acts of transgression are within the purview of G-d's master plan.

> Even acts of transgression are within the purview of G-d's master plan.

The best way to explain these cryptic words is through an analogy. Let us use the example of a father who is teaching his young child how to ride a bicycle. Although the father knows it is inevitable that the child will fall and perhaps, even mildly hurt him or herself; nonetheless, it is all part of his greater plan for the child to learn how to ride the bicycle.

"From this perspective, we can gain some understanding how our occasional failures are not outside G-d's overall master plan. In fact, G-d provided us with a way, through Teshuva— repentance—to undo the error and, even more so, turn it into merit.

"Yes, this world is a place full of obstacles and stumbling blocks, where we all stumble and fall, succumbing to, at least, some of the pitfalls in our path. The *Talmud* teaches, 'There is no human being who never sins.'[92] R' Osher would recount the following narrative when discussing the perils of our world:

"'Rabbi Aryeh Leib of Shpola was known to plaint to the Almighty in the following manner: Master of the universe, what do you want from your children? After all, You have placed them in a benighted world. It is a world where Satan himself entices them, fanning their evil inclination. All the things that provoke fleshly desires are set before their very eyes, while the warnings of retribution lie hidden between the covers of some moralistic tome. You can be certain that if you arranged things the other way around—with the price of retribution right in front of their eyes, and all the fleshly desires hidden away in some learned old book—not a single person would ever do anything wrong!'

"G-d knows that our journey in this world is precarious and, therefore, gave us a great gift; the gift of Teshuva, the power to return.

"Kabbalah teaches that there are sparks of holiness scattered throughout the world. These are bits of holiness that the Kabbalists say fell into our universe prior to its creation from the 'shattering of the holy vessels' of a prior universe that could not contain its great Divine Light. These holy sparks, hints of Divine light that are concealed in material objects, are released through the performance of a Mitzvah with a given object or even by reciting a blessing or holy words of *Torah*. Thereby, the object and its location are elevated closer to G-d. The entire world is elevated in this way to a higher level of spirituality.

"The Baal Shem Tov was accustomed to ask each person he came across in his wanderings, 'How are you?' in order to hear the person say, 'Thank G-d.' The very mention of G-d's name, he taught, freed the sparks of holiness trapped in that place.

"Taking this phenomenon a step further, the Baal Shem Tov asserts that, even in our sins, holy sparks reside. What are these sparks, he asks, 'they are Teshuva,' he answers. When we do Teshuva for a particular

---

[92] Sanhedrin 46b.

wrongdoing, we release and elevate the spark contained within the forbidden act or object. A little piece of repair happens in that moment."

"My goodness, so much to think about" says Jay, "my mind is off in all directions. I obviously want to know more about the concept of Teshuva, but first, I want to make sure that I understand your answer to my question, how one's sins fit into G-d's master plan. So, essentially you are saying, if I could paraphrase, there is general Providence regarding an individual's misdeeds, as opposed to individual Providence. Thus, our sins are somehow inclusive in the Divine overall plan, yet not specifically preordained. It kind of works for me. So, you managed to eke out an answer, after all."

"That sounds about right," I respond, "but, to be honest, because I've never heard it put quite that way, I'm reluctant to say for sure. When discussing Divine characteristics on this high a level, one has to be very careful that he or she be one hundred percent accurate, because the slightest divergence can amount to heresy. So, the best rule of thumb is that you don't accept anything that is not from a credible source. But regardless, Jay, whichever way you phrase it, the idea doesn't change, our misdeeds are not outside the Creator's greater purview and master plan."

26

THE BRIGHT SIDE OF SIN

"The idea that our sins are within the realm of the Almighty's master plan was affirmed in the most unequivocal manner by the late Lubavitcher Rebbe, Rabbi Menachem Mendel Schneerson. His words can be perceived as revolutionary, perhaps even prophetic.

"In a talk delivered in 1992, on the Shabbos of Ki Sisa—the portion containing the sin of the Golden Calf—the Rebbe portrayed sin as part of the Almighty's master plan.

"The Rebbe advances this idea in pondering the connection of the three main events in the Parsha, which are, seemingly, paradoxical. First, the children of Israel are awarded the original Tablets. Then they commit the sin of the Golden Calf, leading to the loss of the Tablets. Finally, a second set of Tablets is granted. How are these three, ostensibly opposite events, connected to each other?

Sin is part of the Divine master plan of creation.

"Our Parsha, says the Rebbe, alludes to three essential elements inherent in creation: The conceptual 'idea' state, followed by the state of implementation, proceeded by the fruition of the original intent—the end state. Every facet of creation comprises these three essential elements.

"For example, let us use the process of building a house. First, there is the desire and conception, followed by the actual construction and finished product. Finally, the house becomes occupied and used, which brings about the fulfillment of the original intent.

"These three elements constitute the very components of our Parsha, which answers the Rebbe's question regarding their connection:

1) *Torah*/Conception: The first tablets, represent *Torah*, for, according to our sages, the entire *Torah* is encrypted within the ten commandments of the tablets. *Torah*, in turn, we're taught, preceded creation and often is referred to as its blueprint and purpose.

2) Sin/Teshuvah: The shattering of the tablets, due to the sin of the golden calf, which resulted in Teshuvah. This component personifies life during the 6 thousand years of world existence.

3) Moshiach/Fruition: The second set of Tablets, signifying the Messianic era—the ultimate redemption—rooted in the origins and purpose of creation. This stage represents the bounty harvested as a result of the descent-sin and repentance.

"We see here, Jay, how the Rebbe weaves transgression into the very purpose of creation, as an inevitable means of transforming the secular into holy and sin into virtue, via the power of Teshuvah.

"The highest levels of spirituality and world transformation are reached when sin itself is reversed, in the words of the Rebbe, 'for sin, too, is needed, because that's the order in which G-d created the world. To quote the words of Rashi: "This was decreed by the King."'

"In this particular talk that, incidentally, was one of the last before the stroke that took away his ability to speak;[93] the Rebbe describes this delicate idea in unusually blunt terms. In all of Chassidus, such words are hardly ever spoken. The role of sin, and where it fits in, is commonly addressed in abstract philosophical terms. Yet, in this particular Sichah (talk) the Rebbe chose to spell it out in the most literal and blatant terms.

"The latter is extraordinary. Perhaps, it is because the Rebbe, acting in the capacity of a prophet, was indicating that this particular way of service, namely. transforming sin into virtue through Teshuvah, is

---

[93] On March 2, 1992, the Rebbe suffered a disabling stroke and was unable to speak in public ever since. A second stroke, on the very same date in the Hebrew calendar (Adar 27—March 10) two years later, left him in critical condition. His soul ascended on high on the 3rd of Tammuz 5754 (June 12, 1994).

especially relevant to our generation; the last vestige of exile, commonly called the 'Heel of Moshiach.'"

"'Heel of Moshiach?' What's the meaning of that, Danni," muses Jay.

"The end of the exile, Jay. The era heralding the coming of Moshiach," I explain, "is called by our sages 'Ikvesa D'moshichah'—the 'Heel of Moshiach.'[94] This is because of its spiritual lowliness due to the 'descent of the generations.'

"Yet, it is also the generation that is specifically connected with Teshuva, as Maimonides states: 'The *Torah* already promised that the people of Israel will return to G-d at the end of their exile and will be immediately redeemed.'[95] Ours is indeed the generation of Teshuvah.

"The prophet Amos' words elegantly describe the proclivity for Teshuvah in the era before the redemption: 'Behold, days are coming, says G-d the Lord, when I will send a famine in the land. Not a famine for bread and not a thirst for water, but to hear the words of G-d.'[96] Indeed the Lubavitcher Rebbe proclaimed our generation to be the Messianic era (the era that will usher in the Messiah). [97]

---

[94] Rashi, Talmud Sotah 49b. Literally: the heel of Moshiach, an expression borrowed from Psalms 89:52.
The simile refers to the final period of Exile (Rashi), when Moshiach will not yet have come; but signs of his imminent arrival will be discerned, as though his approaching footsteps were already audible. Alternatively, a heel, the lowest extremity of the human body, may be used as a synonym for end (see Rambam Deuteronomy 7:12), so that the wording used simply denotes the end of [the period that will usher in] Moshiach (see Rashi to Sanhedrin 97a and to Psalms ibid.).
According to Radak on Psalms (ibid.), the wording used may mean while Moshiach delays. See also Talmud Avodah Zarah 9a and Rabbenu Ephraim al HaTorah, Deuteronomy 7:12.
"The final period in Jewish and world history is referred to in Jewish sources as the era of Acharis Ha-yamim— the End of Days. The period at the end of the Exile, before the Messianic era, is called Ikvesa D'moshichah—on the heel of Moshiach, or Chevlei Moshiach—the birth pangs of Moshiach's coming. The concept of Acharis Ha-yamim includes the eve of the Redemption, as well as the Redemption, itself; whereas the Term 'On the heels of Moshiach' or 'Birth pangs of Moshiach,' denotes only the final days of subjugation— Ikveta D'Meshicha—R. Elchanan Wasssserman.

[95] Yad Hachzaka Hilchos Teshuva 7:5. And as stated in Deuteronomy 30:10: "And it shall come to pass, when all these things are come upon you, the blessing and the curse which I have put before you and you shall return unto G-d your Lord and shall obey His voice according to all that command you this day. And G-d your Lord will return your captivity and will have mercy upon you."

[96] Amos 8:11.

[97] It is noteworthy that other recent Jewish leaders, including the Chafetz Chaim, have declared that we are living in the period of Ikvesa D'Moshicha. See Chafetz Chaim, Shem Olam, part II, chapter 2; Tzipita L'yeshuah, Letters of the Chazon Ish, part I, letters 96 and 111; R. Elchanan Wasserman, Ikveta

"Be that as it may, the Rebbe goes much farther than to merely acknowledge the human's misdeeds as having a place in the greater Divine master plan. He actually presents it as an inevitable part of mankind's journey towards self-perfection and world refinement, the very intent of creation."

"Wow, that's heavy stuff, Danni," Jay declares. "I'm not going to say I fully understand the concept because it is definitely somewhat complex. Nevertheless, in some higher form of consciousness, it seems right to me. For, if G-d sought perfection, He already has the angels; for that He didn't need a lowly and physical universe."

"You are correct in what you say, Jay," I second the observation. "G-d did in fact want to be recognized in this lowly world. This concept is known in Chassidus as 'Dirah B'tachtonim'—a dwelling place [for G-d] in the lower world. Lower, you must realize, is defined not by space, but rather by the level of holiness, or rather un-holiness. Ours is a benighted world prone to transgression, therefore it is dubbed the lowest of all worlds.

> We each have a mission to make a dwelling place for the Divine presence within this world, beginning with ourselves.

"Yet, we each have a mission to make a dwelling place for the Divine presence within this world, beginning with ourselves.

"Our lives begin in a lowly and raw spiritual state, in which we are predisposed to sin and will almost inevitably succumb at one point or another. But that is precisely G-d's desire, especially in this final era of exile, to turn the lowliness of a sin-prone, or even 'sinful', individual, into a dwelling place for His Divine Presence. This, it appears to me, is the meaning of the Rebbe's words."

D'Meshicha; Rabbi Y. Kanievsky, Chayei Olam, Introduction; R. Eliyahu Lopiam, "Sin and Besotting the Heart," Lev Eliyahu.

THE BRIGHT SIDE OF SIN

"But, Danni, there is something wrong with this picture," exclaims Jay. "According to what you're saying, sin should almost be encouraged. It certainly eliminates any good reason to do battle with one's evil impulse in order to avoid transgression.

"One may take the easy path and commit all the desired sinful acts, only to repent. Not only will the individual suffer no loss, but from what you describe, the person may well be ahead of the game. His or her sins, ostensibly, could serve as an opportunity to reach a higher spiritual plane by elevating the mundane and forbidden properties of creation to holiness.

"Accordingly, sin is no longer sinful. This whole notion sounds counterintuitive. It rather seems like a recipe for moral disaster."

"Good point, Jay" I concur. "If not for a few crucial details, you would be one hundred percent right."

"What do you mean by that, Danni," Jay inquires eagerly. "Am I missing something?"

"Judaism," I tell Jay, "certainly did not overlook that gaping loophole. The law is unequivocal that sins committed willfully will elude repentance and bring substantial consequences. In the words of the Mishnah: 'One who says, I will sin and then repent, I will sin [again] and then repent, will not receive an opportunity to repent.' [98] So you see, Jay, one cannot outsmart the system by choosing transgression with the mind of repenting.

"But there is another important caveat in all this, Jay," I note. "Judaism is not content with our learning and growing from our (inadvertent) transgressions, only to move on. It demands that we fix the past by repairing the damage resulting from any sins that we commit."

---

[98] Yoma 8:9.

"But how does one fix the past, Danni," Jay interrupts. "What's done is done. Can one undo something retroactively?"

"Well, Jay, let me introduce you to Chassidus' unique interpretation of the Teshuva process, the path that allows us to rectify the damage done by our sins and become whole with our Maker.

"I'm ready, says Jay, let's do it."

27

TESHUVA

"Regardless of the extent to which our misdeeds are a part of the Divine master plan, there is no ambiguity regarding the price of sin. Judaism is clear that our sins result in punishment and spiritual detachment.

"Fortunately, there is a concept in Judaism called Teshuva—repentance. However, before we get to the idea of Teshuva, I'd like to repeat a joke that was shared at our 'Mornings with the Rabbi' study session.

"Morris comes to the Rabbi and says, 'I committed a sin, Rabbi, and need to know how I can repent.'

"'What was the sin,' the Rabbi asked.

"'I didn't wash my hands and recite the blessing before eating bread. But it happened just once,' Morris assures the Rabbi.

"'Nu, if it really only happened once,' the Rabbi said, 'It's not so terrible. Nonetheless, why, for the sake of curiosity, did you neglect to wash your hands and recite the blessing?'

"'It felt awkward, Rabbi,' said Morris. 'You see, I was in a non-kosher restaurant.'

"The Rabbi's eyebrows arched. 'And why were you eating in a non-kosher restaurant?'

"'Because all the kosher restaurants were closed,' Morris explained. 'I had no choice.'

"'No choice,' muttered the Rabbi. 'So tell me, why all the kosher restaurants were closed,' the bemused Rabbi persisted.

"Morris replied, 'You have to understand Rabbi, it was Yom Kippur, after all!'

"The basic concept of Teshuva refers to a person, who resolves to (re) commit his or her life to G-d and the G-dly way of living; for a Jew, that is the way of *Torah* and its Mitzvos.

"But even of someone whose life is already committed to G-d; someone who is trying to live in accordance with the Divine will, but nonetheless, made a wrong choice, has an obligation to somehow fix the transgression.

"One needs to repair every iniquity committed against the sublime Creator. Our actions toward G-d have consequences, similar to the cause and effect experience that we encounter in our physical lives. The process of restoration is called Teshuva.

"Teshuva is required, because any time we commit a misdeed, we defile our soul and create a separation between ourselves and the Holy One, Blessed Be He. 'For your iniquities have come between you and your G-d,' proclaims the Prophet Isaiah, 'And your transgressions have caused Him to hide His countenance from you; from hearing you.'[99]

Teshuva removes the barrier and brings us closer to Him.

"As long as the impurity persists, one remains distanced from G-d. Teshuva removes the barrier and brings us closer to Him: 'How wonderful is repentance,' declares Maimonides: 'One day a person can be separated from the Lord of Israel, as it is written, "Your iniquities have made a separation between you and your G-d ..." and, on the next day, he can be attached to the Divine Presence, as it is written: "But you who are attached to the Lord your G-d ..."'[100]

"To illustrate the power of Teshuvah, the *Talmud* tells a story of a man by the name Elazar ben Durdaya, who lived in the time of the Mishnah over 1800 years ago. He immersed himself, thoroughly, in one of Judaism's,

---

99 Isaiah 59:2.
100 Laws of Repentance 7:7.

most serious sins: He visited every harlot he could find, anywhere, and paid any exorbitant price that was asked.

"Once, a harlot commented to Elazar that someone like him could never repent for his sins. Her words, penetrated his calloused soul and moved him to penitence. He immediately fled into the wilderness and dramatically beseeched nature itself—the mountains, the heavens, the earth, the sun, the moon and the stars—to pray on his behalf. Then, in a moment of sublime contrition, Elazar wept with all of his heart, and exhaled his final breath in a state of repentance.

"A voice emerged from the heavens and declared, "Rabbi Elazar ben Durdaya has earned a place in the afterlife!" Rabbi Yehudah haNasi, the great sage and leader also known as Rebbe, canonizer of the Mishnah, exclaimed in tears, "Yesh Kona Olamo B'Sha-ah Achas (It is possible for one to acquire his place in the afterlife in just one moment) and the Heavens will even call him Rabbi!"

"G-d, in His abundant mercy gave us the commandment of Teshuva that brings healing to the world and repair to the blemishes caused by our sins. But how can we repair the damage in our relationship with G-d? Can Teshuva make it disappear? No amount of sorrow or regret can undo the monetary loss or fix the physical damage that our actions cause. Then how can Teshuva undo our misdeeds toward G-d?

"In order to answer this question, we must first examine the Halachic mechanics of this important Jewish tenet, as defined by the early codifiers. Maimonides and others[101] agree that the essential properties of repentance are: Regret for the sin, a pledge not to repeat the offense, request for forgiveness, and verbal confession.[102] The components generally break down into two categories: the mental and emotional elements, such as remorse and renunciation and the action-oriented dimension, for example, verbal confession.

---

[101] R' Saadiah-*Emunos Ve-De'os* 5:5. Bachya-*Chovas Ha-Levavos* 7:4.

[102] *Mishne Torah*, Hilchos Teshuva, 2:2.

"But, why must a person confess his or her misdeeds in order to obtain forgiveness? Why aren't regret and renunciation enough? Adding to that question is the edict that the confession specifically must be verbal. Is the Almighty unable to read our thoughts? Does He not know our hearts? Also, why are we not required to verbalize our regret?

"In answer to these questions the Tzemach Tzedek, in his acclaimed work *Derech Mitzvosecha*,[103] shares a profound insight regarding the Mitzvah of Teshuva. He begins with the assertion that every sinful act really has two parts. The first part is the formation of intent, the idea and the desire to act. The second part is the act itself. Therefore, every transgression creates a two dimensional by-product, each a reflection of its respective source.

"The first dimension is ethereal by nature, absent of a physical component, much as the 'soul' of the sin. The second begets a more physical or tangible by-product, akin to its body. Together they comprise the creation of a bad Angel or spirit, so to speak, also known as Klipah, to use the words of the Tzemach Tzedek:

> By negating the observance of a positive commandment or transgressing a negative commandment, a person creates a blemish and brings the light within them [the ten Supernal Attributes] to the external forces, like a person who pierces an organ, causing blood to flow outward.

> This is the mystical secret associated with the verse "My sins are before me at all times," Psalms 51:5, implying that the Klipah which a person brings into existence through his sins continuously stands before him to cause him difficulty. Our prophets affirm this idea: "Your evil will cause you anguish," Jeremiah 2:19, and: "A person will be paid according to his deeds," Job 34:11. The *Zohar* explains: "When a person repents, he must kill the Kelipos to remove them from the

---

[103] Explanations of the reasons for the Mitzvos, according to Chassidus, including the Mitzvos of Tzitzis, Tefillin, prayer, belief in G-d, love of a fellow Jew, having children, building the Holy Temple, and many others. It is a fundamental work of Chabad Chassidus. The late Lubavitcher Rebbe advised many people to begin the study of Chassidus with *Derech Mitzvosecha* that he always referred to as the "Book of Mitzvos," because the style and arrangement are accessible to beginners.

earth, as it is written: "I have wiped away your sins like a cloud," Jeremiah 44:22.

Teshuva is a process that addresses both dimensions through regret and confession. Regret involves removing one's will from the sin, thereby taking away its soul. True repentance occurs when the actor wishes with all his heart that he never acted the way he did and resolves to never repeat it again.

The underlying reason for this is the fact that in the spiritual realms, man is rooted in the Ten Sefiros of holiness. Hence, through his sins, his desire and misdeeds, man is able to draw down a body and a soul [of Klipah] from the nurture of the Ten Sefiros, as explained above. Therefore, in order to withdraw the nurture from the external forces, a verbal confession must accompany one's regret.[104]

"Accordingly, the first step towards repentance is disassociating the action from the actor by removing the desire to act. When the person truly regrets his or her choice, the desire part of the action; the soul of the sin, is reversed.

"Yet, the actor must still do everything in his or her power to undo the action; the body of the sin. To reverse the action requires counteraction; thoughts and feelings cannot repair actions.

"Oops, Jay, I feel another joke coming on: A man gets into an argument with his wife. As a result they gave each other the silent treatment. Suddenly, the man remembers that he needs his wife to wake him at 5:00 a.m. the next morning in order to catch an early morning business flight. Not wanting to be the first to break the silence and 'lose,' he jots down a memo on a piece of paper: 'Please wake me at 5:00 a.m.' He leaves the note where he knew his wife would see it.

"The guy wakes up in the morning only to discover that it is 9:00 a.m. and that he missed his flight. Frantic, he leaps out of bed to see why his

---

[104] *Derech Mitzvosecha*, Maamar Viddui U'Teshuvah.

wife hadn't wakened him. Suddenly he notices a piece of paper near the bed. The paper read: 'It's 5:00 a.m. Wake up!'

"The prescribed counteraction to combat and erase the negative conduct is Viddui—confession. To quote the Tzemach Tzedek once again:

> In order to obliterate the body, a verbal confession is necessary [In this regard,] the movement of one's lips is considered as deed. Through this activity, one obliterates the body [of the Klipah, nullifying its being to the extent that it is] as if it never existed.[105]

---

105 Ibid.

28

TRANSGRESSION INTO MERIT

"The Talmudic author Reish Lakish exclaimed: 'Great is Teshuva, for when the sinner repents, his or her sins are accounted as if he or she committed them unintentionally ... But did not Reish Lakish say', probes the *Talmud*, 'that Teshuva is great because through it a person's sins are accounted as merits... This is not a difficulty', answers the *Talmud*, 'because the first statement refers to repentance out of fear, whereas the second statement refers to repentance out of love.'[106]

"So how are sins turned into merits? When we realize the magnitude of our sins and our deep state of regret over our detachment from G-d, we are propelled to develop a sense of love for Him. So deep is the love that it can only be attained in His absence. The very distance and estrangement serves as the impetus and springboard for the comeback to our source in a stronger way than ever, like the water of a welled up dam, that builds up so much energy, it bursts forth with incredible force and intensity.

"A story is told of R Levy Yitzchak of Berditchev, who was once walking through the streets during the month of Elul and met an individual who was known to be very sinful. R' Levy Yitzchak stopped him and said to him, 'My good man. How lucky you are! When you will do Teshuvah you will have so very many mitzvos, for then all your many wrongdoings will be converted into powerful merits!'

"As previously mentioned, there is no person who does not transgress. In Ethics of the Fathers, we are taught that one who conquers his urges is called a 'gibor'-hero.[107] It's not reasonable to expect heroic conduct from every person one hundred percent of the time. Rabbi Osher Chaimson shared the following anecdote to drive this point home:

---

[106] Yoma 86b.
[107] Ethics of the Fathers 4:1.

"In the early 1900s, in Manhattan's Lower East Side, a local rabbi once ran into an Episcopalian minister, who was not very fond of his immigrant neighbors' ghetto-like lifestyle. 'What a coincidence!' remarked the minister: 'It was just last night that I dreamt I was in Jewish heaven.'

"'Jewish heaven,' mused the rabbi. 'What's it like in Jewish heaven?'

"'Oh!' replied the minister snidely, 'In Jewish heaven, children with dirty faces and untucked, wrinkled shirts play in the dirt. In Jewish heaven, women haggle with vendors, as panhandlers rudely interrupt.

"'In Jewish heaven,' continued the Minister, 'laundry hangs from a maze of clotheslines, dripping water onto the muddy surface. And, of course, there are plenty of rabbis, running to and fro, with large tomes under their arms!'

"'How amazing!' retorted the rabbi, pursing his lips. 'In my dream last night, I found myself, of all places, in Episcopalian heaven.'

"'Really?' muttered the minister. 'I've always wondered what Episcopalian heaven was like. Please tell me what you saw.'

> Only by falling is one able to rise.

"'I must admit,' said the Rabbi with a wide smile, 'It is nothing short of immaculate. The streets glitter as if they were just washed. Homes are lined-up in perfect symmetry, as their fresh paint sparkles in the sunlight. The lawns and gardens are manicured to perfection!'

"'Not at all surprising,' said the pleased, almost giddy minister, nodding in approval. 'But tell me about the people! I'm curious to know what the people are like.'

"'The people,' frowned the Rabbi, as he looked the minister in the eye: 'What people? Not a person could be found!'

"Teshuva was created as a gift to enable us sin prone humans, to work on ourselves when we transgress. Not only can we regain our previous level, but even perfect our character. This is the meaning of the verse:

'A Tzadik falls seven times and rises.'[108] Only by falling, explain the commentaries, is one able to rise. Teshuva raises a person to a point that he or she, otherwise, could not have reached. Rambam lucidly expresses this idea:

> A Ba'al Teshuva should not think that he is less than a completely righteous person because he did transgressions in the past. Rather, a Ba'al Teshuva is beloved and cherished by G-d, as if he never transgressed at all. Additionally, his spiritual reward is great since he tasted sin and abandoned it, and therefore, he rules over his own drives and earthy inclination. The Sages say, "In the place where Ba'alei Teshuva stand, even the completely righteous cannot stand" Berachos 34b. This means that Ba'alei Teshuva achieve greater spiritual heights than those who never transgressed, since they have to exert themselves and take control over their impulses, and thus exercise their power of free will more often.[109]

"Another *Midrashic* statement makes an even more powerful claim about Teshuva: 'Rabbi Abahu bar Ze'ira said, 'Great is Teshuva, for it existed in the world before creation.'[110] Commenting on this *Midrash*, Rabbi Adin Steinsaltz[111] writes:

> The implication of this remarkable statement is that Teshuva is a universal, primordial phenomenon... It is embedded in the root structure of the world... Before we were created we were given the possibility of changing the course of our lives.'[112]

"That was very insightful, really good stuff Danny," says Jay. "there's more, right?" he asks. "There's plenty more," Danny assures him.

---

[108] Proverbs 24:16.
[109] Rambam, Hilchot Teshuvah 7:4.
[110] Genesis R 1:4.
[111] Born 1937 in Jerusalem. Educated at Hebrew University of Jerusalem, Rabbi Adin Steinsaltz or Adin Even Yisrael is a teacher, philosopher, social critic, and spiritual mentor, hailed by Time magazine as a "once-in-a-millennium scholar." He devoted his life to making the *Talmud* accessible to all Jews.
[112] Kol Haneshamah Machzor, p. 8.

29

ELEVATING THE PHYSICAL

"While Teshuvah may have the power to transform the lowliest and unholiest elements of creation—sin itself—into merits, it is nonetheless a circuitous path, applicable only post factum. By no means is it the only medium by which the lowly properties of creation are transformed and elevated to their Divine source. Transforming the lowly and mundane into the service of the Creator is, according to Chassidus, the very essence of creation, and a human being's purpose in this world.

"Before we discuss how this all relates to you, let us explore how Chassidus understands the Jew's mandate to transform the animalistic elements, both within the self, as well as within the world, and the effects it has on the cosmos.

"The lowliest properties, asserts Chassidus, are the most fertile grounds for a Divine revelation. This principle applies to all matters of creation. The rule is that within the lowly elements of creation lies a higher Divine spark and hence spiritual potential. It is, however, only through human action in using the object for a holy cause that its spiritual potential can be released.

"There is a well-known story about Rabbi Schneur Zalman of Liadi, who once received a silver snuffbox as a gift. The Rebbe did not want to put it to its intended use, remarking, 'There is one part of the body that is not constantly seeking gratification—the nose. Should I train it to be a pleasure-seeker too?' Instead, R' Schneur Zalman found a more lofty use for the gift. He detached the snuffbox's cover and used it as a mirror to help him center the Tefillin on his head.

"This incident was once related to R' Schneur Zalman's grandson, Rabbi Menachem Mendel of Lubavitch. In conveying the incident, the narrator stated that R' Schneur Zalman 'broke off' the cover of the snuffbox.' Rabbi Menachem Mendel remarked, 'No, no, my grandfather never broke anyone or thing. He merely removed the hinge-pin that connected the upper part to the lower.'[113]

"'There is deep significance in Rabbi Menachem Mendel's clarification,' observed the late Lubavitcher Rebbe, Rabbi Menachem Mendel Schneerson: 'While R' Schneur Zalman's entire life was devoted to sublimating the ordinary and elevating the mundane, nevertheless, he taught to never repress or crush the lowly, but to gently detach the upper from the lower. The way to elevate is to extract the lofty potential from its lowly encasement by harmonious and peaceful means, therefore, the statement, that Rabbi Schneur Zalman would never have "broken off" the cover.'[114]

"The teachings of Chassidus view breaking the animal traits as a temporary stage in spiritual development. The ideal is to reach the higher level of transforming one's instinctive tendencies into Divine service.

> The way to elevate is to extract the lofty potential from its lowly encasement.

"Chassidus maintains that natural bodily drives possess superior strength over the more holy inclinations. Once they are transformed into the service of the Divine, the vigor of the animal instinct unleashed enables a higher and deeper level of spiritual achievement.

"The Baal Shem Tov derived this principle from the following verse in Exodus: 'When you see the "chamor" (donkey) of your enemy lying under its burden, you might [think to] refrain from helping it; you must [instead] aid it.'[115]

"Playing on the word 'chamor' that can be read as 'chomer' (materiality), the Baal Shem Tov translates the verse homiletically: When you examine

---

[113] Based on *Once Upon a Chassid*, by Yanki Tauber.
[114] Adapted from Sichos of the 2nd Night of Pesach, 5720.
[115] Exodus 23:5.

your 'chomer,' your materiality, for example, natural bodily drives, you will see 'your enemy,' a threat to your Divine soul.

"You may further see it 'lying under its burden,' beleaguered by its efforts to oppose Divine observance. It may occur to you that 'you shall refrain from helping it;' from redeeming it. Instead, you will follow the path of asceticism, to crush the body's resistance to spirituality. Says the *Torah*, 'You must aid it;' you must refine it, rather than break it. You must transform the bodily drives into a vehicle for the essential Divine purpose in creation of the physical, namely, making it into a dwelling place for the Divine.

"Traditional Musar literature often helps a person appreciate intellectual, spiritual, and G-dly matters by shunning bodily and physical pleasures.

Chassidism, on the other hand, maintains that, as much as one might run from materiality, one can never truly succeed, because we live in a physical world.

> Much as one might run from materiality, one can never truly succeed.

"Chassidus teaches that one must fuse the spiritual and physical in order to prosper in the service of G-d Almighty.

"Physicality is not meant to be suppressed, but rather transformed. Consequently, it will not be detached from Divinity, but rather filled with it. Thus, it will lend its unique qualities to spirituality and holiness and thereby, serve it. This could be compared to the energy gained from the harnessed ox.

"In a letter dated 28th of Adar, 5721 (March 16, 1961) the late Lubavitcher Rebbe, Rabbi Menachem Mendel writes:

> Man possesses two apparently contradictory elements, no less incompatible than the incompatibility of matter and spirit, the counterpart of which in the physical world is matter and energy. I refer to the Divine soul and animal soul, or, on a lower level, the Yetzer Tov and Yetzer Harah. But this incompatibility is evident only

in the infantile stage of progress in Divine service, comparable to the plurality of elements and forces that were presumed to exist in physical nature. But just as the appreciation of the underlying unity of nature grew with the advancement of science, so does perfection in the Divine service lead to the realization of the essential unity in human nature, to the point where the Yetzer Tov and Yetzer Harah become one, through the transformation of the Yetzer Harah by and into the Yetzer Tov, for otherwise, of course, there can be no unity and harmony, since all that is holy and positive and creative could never make peace and be subservient to the unholy, negative and destructive. And in this attained unity the Jew proclaims, Hear, O Israel, G-d our G-d, G-d is one.

"That was very intriguing, Danni," observed Jay. "This stuff is really good, there is more, Danni, right?" Jay muses, sporting a look of anticipation. "No worries, Jay," Danni responds. "There is plenty more, it's just a matter of how to structure it.

"Since we are on topic of Teshuva and transforming sin and lowliness," says Danni, "I'm thinking to continue with this subject, exploring the spectrum of this ethos, though it is a diversion somewhat. It's probably still worth it.

"In fact, according to the teachings of Chassidus, Teshuvah pierces the highest of heavens that can be reached by our mortal souls.

"Teshuvah, which is resultant from sin and spiritual decline—the seemingly lowliest and farthermost place from G-d—reaches the foremost primordial source of the cosmos and all of creation; the place of its earliest conception and manifestation.

"This phenomenon is referred to in Chassidic vernacular as "Na-utz Techilasan B'sofon..."-the beginning is wedged in the end and the end is wedged in the beginning. The sum of it all, Teshuvah is most central to the purpose of creation.

30

THE DONKEY OF MOSHIACH

When the soul comes down from its heavenly setting and is invested into a body, it suffers an immense spiritual regression, because the body acts as a formidable obstacle between the soul and G-d. Nevertheless, it is a worthwhile journey for the soul, because the physical world contains, trapped within it, "sparks" of holiness which have a greater spiritual potency than the soul itself. The soul profits from these "sparks" when the body performs Mitzvos with physical objects.[116]

"The prophet Zechariah describes Moshiach's revelation, in the context of 'a pauper riding on a donkey.'[117] According to Chassidus, this imagery is a metaphor for the process that facilitates the arrival of Moshiach. This involves elevation of the material elements of creation to their highest potential and fruition.

"The use of the donkey in Divine service represents the actions and process that prepares the world for the Messianic era.

"Moshiach's donkey surfaces to the fore at key historic intervals in the world's progression towards the Messianic era. Each time, its function is slightly different, reflecting the changes in the status of the world's preparedness.

"The donkey first appeared in the year 2084 from creation (1677 B.C.E.) in the narrative of the 'binding of Isaac,' Abraham's tenth and greatest test: 'Abraham rose early in the morning and readied his donkey.'[118] In preparation for the three-day trek from Chevron to Mount Moriah, in Jerusalem, Abraham loaded his donkey with wood, fire and knife—supplies needed—but no one actually rode on the donkey. "Seven generations later, the donkey reappears when Moses is dispatched on his Divine assignment. As he embarked on his mission to lead the

---

116 Based on Maamar (Chssidic discourse) Az Yashir Yisroel and Ach Begoral 5735, of the late Lubavitcher Rebbe, Rabbi Menachem Mendel Schneerson.

117 Zechariah 9:9.

118 Genesis 22:3.

Israelites out of Egypt—to the Mountain where the Almighty would reveal His Divine creed—'Moses took his wife and children, set them upon 'the' donkey, and set out for Egypt.'[119]

"Based on the definite article 'the,' our sages explain that it denotes the very same donkey Abraham used. Furthermore, they assert that Moshiach, too, will 'come riding' on the very same erstwhile donkey. Accordingly, Abraham, Moses, and Moshiach all employ the same donkey in the fulfillment of their Divine missions. However, the manner in which the donkey is engaged differs with each mission.

"In the case of Abraham, it is merely used to carry the supplies, whereas, Moses places his wife and children upon the animal. By contrast, Moshiach is described as riding on the donkey himself. Why the different degrees in the use of the animal?

"We've already established the Almighty's desire for mankind to refine and elevate the material elements of creation to their highest potential—bringing into full fruition the goodness and perfection inherent in all of creation. This includes, especially, the lowliest creations, such as physical matter.

"Humanity's mission of elevating the material, is a long and involved process. It requires an ongoing effort, in which each generation builds upon the achievements of its predecessors. The process is so encumbered because physical and spiritual matter are worlds apart. Indeed, the very nature of creation is such that a vast gulf divides the two, making them natural antagonists. So, to integrate and elevate the material realm into the spiritual is a gradual cosmic process.

"This explains why Abraham and Moses so differently incorporated the material donkey in their respective missions. As stated earlier, the Hebrew word for donkey is 'chamor,' similar to the word 'chomer'—materiality. The use of 'chomer' in spiritual pursuits represents the material elements harnessed in the Divine service; these physical

___
[119] Exodus 4:20.

177

elements, as they are directed towards higher and loftier ends. But the process is a gradual one.

"Abraham, the first Jew, began the practice of exposing the perfection of the Creator in all things by sublimating the material, thereby, realizing its true potential. But Abraham lived before the revelation at Sinai, before G-d rescinded the decree that divided the world between higher and lower; matter and spirit. In his day, the original order instituted at creation still held sway: The physical and the spiritual were two separate, incompatible worlds.

"The most Abraham could do was harness the physical to serve the spiritual. He accomplished this by using the donkey to carry the accessories of his Divine service. Yet, the physical remained coarse. It could not become directly part of his spiritual life. Nevertheless, Abraham took the first step. He wrestled the holy sparks from their inherent encasement by using the object to assist in his service of G-d, albeit peripherally.

"On the other hand, Moses embarked on the mission that was to culminate in receiving the *Torah*, the medium by which G-d empowered humanity to dissolve the dichotomy between the higher and lower domains. The *Torah* instructs and enables us to sanctify even the most mundane aspects of our lives, to integrate our material selves and environment within our spiritual goals. So, Moses used the donkey to carry his wife and children.

"A person's wife and children are an extension of his own self, in the words of our sages, 'A person's wife is like his own body'[120] and 'A child is a limb of his father.'[121] Beginning with Moses, the material began to play a more central and intimate role in our service of the Heavenly Creator.

"But Moses marks only the beginning of *Torah*'s effect on the physical world. Since then, whenever a person uses a material resource to perform a Mitzvah, for example, giving money to charity or using the

---

[120] *Talmud*, Berachot 24a.
[121] ibid., Eruvin 70b.

energy the body extracts from food to fuel one's fervor in prayer, he or she 'refines' these physical objects, divesting them of their mundane and selfish qualities.

"With each such act, the physical world becomes more holy and in greater harmony with its essence and function. Each such act brings closer the day when our world will finally and completely shed the husk of coarseness that is the source of all ignorance and strife, bringing on a new dawn of universal peace and perfection.

"So, Moshiach, who represents the ultimate fulfillment of *Torah*, himself, rides the material donkey, for he heralds a world in which the material is no longer the lower or secondary element; but is an utterly refined resource, no less central and significant a force for good than the most spiritual creation.

"Very insightful, Danni," observes Jay. "It seems like the concept of elevating the mundane physicality of the world, is a key aspect of the Divine purpose of creation.

There appears to be multiple facets to this important objective, as you have so diligently described. It pertains to the physical objects of the world as well as to the base physical drives of the human being. It involves suppression of the animal soul as well as its transformation. It takes on the form of retrieving the holy sparks, separating the higher from the lower, as well as the use of science and technology, for the sake of spirituality and holiness.

All this is very interesting, but I am particularly curious about the notion of the holy sparks. I am interested in hearing more about this."

" It is indeed a fascinating phenomenon, Jay," agrees Danni. "Chassidus is permeated with this idea. Let me share with you one example, it relates to the Egyptian exile and liberation, which serves as a model for the future and final redemption."

31

MINING THE WEALTH

"The Almighty revealed to our father Abraham in the 'covenant between the halves'[122] that his offspring would descend into Egypt and remain there for 4 hundred years. They would be enslaved and oppressed and eventually leave with great wealth.

"The late Lubavitcher Rebbe, Rabbi Menachem M. Schneerson, observes that money could never compensate for the torture the Jewish people suffered in Egypt. Indeed, the *Talmud*[123] asserts that the Jewish people would have preferred to be redeemed earlier, even at the expense of obtaining riches.

I'm reminded of a legendary joke shared among Soviet Jewry, that captures this very phenomenon:

Q: Rabinovich, what is a fortune?
A: A fortune is to live in our Socialist motherland.
Q: And what's a misfortune?
A: A misfortune is to have such a fortune.

"The *Talmud* compares this to one who is suffering harsh imprisonment and is given a choice to wait another day to be released, and receive a large sum of money, or to leave at once. The person, asserts the *Talmud*, would certainly choose to be freed immediately and forget about the money. What, then, asks the Rebbe, is the big deal that the enslaved Israelites 'will leave with great wealth?'

"According to the Chassidic interpretation, however, there is no quandary. The definition of the word 'wealth' relates to something deeper. It refers to a type of wealth that can justify the descent of the Jewish nation into Egypt with all its slavery and suffering.

---

[122] Genesis, chapter 15.
[123] Brochos: 9b.

"The Rebbe offers, by way of explanation, the Chassidic meaning of 'Egyptian wealth,' and accordingly, the reason it was so important that the Jewish people leave with it. The explanation is based on the Chassidic concept of 'holy sparks.'

"According to Chassidus, there lie great spiritual wealth within material riches—high Sublime sparks—which need to be released from their coarse encasements, and elevated to holiness. It was, hence, not merely material wealth that the Israelites were encouraged to amass, but spiritual riches as well. In fact, these 'Nitzutzos' (sparks) were the primary wealth the Jews were meant to redeem from Egypt.

"Consequently, the reason why the Almighty insisted—upon their departure from Egypt—'that each woman should ask her neighbor for vessels of silver and gold,' even if it meant having to linger in exile, is so that they elevate these holy sparks and acquire their spiritual wealth.

"This, says the Rebbe, was the 'great wealth' that the Almighty promised the children of Abraham; the spiritual riches found within the mundane objects. By taking the affluence of Egypt with them on their journey to the Land of Israel, they would have the opportunity to be partners with the Creator in refining this world.

"This is the inner meaning of the Sages' statement: 'The reason the Israelites were exiled amongst the nations, was so that converts should be added to them.'[124] The convert possesses a spark of holiness even before converting, but it is extremely concealed. It is for this reason that the *Talmud* commonly uses the term 'a "convert" who has converted' and not 'a "non-Jew" who has converted,' because a convert possesses a spark of holiness deep within, even from before. The individual requires Halachic conversion to be considered a Jew, so as to bring the spark into fruition.

"As mentioned before, the process of redeeming the holy sparks applies as much to our exile as to any in the past. Like the gold and silver of

---

[124] Pesachim: 87, 2.

Egypt, the great wealth of our exile is the abundant potential that lies within the dominion of science and technology.

"These energies must be subjugated and used, not just for our physical benefit, but for our spiritual purpose as well. It is the bounty reaped from this long arduous exile that is used for the purpose of preparing the world for the messianic era.

"It is our task to elevate the most advanced levels of science and technology and retrieve the sparks of holiness contained within them to use them for spirituality and Divine purpose.

"This, Jay, is the most important function of our time, the 'Heel of Moshiach', and every Jew regardless of his or her sins and flaws, or perhaps, specifically such individuals, yourself included, have the ability and mandate to bring this about in a complete and speedy fashion.

32

IKVESA D'MOSHICHAH—
HEEL OF MOSHIACH

"So, Jay, can we talk about you now, or do you want to continue changing the topic? Teshuva is the way to go, my friend. Forget the anger; forget the blame; forget the feeling bad for yourself. Focus your energy on self-growth and improvement. Do as Chassidus teaches; turn your past into merits."

"You know, Danni, now you're really beginning to annoy me," says Jay, visibly irritated. "I'm not sure whether you're pretending or just plain clueless, but, for the life of me, I can't understand why you insist on ignoring the elephant in the room."

"The room? The room we're in right now," I say in an attempt to lighten the mood, "is 30 thousand feet in the air, I sure hope there's no elephant in it." I manage to eke a faint grin out of Jay, but my humor fails to do the trick, Jay is still quite upset. "Okay, Jay, tell me about the elephant in the room," I say.

"You mean to tell me, Danni," Jay exclaims, "that you really don't understand the obvious predicament in which I find myself as a result of my marital status? It's easy for you to sit there and preach these hifalutin ideas about Teshuva and turning my past into merits, but I've got to deal with reality, such as a wife and kids.

"So what are you suggesting, Danni? That I do Teshuva, while I remain in the relationship, or do you recommend that I get rid of my family? What do the great Rabbis of Chabad have to say about this situation? Would they favor Teshuva over broken families?"

"I'm sorry, Jay, I really should have been more sensitive to your situation," I concede. "Your predicament is more complex than I seemed to acknowledge, but it was not intentional. I just was not looking that far down the road, but rather at the more immediate picture."

"But is there a long term answer for this type of circumstance, Danni?"

The Torah's laws about intermarriage are over three thousand years old.

"This is an extremely delicate issue, Jay, and I'm afraid there is not a one size fits all answer to this question. Each situation must be considered individually. But Jay, please don't shoot the messenger. Chabad, nor any of the other Orthodox strands, is not the enemy. The *Torah's* laws about intermarriage are over 3 thousand years old. So are the laws regarding conversion; Chabad did not invent them or change them.

"Your predicament, Jay, is a tragic result of an unfortunate state of affairs within the Jewish community, but, of all parties, Orthodoxy is the least to blame."

"Then what does one do, Danni," asks Jay. "You know how little control I have over the situation at this point. I can't make the kids be any more Jewish. I certainly can't make Arlene. To be honest, I don't even feel like I have the right to request it from her. So, what am I supposed to do, Danni?"

"You really want to know, Jay," I ask."

"No, I don't really want to know, Danni," he sarcastically remarks. "I'm just trying to make conversation, because we've hardly talked to each other during this trip... Of course, I want to know."

"Well then, I'll tell you Jay," I assert. "Leaving aside for now the possibility of an Halachic conversion that, of course, should be part of any plan, the answer is that you should do whatever you can to align your life with G-d and *Torah*. The rest leave up to G-d. Remember the Hashgacha Pratis concept, G-d has a master plan and nothing is outside its purview, even your situation. So don't try to run the world, because you'll put G-d out of a job, and who knows where that could lead."

"Oh I see, so now you want me to turn into a hypocrite," Jay protests. "I should have two lives, Jay the sinner and Jay the saint. Are you really serious, Danni? Can one really serve G-d and transgress at the same time? What about Teshuva?"

"You raise a good point" I tell Jay, "In a different era, you might have been 100 percent right; but our generation is unlike any other, especially regarding the issue of hypocrisy. You see, Jay, each generation in history has its unique mission and set of challenges that call for a corresponding response. In that regard, Judaism is not a static religion, but rather a living breathing organism. Incidentally, this may explain Judaism's mysterious ability to survive against overwhelming odds.

> Can one really serve G-d and transgress at the same time?

"Be that as it may, much as the Baal Shem Tov acted in response to the crisis of his time, the Supra Leaders of each generation are charged with the responsibility to identify and contend with the unique threats facing world Jewry in their time. This is why Judaism places such great prominence on leadership in conjunction with the law. The Tzadik is called 'the eyes of the community.'[125] He possesses the vision to not only see the immediate, but also the larger picture. In fact, there is 'an extension of Moses in every generation'[126]

"The Moses of the day maintains the Divine spirit and authority to make necessary adjustments within *Torah* observance.[127] Such adjustments include the emphasis, or de-emphasis, of a given law or set of laws and practices. Even the temporary suspension of certain commandments is placed in his authority and judgment. In some cases, the generational

---

[125] Rashi, Taanis 24a.
[126] *Tikkunei Zohar*, Tikkun 69
[127] *Talmud* Sotah 47-48.

leader relies upon the power of prophecy to mark a shift in the national direction."

"From what you describe, Danni," interjects Jay, "the revelation of *Torah* is kind of an ongoing phenomenon, what might be referred to as 'real time' in today's vernacular. It's almost as if the *Torah* continues to adapt through its leadership, in accordance with the characteristics of each generation."

"Indeed, that is the case, Jay," I affirm. "From its earliest inception, Judaism placed the highest value on spiritual leadership, beginning with Moses of whom the *Torah* states, 'And they believed in G-d and in Moses His servant,'[128] thus placing G-d and Moses in the same phrase.

"Leadership and supra-leadership are a constant within Judaism, from the age of the prophets to the Judges and from the authors of the *Talmud* to the Chassidic masters. The function of leadership and, especially, supra-leadership is to reveal, adjust, and apply proper Jewish observance, in accordance with the time and circumstance.

"Our generation was fortunate to have its own such Moses, the late Rebbe of Lubavitch, R' Menachem Mendel Schneerson, known simply as the 'Rebbe.' For our generation, he identified and confronted the momentous trials and conflagrations.

"World Jewry at the time of his ascendance to leadership, the immediate post holocaust era, was in a ravaged state. The events of the first half of the 20th century left a majority of Jews victims of ignorance, through no fault of their own. Jewry found itself vulnerable as the winds of change swept the world and world Jewry in particular.

"Our 3 thousand year heritage was showing signs of fatigue as a result of the long and bitter exile. The culture that nurtured the people for centuries came under siege on many fronts.

"The dynamic Rebbe of Lubavitch declared our age to be the long

---

[128] Exodus 14:31.

186

anticipated era of 'Ikvesa D'Moshichah'—a degenerate yet opportune time, known as 'Heel of Moshiach'—when Moshiach's approaching footsteps can practically be heard.[129]

"The commentaries explain that when we observe the *Torah* and its Mitzvos during the time of Ikvesa D'moshichah, G-d will keep His promise and bring the redemption. This promise is implied in Deuteronomy by use of the word 'Eikev:' 'And it will be, "Eikev"- because you will heed these ordinances and keep them and perform them, that the Lord your G-d, will keep for you the covenant and the kindness that He swore to your forefathers...' The word Eikev, assert the commentaries,[130] also means 'heel,' as in 'Heel of Moshiach.'

> ... The lesson that one who completes a mitzvah is credited with it (Rashi, Deuteronomy 8:1), is particularly apt for our generation. For according to all the signs which were given by our Sages, we are presently in the last generation of exile, which will become the first generation of redemption. Thus, it is greatly encouraging to know that, despite the fact the *Torah* study and observance of Mitzvos in previous generations greatly surpassed that of our more humble efforts, nevertheless, one who completes a mitzvah is credited with it. Moshiach will come in the merit of our Mitzvos, which are performed in the last moments of exile.[131]

"Implied here is that there is something unique about our observance of *Torah* during the stage of the 'heel' that will precipitate the redemption. What is so unique about the time of the heel? The explanation lies in its unique character.

"When one wants to enter a very hot bathtub or cold swimming pool, which limb does he or she put in first? The answer is the foot. Despite and because of the foot's reduced sensitivity compared to the more refined limbs of the upper body, it responds more readily to our will.

"The very 'lowliness' of the foot is its strength, enabling it to withstand

---

[129] See footnote 94 & 97.
[130] Deuteronomy 7:12.
[131] Based on *Likutei Sichos* vol. 19, pp. 104-5.

harsh conditions and keep soldiering on. Similarly, although our generation may lack higher qualities and spiritual refinement associated with previous generations, like the heel, we are able to show a deeper commitment to the fulfillment of the Divine will. It is the action of the heel that brings fruition to the ultimate purpose of creation.

"So Jay, are you starting to get the picture? Unlike in previous generations, the service of our particular moment in history is about the heel—the remnant souls that may have many blemishes—that might be entangled in matters not compatible with *Torah*. Nevertheless these souls, through their fulfillment of a single Mitzvah help bring an end to this dark and bitter exile."

"But Danni," muses Jay, "why would G-d want the Mitzvah of a lowly, even sinful individual?"

"Well," I tell Jay, "this speaks to the essence of the entire purpose of creation; G-d's desire to be found in the farthest and lowliest of places. We will get to this phenomenon shortly, but let me first present an overall schematic of the cosmic existential properties."

33

Three Stages in Cosmic Existence

"The cosmos mirrors the days of creation, states the *Talmud*.[132] Just as the weekly cycle consists of 7 days, so too, the universe will exist for 7 millennia. The *Talmud* continues to note that much as the 7th day of creation is Shabbos, so too, will the world as we know it exist for 6 thousand years, followed by a grand Shabbos. This millennial Shabbos will usher a new era for all of humankind; an entirely novel existence with the coming of Moshiach and the Final Redemption.

"The *Talmud* continues to assert that the 6 thousand year cycle is divided into 3 periods: The first 2 thousand years are known as the era of 'Chaos.' The next 2 thousand years are called the epoch of '*Torah*,' and the last 2 thousand years are reckoned to be the age of 'Moshiach.'

"The first 2 thousand years, prior to Abraham's debut, are called 'chaos,' because, in absence of a Divine creed, the world floundered in darkness, bereft of any and all direction, civility, and purpose. Lacking a spiritual Deific code or any morality, debauchery and turmoil reigned supreme.

"Following the years of chaos were 2 thousand years dedicated to *Torah*, beginning with Abraham's endeavor to disseminate its principles and sacred teachings. Born 1,948 years after the creation of Adam and Eve, Abraham was about 52 years old in the year 2000, when he began reaching out to people.

"In his commentary on the aforementioned Talmudic statement, Rashi explains how the year 2000 could have begun the epoch of *Torah* through Abraham, despite the fact that the *Torah* was not yet revealed. 'We have a tradition,' asserts Rashi, 'that our Forefathers knew the *Torah*

---

[132] Sanhedrin 97a.

principles and were able to relate them to the world before it was handed down to the nation of Israel on Mount Sinai as a binding covenant.'[133]

"Between the time that Abraham started to spread the *Torah* until the destruction of the Second Temple, 1,828 years elapsed. Adding another 172 years until Rabbi Yehudah Hanassi completed the recording of the Oral Law, known as the Mishnah, the epoch of *Torah* came to an end and the era of Moshiach began.

"During the 2 thousand years of *Torah*, the entire framework of *Torah* was laid out, beginning with the written *Torah*, including the Five Books of Moses handed down in the year 2448. Scriptures known as '*Tanach*' and the corpus, comprising the foundation of Oral *Torah*, known as Mishna, also were transmitted during this time frame.

"The year 200 C.E., 4 thousand years from world creation, dawned the 3rd epoch of the cosmic cycle, the age dedicated to the Final Redemption and the coming of Moshiach.

"The actual end of the Exile and the ultimate date of redemption is meant to be a mystery to humankind. This notion is affirmed in the book of Daniel, 'But you, Daniel, close up the words and seal the book until the time of the end.' [134]

"The above, notwithstanding, the latest possible date by which the redemption must occur, was always known to our sages, as the *Talmud* asserts, "Six thousand years shall the world exist and in the seventh it shall lie in ruin." [135] This dictum was understood to mean that Moshiach must come by the end of the 6th millennium. But that doesn't preclude his coming before.

"In fact, throughout the long and arduous exile, many of our leaders have attempted to calculate the end of the exile at some earlier date. This practice is based on the following Talmudic statement:

---

[133] See, for example, Yoma 28b; Rashi to Bereshit (Genesis) 26:5; Rashi to Bereshit (Genesis) 32:5.

[134] 12:4.

[135] Sanhedrin 97a.

THREE STAGES IN COSMIC EXISTENCE

R. Alexander said: R. Yehoshua Ben Levi pointed out a contradiction. It is written, "In its time [will the Messiah come]," whilst it is also written, "I [the Lord] will hasten it!" (Isaiah 60:22). If they are worthy, I will hasten it: If not, [he will come] at the due time.

"According to this Talmudic dictate, the seemingly conflicting verses, regarding the nature of Moshiach's arrival, imply the potential for more than one possibility. In that light, the sages surmise that, although the deadline for Moshiach is the end of the 6th millennium, should Israel be meritorious, his arrival could be hastened. The nature of his arrival, whether in its set time or hastened, signifies the dual possibilities.

"It's apparent from the above that, according to Chassidus, the world is a living organism; a work in progress, constantly evolving. Notably, the evolutionary nature of our universe is designed as a means to an end; an end that is affected by our actions. This makes life that much more meaningful and consequential, since the narrative is still being written and we are in the cast.

"As has been established earlier, cosmic existence is divided into 3 pairs of 2 millennium, followed by a millennial Sabbath. The preceding 6 thousand years serve as a preparation and enabler for the advent of the Moshiach—a major component of the millennial Sabbath. Moshiach's coming, as we just learned, can be hastened. It is where our efforts come in.

"Through our actions, we turn this world into a G-dly domain, what is referred to in Chassidic vernacular as Dirah B'tachtonim-a dwelling place for G-d in this world.

"Dirah B'tachtonim is the ultimate objective of the first 6 thousand years of creation, the drawing down the Divine presence into this lowly world. This is accomplished through our transforming physical mater back to its Divine essence, as discussed. The latter in turn, amongst others, hastens to arrival of Moshiach.

34

MAKE FOR ME A DWELLING PLACE

"Dirah B'tachtonim'—G-d's desire for a dwelling place in this lowly world—is a central principle expounded upon in Chabad Chassidus. At our morning study session, R' Osher began this lesson with the humorous tale about the man who brings some fine material to a tailor and asks him to make a pair of pants. When he comes back a week later, the pants are not ready. Two weeks later, they are still not ready. Finally, after 6 weeks the pants are ready.

"The man tries on the pants, they fit perfectly. Nonetheless, when it comes time to pay, he can't resist a jab at the tailor. 'You know,' he says, 'it took G-d only 6 days to make the entire world. And it took you 6 weeks to make just one pair of pants.'

> It all began with G-d's desire for a dwelling place in a remote and lowly world.

"'Ah,' the tailor rejoins, 'how could you even compare? Just look at G-d's world, and look at this pair of pants!'

"It all began with G-d's desire for a dwelling place in a remote and lowly world for His G-dly eminence to be recognized and exposed in a universe that is outwardly detached from Him. In other words, G-d wanted His holy eminence—masked by a world of materialism—to be made to shine by the efforts of humankind.

"Dirah B'tachtonim means that, despite the inclination of the Divine servant to become closer to his or her maker by withdrawing from the materialistic world and mundane matters, one must temper this desire in recognition of G-d's overarching objective—the mandate to make a home for His glory here on earth and to serve Him in this world. Contrary to logic, this is the way that one can ascend upward and become closer to his Creator. The late Lubavitcher Rebbe succinctly summarizes this idea in his *Hayom Yom*:

> Refraining from deriving pleasure—in the fullest sense—from this world is only a fine preparation for avoda (Divine service). Avoda itself is transforming the physical into a vehicle for G-dliness.[136]

"King David asserts in the book of Psalms, 'The heavens are the heavens of the Lord, but the earth He gave to humankind.'[137] The meaning of this declaration is that, from the time of creation, the higher (spiritual) and lower (physical) domains were segregated and non-fusible.

"The *Midrash* uses the following parable to explain the significance of the event: 'Once there was a king who decreed, "The people of Rome are forbidden to journey to Syria, and the people of Syria are forbidden to journey to Rome." Likewise, when G-d created the world, He decreed: "The heavens are for G-d, and the earth He has given to humankind."' [138]

"The *Midrash* further expounds: 'At the time of the giving of the *Torah*, the Almighty annulled this decree: "The lower realms shall ascend to the higher, and the higher realms shall descend to the lower," as it is written in the *Torah* (Exodus 19:20) "The Lord descended upon Mount Sinai, to the peak of the mountain and the Lord summoned Moses to the peak of the mountain and Moses ascended."'[139]

"In elucidating this *Midrash*, Chassidus offers the following insight: In the original modality of creation, the material and spiritual realms were discrete planes that never converged. Only when G-d descended on Mount Sinai, was the wall between spirit and matter breached. The *Torah* was given to the people, so as to enable them to sanctify the mundane—to express and make known the all-pervading truth of G-d within and via the material world.

"G-d's ultimate intent of creation is, hence, for His underlying essence

---

[136] *Hayom Yom*, 17 Sivan.
[137] Psalm 115: 16.
[138] *Midrash Tanchuma*, Va'eira 15.
[139] Ibid.

to be brought to the surface to manifest itself in our material world. This process was initiated with the giving of the *Torah*, while its completion will take place in the era of Moshiach—when the spiritual nature of all existence will be manifest.

"Ever since the revelation at Sinai, this mission is accomplished through the Divine precepts that were presented at Sinai. Thus, the Mitzvah serves as a means of refining and elevating the material realm of creation, thereby, bringing into fruition the ultimate G-dly intent.

"A dwelling for G-d is, then, created by using everyday life experiences and possessions for the sake of Heaven. These acts remove the mask that conceals the true creator as proprietor of the world and allow Him to be known. This type of interaction refines and elevates the elemental universe, turning it into a fitting place for G-d to dwell.

"Thus, despite all the spiritual rationale and calculations, one may not retreat from acting and interacting with the world. One's mission is to be inclusive, not elitist.

"Often, Chassidus gleans delicate lessons regarding a person's higher Divine service from a *Torah* narrative that seems to depict loathsome conduct and rebellious characters. The fine insights and traits, couched in these unassuming narratives, are brought to life through the inner dimension of *Torah*. One such lesson, found in the *Torah* reading of Sh'lach,[140] captures this very point.

"Of the twelve spies that Moses sent to scout the land of Israel, ten returned with a negative report, defaming the Promised Land as 'A land that consumes its inhabitants.'[141] They implored the Israelites to abandon their mission of conquering the land. Only Caleb and Joshua insisted that the Jews can and must proceed with the Divine directive. Convinced that G-d betrayed them, the people of Israel responded with a night of wailing and mourning over their awful plight.

---

[140] Numbers 13:1-15:41.
[141] Ibid. 13:32.

"On the surface, this is a simple story about loss of faith and rebellion. In light of the negative report, the Israelites, in spite of all the miracles they experienced, lost faith in G-d and His ability to deliver them into the land of Canaan. However, Chassidus ascribes entirely new meaning to this narrative.

"According to the teachings of Chassidus, these people were not cowardly ingrates. Quite the contrary, they were a highly pious generation, infatuated with Divine service. What these spiritual souls feared most was jeopardizing their intense relationship with G-d, not a physical defeat by the Canaanites.

"Sheltered by the Clouds of Glory, fed by Manna from heaven and water from a miracle rock, they experienced an angelic existence, immersed in Divine wisdom and service. Given the spiritual existence to which they became accustomed, the notion of leaving their desert paradise to settle a land and eke earthly bread out of its soil was inconceivable.

"Here in the desert, they argued, our souls are free to ponder the Divine. There, we shall succumb to the mundane, intrinsic to an earth-bound existence. 'It is a land that consumes its inhabitants,' they warned the people. Why abandon our spiritual idyll for a life subsisting off the land?

"But humankind, the crown of G-d's creation, is meant to execute the G-dly purpose of creation; His desire is for 'a dwelling below'—a home in the physical world. A person's function is to fuse the spiritual and physical in the service of the Divine, for he or she alone, is fashioned of both spirit and matter.

"The spies erred in confining the purpose of creation to the realm of the spirit, in effect, rejecting Israel's true mission: to conquer and settle the land of Canaan and use its physical matter and potential for holiness and sanctity.

"Herein lies a significant message regarding our true identity and purpose. Our essential quality is not to cleave to G-d by shunning the body. Quite the contrary, our true mission is to elevate and refine the world by enlisting the physical in the higher service of the Divine. Asceticism is not the Jewish path to self-realization and purpose. In the words of the late Lubavitcher Rebbe regarding G-d's command to Noach to leave the ark:

> A person might be tempted to lock himself away in an "ark" of personal spirituality; the *Torah* however teaches a Jew that he "most go out of the ark…" and take responsibility for the world around him. [142]

"Among the many religions that have come and gone, some relegated G-d to the heavens of heavens and others turned Him into wind and sand. None ever dreamed of fitting an elusive, holy, and infinite G-d into a lowly and finite vessel. However, according to Chassidus, this is precisely what Judaism is all about, indeed, what creation is all about.

> Asceticism is not the Jewish path to self-realization and purpose.

"With such an approach, one cannot remain a smugly reclusive individual, aloof from one's environment. One is impelled to do everything in his or her power to bring Heaven down to earth, to reach out and affect others to help them find their place and to make this world a better and more holy dwelling—a 'dirah' for the Divine presence. The mandate to make this world into a dwelling place for G-d, perhaps, is the most driving force behind Chabad's global outreach campaign.

"It is important to note that turning the world into a dwelling place for the Divine Presence, includes making ourselves into a dwelling place for Him. Let's talk about this some."

---

[142] *Likutei Sichos* vol. 25

THREE SCHOOLS OF THOUGHT:

Hayom Yom, Rabbi Menachem Mendel Schneerson

1. The discipline of nullification of the material by indicating the repulsive and abhorrent nature of all that is bodily and material. This is the school of Mussar.

2. The school of recognition of the superiority of the "Inner form"[1] and the spiritual—the dimension of character-traits and intellectuality[2]— and instruction as to how one may come closer to attaining these. This is the school of Chakira, philosophy.

3. The discipline of predominance of form over matter. This school teaches the unique quality of the material when it is purified, and the unique quality of "Form" when integrated with the material; the two are to be so thoroughly fused that one cannot detect where either of them begins or ends—for "Their beginning is wedged into their end, and their end into their beginning."[3] The One G-d created them both, and for one purpose—to reveal the light of Holiness of His hidden power. Only both of them together will complete the perfection desired by the Creator. This is the school of (the teachings/instruction of) Chassidus.[4]

Hayom Yom, was compiled and arranged by the Lubavitcher Rebbe, Rabbi Menachem Mendel Schneerson, in 5703 (1943) from the talks and letters of the sixth Chabad Rebbe, Rabbi Joseph Yitzchak Schneersohn, of righteous memory.

---

[1] Heb. tzura, 'form,' as opposed to chomer, 'matter,' that is, the body's life-force—the soul—is its 'form,' its inner spiritual dimension; the body, itself, is the outer physical dimension, the 'matter.'

[2] As opposed to the dimension of bodily matters.

[3] See 16 Adar I Footnote.

[4] See also On the Teachings of Chassidus (NY: Kehot) chapters 11-18 where these three schools of thought are discussed at length.

35

AND I SHALL DWELL WITHIN THEM

"There is a well-known story of the great Chassidic master, Rabbi Menachem Mendel of Kotzk.[143] He asked his students, 'where is the dwelling place of G-d?' Amused, they responded, 'what a thing to ask! Is not the whole earth full of G-d's glory?' R' Mendel then answered his own question: 'G-d dwells wherever we let Him in.'

G-d
dwells
wherever
we let
Him in.

"It is known that the Tabernacle that the Almighty commanded the Israelites to build in the desert was but a prototype of the temple that each one of us is commanded to build on a microcosmic level.

"Many commentaries note the textual anomaly inherent in the phrase 'V'asu li Mikdash V'shachanti 'B'socham'— and they shall make for me a Mikdash (sanctuary)—and I shall dwell within 'them,'[144] rather than 'B'socho' within 'it.' G-d tells the Israelites that if they build Him a sanctuary, He will dwell within them. The goal of the Mikdash is the resting of the Divine presence in each and every member of Israel.

"The Shechinah's presence, seen by all in the Mikdash, served as a potent reminder of the goal of creation: For G-dliness to permeate all creation and especially human beings, the pinnacle of creation. A holy place is within a heart moved to open.

"In summary, we are enjoined to refine and elevate the material realm within the universe; as we are enjoined to fuse the heavenly and earthly

---

[143] Menachem Mendel Morgensztern of Kotzk, better known as the Kotzker Rebbe (1787–1859) was a Chassidic rabbi and leader. Born to a non-Chassidic family in Goraj near Lublin, Poland, he was attracted to Chassidism in his youth. He was known for having acquired impressive *Talmudic* and Kabbalistic knowledge at an early age. He was a student of Reb Bunim of Peshischa and, on the latter's death, attracted many of his followers. Morgensztern was well known for his incisive and down-to-earth philosophies and sharp-witted sayings. Apparently, he had little patience for false piety or stupidity.

[144] Exodus 25:8.

within ourselves into the service of the one true Creator. According to Chassidus, this is the meaning of the most renowned Jewish prayer, 'Hear, O Israel, the Lord is our G-d, the Lord is One.'

"In this regard, Chassidus draws a lesson from the *Torah* portion of Ki Sisa.[145] G-d commanded Moses to take a census of the Jewish people. He was instructed not to count the Jewish people, but rather to collect a poll tax consisting of a half shekel. All who were to be counted were obligated to pay this tax. 'The rich shall not give more and the poor shall not give less than half a shekel, when giving the contribution for G-d to atone for your souls.'[146] The half shekel served as atonement for their involvement in the incident of the Golden Calf.

"Rashi asserts that G-d actually showed Moses a fiery coin weighing a half shekel, saying, 'This is what everyone counted shall give, a half shekel of the sacred shekel.' But why did Moses need to be shown a half shekel?

"True, we know that Moses also was shown a Menorah (candelabrum) as a prototype before its construction. However, considering how complicated the Menorah was—with all of its buttons, flowers, and details—it is understandable why it was needed to be seen. On the other hand, a half shekel doesn't seem that complicated. And what about the fire? Why not show him an ordinary half shekel instead of one that was on fire? Here then, is the Chassidic insight on the 'coin of fire:'

> Occupation with materiality is as holy an endeavor as the most transcendent flight of spirit.

"Moses was familiar with a half shekel all along, what he didn't understand was how it could cause 'atonement for the soul.' The notion that a mere piece of silver could redeem a soul from so severe a sin, left Moses perplexed.

---

[145] Exodus 30:11-34:35.
[146] Exodus 30:13-15.

"Seemingly, silver and soul are polar opposites; the soul epitomizes the metaphysical, while silver epitomizes earthliness. Not only is silver taken from the earth, which is the lowest of the four fundamental 'elements'—fire, water, air, and earth—usually it is found deep within the earth, the lowest of the low. Given that the soul needed redemption, because it succumbed to earthliness, how is it that earthliness is prescribed as the cure for the very ailment of earthliness?

"So, now that we understand the question, how is it explained through the sighting of the half shekel?

"In displaying a half shekel of fire, G-d sought to demonstrate that opposites can be fused. Silver, the earthliest of the elements becomes fire, the most ethereal of the elements. The point is not that the 'source' of the half shekel is spirituality, for that is true of every physical object. Nor is the point that the half shekel becomes a vehicle for spirituality, for all objects used in a Mitzvah are meant to achieve that end.

"Rather, the idea here is that the actual earthly half shekel can be transformed into 'fire.' Therein lies the answer to Moses' perplexity—the ability of a physical coin to redeem a tarnished soul.[147]

"More specifically, the individual's occupation with materiality can be as holy an endeavor as the most transcendent flight of spirit. Indeed, our sages consider one's sanctification of material life the ultimate objective of creation. G-d, as stated above, desired a dwelling in the lowly realms.

"'This is what man is all about; the purpose of his creation and the creation of all worlds, supernal and terrestrial,'[148] says Rabbi Schneur Zalman of Liadi, in his acclaimed work *Tanya*, regarding this matter.

"The transformation of earthly matter occurs by virtue of our soul's essence that is an actual sliver of G-d. The soul's essence never sins. Only the superficial dimension of the soul that is manifest in the body is susceptible to the temptations of the evil inclination. By

---

[147] *Likutei Sichot*, vol. 1, pp. 180-181.
[148] *Tanya* Chapter 36.

engaging our soul's essence in what we do, we fuse fire and silver in a harmonious blend.

"Earthly objects and activities can be cold and unremarkable. But when imbued with warmth and enthusiasm of the soul's essence, they become alive and permeated with spiritual meaning. Therefore, they can atone for the gravest of sins—the severe sin of the golden calf—transforming them into good.

"Chassidus uses a parable (that some attribute to the Baal Shem Tov) to make the point: A goldsmith apprentice learned all the details necessary to become an expert. But, assuming the obvious, the teacher never taught him to light the fire. This is the message of the fiery coin shown to Moses.

"Vitality and enthusiasm make all the difference between earthly objects and spiritual substance. Fire, as it soars upward, represents excitement and emotion—rising above.[149]

"So, you see Jay, once again, Chassidus emphasizes the unique fire-like quality of the Jewish soul and its uncompromising relationship with its Divine source, regardless of any mitigating circumstances."

---

[149] *Likutei Sichot*, vol. 3, p. 925, vol. 26, pp. 231-237.

36

THE 7TH GENERATION

"The process of bringing Divine presence into our benighted and physical world, and the lowest realms within the physical, essentially, is a gradual one. With every subsequent generation, the Shechinah descends a little further. As holiness penetrates increasingly lower levels of existence, our mission becomes more outward oriented. At some point, this process increases exponentially. That period is what we refer to as Ikvesa D'moshicha—the 'Heel of Moshiach.'

> With every subsequent generation, the Shechinah descends a little further.

"You see, Jay, the earlier generations correspond to the 'brain' of the cosmic matrix, while the final generations correspond to its 'heel'. The brain, or head, which is the seat of the intellect, is far more delicate than the foot.

"Maintaining the integrity and wellbeing of the brain—protecting its delicate complex mechanism, both neurologically and physiologically—requires greater care than that of the relatively coarse foot. We see this patently reflected on a daily basis, in the fact that helmets are commonly worn on the head rather than on the foot.

"As part of the cosmic 'head,' our forebears had the great responsibility of interpreting the *Torah* and establishing the law for all of time. This required a helmet, in the form of increased inward focus, and limited exposure to the 'outside' elements. Thus, they were unable to engage the lowly and coarse elements that are common in the generation preceding the advent of Moshiach.

"Even in the time of R' Schneur Zalman of Liadi, the 18th century author of *Tanya* and founder of the Chabad movement, the Divine servant found himself withdrawn from the materialistic sphere.

"Expected to study vast amounts of *Torah* and pray with utmost fervor and concentration, while expressing the ultimate in character refinement, the seeker of holiness had little capacity for involvement with the secular and mundane elements of life. After all, that generation had the sacred task of laying the foundation and framework of Chassidic ideology.

"But now that we reached the final quarter of the 5th millennium since creation, well into the stage known as the 'Heel of Moshiach'—indeed the very end of the heel—we possess the unique ability and mission to confront and transform the darkest vestiges of exile, our generation's limited spiritual capacity notwithstanding.

"Chabad sees a critical parallel between the advent of the Chassidic movement and the period of the heel. In fact, Chassidus is seen as the armor, or intelligence, for this final foray. Our mission entails completing the process of drawing down the Shechinah to earth.

> The sixth Chabad Rebbe, R' Yosef Yitzchak Schneerson, took the process to a new level.

"We must draw down the Shechinah, not just to the lower levels, but to the very lowest level—the farthest and the darkest corners of the universe—thereby clearing the path for the ultimate redemption.

"Chabad culture maintains that, with the advancement of time and the proliferation of more potent forms of Chassidus and their more illustrious articulation, the implements are provided to complete the work of turning this world into a dwelling for the Divine presence. Through the progression of Chabad Rebbes and the translation of the deepest concepts of *Torah* into every spoken language, we are ready to penetrate the farthest and innermost layers of exile.

"The anticipation of the final redemption in this age of Ikvesa D'moshicha is not limited to the cognitive intellectual realm; it finds expression in the practical arena, as well. Through its army of Chassidim and

Shluchim, Chabad sees its role as being the vanguard of this mission—
'the boots on the ground.' Chabad's goal is to use every method of
outreach to bring *Torah* to every man, woman, and child alive today.

"Although this final endeavor began with the Baal Shem Tov and R'
Schneur Zalman of Liadi, the farthest corners remain reserved for the
last generation to elevate. The sixth Chabad Rebbe, R' Yosef Yitzchak
Schneerson, brought the movement to the West and took the process to
a new level, by extending it to people and places that were, previously,
unable to even relate to the process.

"Through his Yiddish translations of Chassidus and illustrious memoirs,
R' Yosef Yitzchak enabled the mind of the ordinary person to grasp
and internalize the transcendent spirituality of basic Chassidism and
Kabbalah.

"However, the greatest expansion came with the advent of the late
Lubavitcher Rebbe, Rabbi Menachem Mendel Schneerson, the
'seventh generation' of Chabad leadership. His teachings include
Kabbalistic philosophy and theology, recorded for the most part in his
Likutei Sichos.[150]

"Chabad believes that the final step of bringing the Shechinah down to
earth, so that the 'lower world' itself becomes a source of illumination,
belongs to the Rebbe of the 'seventh generation.'

"Upon accepting the mantle of leadership, in his inaugural discourse—
'Basi L'Gani—on the 10th of Sh'vat 5711 (January, 1951), the Rebbe
clearly stated as much:

> It is required of each of us, the members of the seventh generation
> about which it states 'All sevenths are beloved,' *Midrash Rabba* Vayikra
> 29,[151] to complete the process of drawing down the Shechinah [to

---

[150] *Likutei Sichos* (literally, "Collected Talks") contains both the scope and the core of the late Lubavitcher Rebbe Rabbi Menachem Mendel Schneerson's teachings, and is the most authoritative source text for the Rebbe's unique, original, and often revolutionary explanation of Judaism. These talks represent the legacy of the Rebbe's teachings to the world.

[151] More than any other number, seven is the protoplasm, the very building block of Jewish time. The Jewish week is known as Shavuah (seventh) and is composed of 7 days. The Kuzari notes that it

earth] and not just the Shechinah, but the 'Essence' of the Shechinah and precisely to the lowest levels.

...The fact that we are of the 7th generation is not by our choice or in the merit of our own 'Avoda'— service. In many respects, it even may be against our will. Nonetheless, 'All sevenths are beloved,' and we are now in the period known as Ikvesa D'moshichah, we are in fact at the very end of the heel.

"To bolster its assertion that 'Kol Hashviim Chavivim'—all sevenths are beloved—the *Midrash* provides historical proof by listing a surprising array of generations and sequences that peaked on the seventh; the seventh of a cycle or sequence is its climax and completion. The very etymology of Sheva—seven—relays the above idea. The Maharal[152] correlates Sheva to Sova—satisfaction—after seven, we completed whatever we set out to do. Hence, we are satisfied.

"Intriguing thought, Danni," says Jay, "But I have no idea where you're going with it. How does this relate to my spiritual quagmire resulting from my marital situation?"

---

did not have to be that way. Society could have structured weeks composed of sequences of eight, ten, or any other number of days. Our 12-month calendar all heeds the cycle of 7. In his Collected Writings, Rav Shimshon Rafael Hirsch notes that our 2 festive months, Nissan and Tishrei, are at 7-month intervals from each other. Some other manifestations of this maxim are the 7 year (Shmitta) sabbatical of the land cycle, the 7 day duration (in Israel) of the festivals of Pesach and Sukkot and the 7 day cycle of ritual purification.

The Vilna Gaon in Divrei Eliyahu, Parshat Emor, even compiles a list of 7 days that the *Torah* forbade work: the first and last days of Pesach and Sukkot, Shavuot, Rosh HaShana, and Yom HaKippurim. Seven is distinct, even from a mathematical standpoint. Of all the basic numbers—one through ten—only seven is both non-divisible (in contrast to six, for example, that can be divided by two or by three). Yet, neither can it be multiplied and still remain within the realm of basic numbers (one through ten). Seven cannot be fragmented into equal whole numbers (unlike four, six, eight, nine, or ten), and it is a number so perfect that it doesn't have to duplicate itself to achieve greatness (for example, if we multiply seven, we leave the realm of basic numbers, unlike one, two three, four, and five). Seven symbolizes the fulfillment of our potential; being completely developed; being fully able to stand on our own two feet without any assistance. Therefore, our mundane day-to-day lives are structured in sequences of seven.

[152] Judah Loew ben Bezalel (c. 1520–17 September, 1609), widely known to scholars of Judaism as the Maharal of Prague or simply The MaHaRaL, the Hebrew acronym of the initials of "Moreinu Ha-Rav Loew" ("Our Teacher, Rabbi Loew"), was an important *Talmudic* scholar, Jewish mystic, and philosopher who, for most of his life, served as a leading rabbi in the cities of Mikulov in Moravia and Prague in Bohemia. Within the world of *Torah* and *Talmudic* scholarship, he is known for his works on Jewish philosophy and Jewish mysticism and his work Gur Aryeh al Ha*Torah*, a supercommentary on Rashi's *Torah* commentary.

"Don't worry," I assure Jay, "It will all come together. The key idea is that the times we live in—the 'Heel of Moshiach as well as the 7th generation—present enormous bearing on the status and service of today's Jew, creating an entirely unique paradigm.

"A wise person once observed that when a Jewish child is born, he or she is 2000 years old, because he or she is the product of 2000 years of Jewish exile and thus shoulders that burden. A Jew belonging to the epoch of the heel, is one who survived 2 thousand years of bitter exile. The connection to G-d and Judaism of such a person is not based on intelligence or logic. Neither is it based on his or her status regarding religious perfection or even mitzvah observance. You see where all this is heading, Jay?"

> A Jew belonging to the epic of the heel is one who survived 2 thousand years of exile.

"Wow Danni, well said," Jay notes, "you're starting to sound convincing now, and that's a frightening thought," he quickly adds in jest.

"Can I ask you a more technical, or personal, question Danni," asks Jay. "It's about the central role that Chabad sees itself, and that of its leaders, in effectuating what you call, the ultimate purpose of creation. I mean no disrespect, but I'm curious how this compares with historic Judaism? Is it historically common for Jewish factions to single themselves out as being at the center of the Divine cosmic mission? How does this go over with other sects within the broader Jewish community?"

"Let me address your second issue first," I tell Jay. "It's a fair question, although a quite loaded one. To be honest, I don't profess to have the answer. I'm not a historian and can't tell you statistically how common this phenomenon was culturally. Nor do I know how other strands feel about it, because I never really discussed the matter with any of them. What I can share with you is my own take on the subject.

"With respect to the historic prevalence, it appears that the possession of a clear perspective, regarding the overall and ultimate cosmic mission—not to mention a defined method and modus operandi in bringing it to fruition—was not a likely phenomenon in earlier generations.

"In those early stages, people mostly were focused on smaller and more immediate pieces of the puzzle and could not yet see the greater picture. In fact, I don't believe that until our very own times, was such a phenomenon heard of.

"During the first 2 thousand years of chaos, the revelation of Moshiach and the messianic era weren't even a possibility, let alone the overriding focus. During the next 2 thousand years of *Torah*, while Moshiach was a possibility, the predominant focus, as stated above, was on the revelation and expounding of *Torah*. Those 20 generations would have understood their mission in that limited context.

"It is only in the last 18 hundred years that this type of mindset could be imagined. Yet, in these years, the long and sharp talons of exile were just beginning to sink in. While the Jewish people undoubtedly longed and prayed for Moshiach, they could certainly not visually perceive the messianic onset and the process of Dirah B'tachtonim through gradual world transformation.

"It is only in recent times, that we are fortunate to experience this. What they saw was a world from which the Divine presence was being driven out by unimaginable godlessness and evil, not a world of spiritual transformation.

"This should answer your question. There is probably no historic parallel of a particular segment of Jewry regarding themselves as the vanguard of the ultimate Divine mission of creation.

"Was there competition among the diverse strands within the Jewish world regarding the specific Divinely ordained path? The answer is yes, of course. In fact, every religious faction tends to believe that their method and approach is superior to all others. They belong to that particular system for that very reason. Misnagedim, for example, consider their system superior to Chasidism, and Satmar Chassidim believe that their approach is superior to Chabad, and so forth.

"This answers the other part of your question, Jay, as to how other sectors of the Jewish community feel about Chabad's belief in holding the secret of the Divine intent. The answer is that each sector believes that their path is the most accurate.

"So, in essence, Chabad has not changed the intersect dynamics, but has upped ante.

"At this point, I think we could finally address what you asked way back in the beginning of our conversation, about why it took all these millennia for Chassidus to come into fruition."

37

WHY NOW?

"A fascinating insight found in the holy *Zohar*,[153] corroborates our assertion regarding the extraordinary potential and merit of our age— the 7th generation—according to R' Osher Chaimson. It comes as an answer to the question as to why the 'inner dimension' of Torah was propagated only in the latter part of our almost 6 thousand years of world history. It also sheds light on how this occurrence coincides with the explosion of scientific knowledge and the onset of the Messianic era.

"'The explanation must be prefaced,' says R' Osher, 'by noting the disproportionate scientific progress that civilization achieved in the last several hundred years, compared to the first 55 hundred years following creation. There is an obvious paradigmatic shift from the early years of civilization until the 1800s C.E. and from 1800 C.E. until now. This phenomenon is quite astounding. But even more astounding is that Kabbalistic writings predicted this phenomenon, thousands of years prior to its actualization.

"'Two thousand years ago, the holy *Zohar* forecasted the great explosion of knowledge in a homiletical interpretation of a biblical verse recounting the flood in the time of Noach: 'In the six-hundredth year in the life of Noach... all wellsprings of the great deep burst open, and the windows of heaven were opened...'[154]

"'The *Zohar* interprets this Biblical statement along the following prophetical lines: 'In the sixth hundred year of the sixth millennium the gates of knowledge above and the fountains of knowledge below will be opened and the world will be prepared to enter the seventh millennium, just as man prepares on the sixth day to enter the Shabbos when the sun is about to set...'[155]

---

[153] See footnote 24.
[154] Genesis 7:11.
[155] *Zohar* I,117a.

"'The 6th century of the 6th millennium in the Jewish calendar is the Hebrew year 5600 that corresponds to the secular year 1840. The 'gates of knowledge above' refers to the revelation of the esoteric dimension of *Torah*, specifically Chabad Chassidus, that came into blossom during the late 1700s and early 1800s. The 'fountains of knowledge below' refers to secular knowledge, specifically the industrial revolution that occurred in the early 1800s.

"'Indeed,'" continues R' Osher, "'the 56th century from creation (1740-1840, in the secular calendar) was a time of great discovery and accelerated development, both in the supernal wisdom of *Torah* and in the earthly wisdom of secular science.

> The gates of knowledge above and the fountains of knowledge below will be opened.

"'The *Zohar* actually uses the term 'lower' for earthly wisdom, in line with the usual metaphysical axiom of 'above' corresponding to spiritual matter and 'below' to physical matter. So, lower wisdom refers to science and higher knowledge to the inner dimension of *Torah*.

"'This is a big deal, because the industrial revolution was an extraordinary occurrence and the revolution brought on by the revelation of Chassidus is even more spectacular. The improbability of these two events coinciding is exceeded only by their 2 thousand year prior prediction. Is there another example of such coincidence and prognostication?

"'The *Zohar* explains that this 'expansion' of physical knowledge is for the purpose of 'preparing' the world for the 7th millennium, the 'Shabbos,' or period of rest for humankind and the earth. The Shabbos according to the Hebrew calendar is the millennium 6000-7000.

"'We live in a world that is changing so rapidly' continues R' Osher, 'that what was new yesterday is obsolete today. The benefits brought on by modern science are wonderful; but, modern technology must be viewed from the perspective of Divine intent, for the entire world and the creations therein, only have one purpose—to be used in our service to G-d. Hence, the products of secular science should not be looked on indifferently or, worse yet, with hostility simply because they are modern.

"'On the contrary, modern technology must be used to serve the Sublime Creator. In our age, there is the obligation to use all modern advances for the propagation of Chassidus. The technological advances of the last few centuries occurred, according to the *Zohar*, entirely for the purpose that, together with the revelation of the *Torah*'s inner dimension; the world should become ready for the Messianic age.

"'This begs the question: One can appreciate why the dissemination of mystical thought would be a preparation for redemption, since with the coming of Moshiach, 'the earth will be filled with the knowledge of G-d,'[156] of which Kabbalistic teachings are a foretaste. But why is the development of scientific and technological wisdom a prelude to Moshiach?

Why is the development of scientific and technological wisdom a prelude to Moshiach?

"'The answer is yes. It is the bounty reaped from the dark and arduous exile, which serve as instruments in bringing about the coming of Moshiach.

"'One of the prophecies regarding the time of redemption is that, 'The glory of the Lord will be revealed; and all flesh together will perceive it, for the mouth of the Lord has spoken it,'[157] in example, that G-d's presence will be discernable to the physical senses. Scientific developments over the past 150 years have brought to our senses phenomena that were previously deemed to be supernatural. In the words of the late Lubavitcher Rebbe:

> This explosion of knowledge in the secular sciences and the propagation of Chassidus, ensures the fulfillment of the promise that

[156] Isaiah 11:9.
[157] Isaiah 40:5.

'The earth will be filled with the knowledge of the Lord as the waters cover the sea,' (Habakkuk 2:14).

For example, through television, radio, and the telephone, man is able to see and hear from one end of the world to the other instantaneously. So now, the concept that there is, 'an Eye that sees, and an Ear that hears, and all your deeds are recorded in a book' (Avos 2:1), is no longer something left for the imagination alone to appreciate, for now our physical senses can begin to appreciate this phenomenon too.

This was the *Zohar's* intention in connecting the scientific revolution with the coming of Moshiach. Modern technology has brought unimaginable phenomena to our senses which help us to envision the time when, 'all flesh will see together that G-d is speaking (Isaiah 40:5)'.[158]

"'The latter' concludes R' Osher, 'is why it is particularly in our times that the revelation of the most inner dimension of *Torah* was revealed.'

"Extremely interesting," proclaims Jay, somewhat amazed, "there is so much to digest. I feel like I'm being exposed to a whole new world that I had no idea existed. Did the *Zohar* actually predict the technological revolution as well as the inner part of *Torah*?"

"Well, I read you the quote" I say, "I didn't make it up. What do you say? Was that a clear enough prediction?"

"From what you read, it seems pretty clear," Jay agrees.

"There you have it. I didn't change a word," I assert.

"Now that's mindboggling stuff," declares Jay.

"But, hold on, there is more to the uniqueness of our 7th generation, which is really where you come in."

---

158 Based on *Likutei Sichos* vol. 15.

38

TINOK SHENISHBA

"Once, I remember seeing a cartoon showing a father examining his young son's report card that was filled with D's and F's. As the father scowled, the boy asked, 'Dad, do you think the problem is heredity or environmental?'

"Perhaps the most revolutionary measure taken by the Chabad leader of our time—the late Lubavitcher Rebbe, Rabbi Menachem Mendel Schneerson—was to classify all non-*Torah* educated Jews in our times as Tinok Shenishba, literally 'captured infant.' This ideology was based on the approach of his father-in-law, the sixth Lubavitcher Rebbe.

"Tinok Shenishba is a Talmudic term that refers to a Jewish individual who inadvertently sins as a result of being raised from infancy among gentiles and, therefore, has no understanding of Judaism.[159] Raised without an appreciation for the ideology and practice of Judaism, by Talmudic law, one is not held accountable for failing to live in accordance with *Torah*. In this case, Judaism absolves the person because he or she cannot be blamed for his or her lack of belief and observance.

"At the end of a long letter, in response to a certain individual, the sixth Lubavitcher Rebbe, Rabbi Yosef Yitzchak writes:

> ...The Sages tell us that even when one sins, he or she is still called a Jew. Even one, who discards Judaism and becomes—Heaven forfend—an apostate, remains a Jew. To stop being a Jew is impossible (Sanhedrin 44a). Whether he or she wants to or not, one who is born a Jew remains a Jew and sooner or later will feel the sentiment expressed at Sinai: 'We will do and we will hear,' (Exodus 24:7) because the Pintele Yid—the essence Jewish soul—always remains whole...[160]

---

[159] Shabbos 68b; Shavuos 5a.
[160] Igros Kodesh of the Previous Rebbe, Vol. 2, p. 526.

"The late Lubavitcher Rebbe crystalized this philosophy throughout his 50 years of leadership. Expounding on the theme of Tinok Shenishba at a Shabbos gathering of Parshas Vayechi,[161] the Rebbe stressed that, in our generation in particular, we must always relate to our less observant brethren in the context of Tinok Shenishba. Furthermore, our relationship with such individuals should be one of inspiration and encouragement towards observance, if only one Mitzvah at a time:

> ...This long exile, which because of its length is much more difficult than all other exiles; therefore, it becomes more necessary to give strength and encouragement... To emphasize the true level of each and every Jew—the seed of Yaakov—that he is a 'Jew;' therefore, notwithstanding his status and revealed situation, he can and must reveal his true level through doing Teshuva and keeping *Torah* and Mitzvos. That is the way to strengthen and encourage... This is all important in this generation in which those who are until now non-observant are in the category of a Tinok Shenishba and their status is as clearly ruled by Maimonides who says: 'It is correct to bring them to do Teshuva and to draw them with peaceful words until they return to the strength of the *Torah*' (Rambam, Hilchos Mamrim 3:3).

When a Tinok Shenishba keeps even one Mitzvah, this is surely very precious and beloved by G-d.

> ...'*Torah* exempts one who is forced to transgress' (*Talmud* Bava Kamma 28b). On the other hand, when a Tinok Shenishba keeps even one Mitzvah—and definitely one who keeps many Mitzvos—as the Sages have testified (*Talmud* Chagigah end) that there is no man of Israel who has not kept many Mitzvos[162]—this is surely very precious and beloved by G-d.[163]

---

[161] 5751 (1991).

[162] See *Torah Or*, Mikeitz p. 31c: "Now there is no Jew who has not honored G-d to that extent at least; every Jew is thus deserving of all the good things of this world. Nebuchadnezzar merely took three steps out of deference to G-d and he and his descendants were granted sovereignty over the whole world for three generations, how much more so is the worthiness of the Jew." See also Iggeres HaShmad of the Rambam, Chapter 3.

[163] At the Shabbos gathering, Parshas Vayechi, 5771 (1991).

"So you see, Jay, the Rebbe repeatedly advocated that, due to the depth of the exile in our times, a Jew who failed to receive a proper Jewish education pleases G-d with a single Mitzvah, even though he or she may not keep the other six hundred and twelve.

"The Rebbe maintained that the unique character of the Jew reaches beyond the observance of Mitzvos. It is rather something intrinsic and soul related. In a talk regarding the *Torah* portion of Kedoshim,[164] he argued this point:

> A unique quality of Parshas Kedoshim is that it was said directly by Moses to the people, unlike the other laws of the *Torah*, which were first taught to Aharon and the elders. As Rashi states in the opening of the Parsha, 'This Parsha was said to the assembled [congregation of Israel] because most of the basic teachings of the *Torah* depend on it.' (Rashi, Leviticus 19:2)
>
> The first thing that the Jewish people were told after being assembled was 'You should be holy because I, G-d your G-d, am holy.' (Leviticus 19:2)
>
> Now, we might have thought that when addressing the public about 'the basic teachings of the *Torah*,' the first thing to do would be to warn the people about keeping the Mitzvos and the grave consequences of their non-observance. And only then would it be appropriate to stress the positive side of the Mitzvos, such as the great merit that the Jewish people have to be given these laws. Moses would thus have followed the sequence of the verse, 'Turn away from evil, and do good.' (Psalms 34:16)
>
> In fact, however, Moses did the very opposite. First, he stressed the positive aspects of being Jewish and observing the Mitzvos—'You should be holy because I, G-d your G-d, am holy,'—that the holiness of a Jew is connected with the holiness of G-d Himself. And, only after this positive introduction did he begin to stress the seriousness of the Mitzvos, etc...

---

[164] Achrei-Kedoshim 5748.

And, even though the verse seems to suggest that the negative must come first ('turn away from evil, and do good'), we could nevertheless interpret the verse as follows: In order to turn away from evil, simply do good and the evil will take care of itself.[165]

"The Rebbe was displeased with those who made a habit of speaking ill of the Jews of our generation, regardless of their level of observance. In another talk, he added the following point:

> There are those who wish to suggest that a path of rebuke and citation of punishment, retribution, etc., is authentic as it is the path of the Musar Movement. This is how the Maggidim of old used to rebuke their congregations. They further add that all the writings of the Prophets are full of such rebuke.
>
> The holiness of a Jew is connected with the holiness of G-d Himself.
>
> In addition to the fact that in recent generations the way of Chassidus has been embraced in most Jewish circles, the Tinokos Shenishbu (plural for Tinok Shenishba) of this generation who, when spoken to sharply are turned off; whereas when spoken to warmly, show interest.
>
> Chassidus has been demonstrated to be the most effective way to draw the hearts of Jews to our Father in Heaven—the saying of Musar also has to fall within the parameters of *Torah* as demonstrated by all the Gedolei Yisrael— great Jewish leaders—who walked in that path. [166]

"So Jay, to summarize, our Jewishness is not dependent on our level of religiosity or observance. It is intrinsic; part of our DNA.

Every Jew is dear to G-d, like an only child, every Mitzvah is cherished by Him regardless of what he or she has done before and after. Let us explore this intriguing phenomenon.

---

[165] Based on the Sicha of Shabbos Parshas Acharei-Kedoshim 5748.
[166] Shabbos Parshas Shemos 5751. See similar Sicha in *Likutei Sichos*, Vol. 24, p. 308.

39

FAST FOOD, JEWISH STYLE

"Chassidus further explains that we are getting closer every day to the Redemption, the era of peace, prosperity, and wisdom, promised by G-d and foretold by the prophets. Therefore, we shouldn't spend time contemplating the menu of Mitzvos. We no longer have time to sit and wait to perform certain Mitzvos because we haven't first committed to other Mitzvos.

"Our sages suggested that we implement the fast-food mentality into our lives, though with a Jewish twist of course: 'Grab and eat, grab and drink,' said Rabbi Shmuel to his student, Rabbi Yehuda Shenina, as related in the *Talmud*, 'for life is like a party that will soon be over.' [167]

"Far from espousing a hedonistic attitude, Rabbi Shmuel was conveying the proper mentality towards Judaism and its commandments. Chassidus likens Mitzvos to food and *Torah* to water. 'Grab and eat, grab and drink whatever Mitzvah comes your way. Grab every Mitzvah you can, study as much *Torah* as you are able,' was R' Shmuel's advice, 'for life in this world will soon be over and, in the World to Come, the opportunity for Mitzvos and *Torah* study will no longer be available.'

"To put this into practical perspective, asserts the Rebbe, some ask about themselves, some about others: 'What's the point of putting on Tefillin? What's the use? If we want to come closer to Judaism, shouldn't we first take the time to learn what *Torah* is, what G-d is and what Tefillin are and, only after we master all that, put on the Tefillin?' The answer is no. We start with action and actually accomplish something.

"The Jewish fast-food mentality means seizing every opportunity to do a Mitzvah, regardless of whether we think it should be the next one in our repertoire or whether we're worthy enough. There's no time for,

---

[167] Eruvin 54:a.

'How can I light Shabbat candles if on Saturday I...?' Or, 'Why put on Tefillin if I don't...?' Grab and eat, grab and drink means that these last few moments before the Messianic era need to be filled with action, not contemplation, for soon the party will be over. It's not a time for calculations of any sort regarding the status of the Mitzvah or the doer of the Mitzvah.

"In fact, to take it a step farther, according to Chassidus the exile is likened to a state of sleep: 'When G-d will return the exiles of Zion, we will have been like dreamers,' says the Psalmist.[168] When we will be redeemed from exile, the experience will be like awakening from a long sleep.

"A dream consists of eccentric, even conflicting ideas. In a dream, one can visualize things that are logically impossible. Fire can be cold, snow can be hot, and elephants can pass through the eyes of needles.

> Every spiritual success is real and permanent.

"Life, thus, has a paradoxical quality in the present time of exile. For example, one moment while praying, we can be aroused with love for G-d. The very next moment, the love vanishes and we're back to our material, mundane self.

"Yet, this does not mean that our spiritual service, while in exile, is of no value. Even if the inspiration tends to be sporadic and fleeting, in truth, every spiritual success is real and permanent. Our G-dly soul is always complete and its accomplishments should not be underestimated; it can never be erased.

"The fact that we are in a 'dream-state' actually has a positive component. It means that we are able to overcome boundaries that to our lucid, rational mind would be considered insurmountable. It is specifically during exile that the essential power of a Jew is revealed. When times are tough, the soul's overdrive is activated.

---

[168] Psalms 126:1.

"While awake, our sensible mind tells us that we must progress in an orderly, systematic fashion. We mustn't think too big or get ahead of ourselves. However, in a sleep state, we ignore all these limitations and have the ability to make huge spiritual leaps, disproportionate to our previous level.

"In our dream state, our observance does not have to follow the rules of rationality or rational order; we can make quantum spiritual leaps.[169] In the absence of the conscious, the subconscious emerges. Thus, according to the Kabbalah, the soul's essential powers are in fact strengthened and more apparent while one is asleep. Here is how Rabbi Adin Steinsaltz[170] describes the exile/dream phenomenon:

...In many ways, life in exile is unnatural, cumbersome and full of suffering. Yet life in exile also contains an unexpected sort of freedom.

Peoples living in their homelands behave in a normal way in whatever they do: Their thinking, their political activities, their daily conduct all are governed by some kind of rational law, which is taken for granted and never questioned. Thus, free peoples living in their native lands are, in a sense, doubly limited: they are limited both by the physical boundaries of their native countries and by the patterns set by the normal flow of everyday life.

In exile, on the other hand, people live an abnormal life, which is in a way like a dream. And what is a dream? Dreams are made up of real elements—one cannot dream about things that are outside of reality—which are however combined in ways that do not exist in reality. Thus, in a dream one can do things that would otherwise be impossible.

Although even in exile one certainly cannot do things that are not doable, one can create there combinations that do not exist in the "Real" world. A person who is objectively outside of his homeland, even if he feels that he belongs to another place is, in fact, living deeply within this combination of fantasy and objective reality; that

[169] *Torah Or,* Vayeishev, p. 28c.
[170] See footnote 120.

is, he creates a dream. Thus, exile sometimes produces individuals who are very creative in ways that they could never have been in their homelands, because they are not bound by the laws and limitations of the country in which they live. One such example is Napoleon: had he remained in Corsica, he would not have gained the throne of France. Or Pushkin's grandfather: What could he have become in his historical homeland? It was only in distant Russia that he became a general in Peter's army, and the grandfather of a famous poet...[171]

"On the surface, irrationality occurs in dreams because the rational mind does not control imagination during sleep. Similarly, during exile our 'rational mind,' our appreciation and understanding of Divinity, is feeble.

> The irrationality of dreams and exile are both rooted in transcendent, infinite Divinity that defies logic.

"On a deeper level, however, the irrationality of dreams and exile are both rooted in transcendent, infinite Divinity that defies logic and allows contradictions to coexist. However, when this transcendence manifests itself in dreams and exile, its infinity is hidden beneath a cloak of confusion and exilic chaos.

"This explains why dreams were a major channel in bringing the Jews into Egyptian exile. Joseph's dreams were a catalyst in leading the Israelites into Egypt. Pharaoh's dreams played a role in bringing about the state of exile.

"This is the deeper significance of Joseph's interpreting Pharaoh's dreams: By reaching above the external contradiction of Pharaoh's dreams, Joseph gave the Jewish people the strength to go past the external contradiction of exile; to see its root in Divine infinity. This phenomenon is completed in the Messianic age, when the inner light of G-dliness will be revealed.

"Accordingly, because of the unique nature of exile, there is an

---

[171] Interview with Rabbi Adin Steinsaltz for Magisterium.

advantage in our spiritual achievement during the 'dream' of exile over our achievement during the days of the Holy Temple; when we were 'awake' and things went in accordance to an orderly system.

"Speaking of reaching beyond the constraints of logic, I'm reminded, Danni, of a joke regarding the case of using super-logic:

"A Talmudist from Odessa who finally obtained permission to visit Moscow after months of negotiation with the authorities, boarded the train and found an empty seat. At the next stop a young man got on and sat next to him. The scholar looked at the young man and he thought:

"'This fellow doesn't look like a peasant, so if he is no peasant, he probably comes from this district. If he comes from this district, then he must be Jewish, because after all, this is a Jewish district.

"'But on the other hand, being that he is a Jew, where could he be going? I'm the only Jew in our district who has permission to travel to Moscow.

"'Ahh, wait! Just outside Moscow there is a little village called Samvet and Jews don't need special permission to go to Samvet. But why would he travel to Samvet? He is surely going to visit one of the Jewish families there. But how many Jewish families are there in Samvet? Aha, only two: the Bernsteins and the Steinbergs. Given that the Bernstein's are a strange family, such a nice looking fellow like him must be visiting the Steinbergs.

"'But why is he going to the Steinbergs in Samvet? The Steinbergs have only daughters, two of them, so maybe he's their son-in-law. But if he is, then which daughter did he marry? They say that Sarah Steinberg married a nice lawyer from Budapest and that Esther married a businessman from Zhitomer. So it must be Sarah's husband, which means that his name is Alexander Cohen, if I'm not mistaken.

"'But if he came from Budapest, with all the anti-Semitism there, he must have changed his name. What's the Hungarian equivalent of Cohen? It is Kovacs. Because they allowed him to change his name, he must have special status to change it. What could it be? It must be a doctorate from the university. Nothing less would do.'

"At this point, the scholar of *Talmud* turns to the young man and says, 'Excuse me. Do you mind if I open the window, Dr. Kovacs?'

"'Not at all,' answered the startled co-passenger, 'But, how is it that you know my name?'

"'Why,' replied the Talmudist, 'It was obvious!'

"During the Temple era, the conscious capacities of our souls operated soundly. During exile, these capacities are asleep. Ironically, this provides us greater access to our subconscious capacities that transcend limitations.

"For example, in Temple times, a ritually impure person could not experience holiness. Today, however, we transcend such limitations and can experience holiness even in the midst of our impurity.[172]

"In 'Normal' times, we must follow 'Normal' conventions, such as ascending the spiritual ladder one step at a time. In exile, however, we can tap into lofty spiritual opportunities that by normal standards are outside our realm. For example, in previous generations, we could not study the inner dimension of *Torah* without having undergone numerous preparations. Today, however, we can—and, therefore, must—study the inner dimension of *Torah*, regardless of our limited knowledge and spiritual level. However, most important, we must grab any Mitzvah we can, irrespective of our station in life.

"So, Jay, this should put an end to your beating up on yourself. You clearly fall into the category of Tinok Shenishba. You also belong to the age of Ikvesa D'moshichah and the 7th generation. What the Rebbe wants from you is to learn as much *Torah* and do as many Mitzvos as you can and leave your destiny in G-d's hands."

---

[172] See Leviticus 16:16.

"But Danni," exclaims Jay, "You just don't seem to get it. To adapt a familiar refrain: It's the 'family,' stupid!

"You know, I brought children into the world, and I want them to share the same identity and purpose with which I was blessed.

"It's nice to know that there is redemption for my soul through the ways of *Torah* and Teshuva, but I would like my family to share the beauty and depth of the path on which I hope to embark—the Jewish way of life. Is there redemption for them as well?

"Earlier, you spoke about Hashgacha Pratis, the bigger Divine picture to which everything belongs. It made a lot of sense, but does it apply to them as well?"

"Let me assure you, Jay, that regardless of your family's religious status, they are undoubtedly the products of Divine Providence. Souls do not enter this world by mistake, at least not on the part of G-d.

"There is a reason for your relationship with your wife Arlene, and you can be sure that it includes the children you brought into the world together.

"Regarding your question concerning the family's status that you refer to as their 'redemption,' let me preface my answer with a lesson on the lineage of two great icons within Judaism: the legendary King David and his impending most prominent descendant, King Moshiach—Messiah.

40

THE MYSTIFYING LINE OF MOSHIACH

"The lineage of King David, founder of the Jewish royal dynasty and progenitor of Moshiach, is rather mystifying. David belonged to the tribe of Judah. He descended from a union between Judah and Tamar that, on the surface, appears an unlikely source for the Davidic dynasty.

"In the book of Genesis,[173] we find the narrative of Judah's puzzling descent. After leaving his brothers, he becomes involved with the surrounding culture, where he marries, loses two sons and eventually impregnates his daughter-in-law Tamar.

"After learning that Tamar was pregnant, the family sought to have her killed, thinking she had violated family honor. At the last minute, Judah realizes her innocence. He admits that she was in fact 'More in the right than I.'[174]

"Tamar had been married to two of Judah's sons, Er and Onan, who both died before producing any children. According to the Jewish law of Yibum—levirate marriage—the widow of a man who dies childless marries his brother, so as to produce and raise a child in his brother's name. This child stood to inherit the deceased brother's land.

"The twice-widowed Tamar was expected to wed Judah's third and youngest son, Shelah. However, Judah, who thought of her as a black widow because both of her husbands died, did not wish to give his youngest son to her as a husband. He postponed the marriage by telling her to wait until Shelah got older.

"But Tamar, aware that the royal lineage was destined to result from her union with Judah, would only wait so long. Upon learning that the newly widowed Judah was traveling to his sheep as a means of consolation,

---

[173] Genesis 38.
[174] Genesis 38:26.

she disguised herself as a prostitute. Waiting at a crossroads, she enticed Judah into a liaison that produced twin sons, Peretz and Zorach. From Peretz descended Yishai, father of David.

"The *Midrash* relates that as Judah approached the crossroads, he did not pay the lady in disguise any heed. But a heavenly angel called out, 'From where shall the kings come?'[175] This question from On High prompted Judah to accept her services. The *Talmud* states that because Tamar committed an act of adultery with noble intentions, she merited propagating the Davidic Dynasty.[176]

"Our sages assert that, with the birth of Peretz, the Almighty created the 'light of Moshiach.' The *Midrash* notes that 'before the first enslaver of Israel was born, namely, Pharaoh, the ultimate redeemer of Israel, Peretz, who is Moshiach, was already born.'[177]

"Thus, G-d delivered the remedy before the affliction; before the Egyptian exile and the exiles that followed thereafter—including our present one. This light of Moshiach confers on Israel the strength and ability to succeed in their exiles to 'break through,' as the name Peretz indicates, all obstacles and impediments to the coming of Moshiach.

"But why should David and Moshiach be the products of such a line? True, the relationship occurred before the *Torah* was given and, hence, before its restriction. Nevertheless, it seems odd that Jewry's most respected family, the house of David, would be established through a relationship that would later be forbidden.

"Tamar was not the only perplexing link in the chain of David's ancestry. His great-grandfather, Boaz, married Ruth in a levirate marriage, as well. Ruth was a convert from Moab, a nation with whom Jews, ostensibly, were forbidden to intermarry.

"Similar questions pertain to other links in King David and Moshiach's

---

Bereishit Rabba 85:8.
[176] Nazir 32b.
[177] Bereishit Rabba 85:1.

lineage. For example, his son and successor, King Solomon, was born from his union with Bathsheba. Attracted to Bathsheba, David sent her husband Uriah to the front lines of war. After Uriah died in battle, David married his widow. While our sages maintain that David did not sin in this relationship, would it not be preferable for David's successor to be the product of a more honorable union?

But why should David and Moshiach be the products of such a line?

"The mysterious line of the Davidic ancestry reaches considerably farther back in Biblical history. In fact, it traces back to the descendants of the illicit union between a man and his two daughters.

"The *Torah* relates that, after Lot and his two unmarried daughters survived the destruction of Sodom, they lived together in a cave. The two sisters thought that the world was destroyed and that they were the only remnants of humankind. Therefore, they decided to impregnate themselves from their father in an effort to repopulate the world. For two consecutive nights, the women intoxicated their father Lot and on each night, one cohabitated with him.

"The eldest daughter, who was with her father the first night conceived and bore a son whom she named Moab, meaning 'from [my] father.' The younger daughter also conceived and, in time, bore a son whom she named Ben Ami, meaning 'son of my nation.'

"The *Talmud* states that, because of the noble intentions of these women in committing their acts of incest, they merited the reward of becoming the ancestors of the Davidic dynasty.[178] Hence, the lineage of the eternal king of Israel, David and the ultimate redeemer of Israel, Moshiach, is manifestly of unusual character in many respects.

"G-d established the Davidic dynasty in a surreptitious way. At every step, the unnatural occurred. Why is it that, of all things, the dynasty

[178] Nazir 23a.

of King David and, ultimately, the Messiah should spring from such unbecoming origins?

"The *Talmud* explains that, by establishing the Davidic dynasty as the only legitimate heirs to the throne, G-d insured that no king would rebel against Him. All descendants of King David could be suppressed easily should they revolt against Him by being reminded of their dubious lineage. This is why G-d specifically founded the Israelite kingdom through the man of tainted progeny, King David.[179]

"Kabbalah goes further in teaching that the soul of Moshiach is of such a high source of holiness that Satan strenuously tried to block his descent to this world. Therefore, G-d had to conceal this soul, cloaking its birth in a series of seemingly unholy alliances. Surely, Satan would not think to look in such lowly places for the birth of the future redeemer. And so, the dynasty of David and Moshiach was ushered in a stealth manner, unnoticed and unhampered by the forces of impurity.

"A similar idea is found in the *Midrash* regarding the relationship between Judah and Tamar. Judah sought to marry a wife to create his family, while G-d was busy creating the Messiah, King David, and his monarchal dynasty.[180]

"But why should David and Moshiach be the fruit of such a family tree? Three women, who are not Israelites; three women—who, in seeking the 'redeemer' of levirate marriage—themselves become redeemers, redeeming into righteousness what would otherwise be questionable within the legal code, and act with utter vigor and determination to redeem their family's destiny.

"It is as if the *Torah* is suggesting that should the Messiah be the redeemer of the entire world, he must descend from the broadest and most eclectic line. If Moshiach is to transform the subversive darkness in the world, a tinge of it would have to be part of his core essence and lineage.[181]

---

[179] Yoma 22b.

[180] Bereishis Rabbah 85:1.

[181] A similar idea is found in the Discourse called Shoresh Mitzvos Hatfillah in *Derech Mitzvosecha* of the

"Incest and harlotry are not the means (Heaven forbid) of bringing the Messiah, nor will they be celebrated afterward. So it is not prostitution that gives birth to Peretz, but what might be mistaken for prostitution before the assertion of levirate marriage.

"In the *Torah*, the story of Joseph contrasts the episode of Judah and Tamar. Joseph and Judah face similar challenges.

"In fact, the narrative of Judah and Tamar is inserted at a critical spot within Joseph's drama in the house of Pharaoh. It is not even consistent chronologically. While Judah is considerably aged, Joseph is a seventeen-year-old. The juxtaposition of the two stories that, in modern cinematic terms we might call crosscutting, is meant to contrast the two dominant descendants of Jacob.

> Judah symbolizes the route to achieve atonement and transcendence.

"Chassidic commentators explore the metatheory regarding the contrasting archetypes of Joseph and Judah. The paradigms of Joseph and Judah represent the two ways of spiritual achievement.

"Joseph holds fast against the advances of Potiphar's wife. Despite being exploited, he withstands temptation. Joseph is the 'righteous one.' He is a saint from birth, who intrinsically safeguards himself from temptation. Judah, on the other hand, does not fare as well in his test with Tamar, though, in the end, he confesses and owns up to his fault.

"Joseph represents spiritual perfection. It is part of his psychological makeup to be distant from sin and connected to G-d. Much like his mother, Rachel, who, in contrast to Leah, is described as perfectly beautiful, Joseph, too, symbolized spiritual perfection and beauty.

Tzemach Tzedek that discusses how sometimes a high level of Chesed-kindness must enter the world through the medium of Gevurah—stringency. The Kabbalistic term for this phenomenon is "Achlifu Duchtiehu"—interchanging of the vessels.

"Joseph represents conformity to the full letter of the law. He sees the world, as though through G-d's eyes.

"On the other hand, Judah symbolizes the route to achieve atonement and transcendence. Judah sins, but learns from his mistakes; he discovers that, despite his initial impression, in reality, 'She was more in the right than me.' He was able to recognize that he was the flawed one and needed to correct himself.

"As it happened, his descent was an opportunity for him to achieve his maximum potential, to reach the high-point of his life. This very admission gave Judah his claim to fame, as Jacob later said, 'Judah, you, your brothers will acknowledge.'[182]

"As part of the blessing that he gave to Judah, Jews, regardless of what tribe they are from, are called by his name 'Yehudim.' We are all spiritual descendants of Yehuda-Judah.

"So, Jay, need anything more be said? Does this not speak to your personal situation? Just think about the history of King David and Moshiach. Do you find any inspiration regarding your predicament? I think you ought to give this matter some serious thought.

"True, the choice is not in your hands, it is rather in the hands of your family; but should they so choose, there is room in Judaism not just for their acceptance, but for greatness as well. You cannot control the outcome, that is the unfortunate reality, but you can be a shining example of what is at stake.

"The most important thing you can do is pray. Pray that the Almighty bestow upon them an inspiration from above to recognize the beauty and advantage in the Jewish way of life. G-d, as you surely know, listens to our prayers, especially those that come from the heart."

At this time, the captain announces the initial descent to Atlanta's Hartsfield Jackson International Airport. We were both caught by surprise, shaken out of our trance and drawn back into reality.

---

[182] Ibid. 49:8.

The discussions were intense; they could easily have gone on for many more hours. But soon Jay and I would part, each reporting to our separate gates for the final leg to our respective communities. There was a sense of mutual disappointment.

"This can't be the end," declares Jay. "There is so much more to discuss. There are so many unfinished issues!"

"I agree with you," I tell Jay, "This must not be the end; we really ought to keep these discussions up. We can talk by phone once a week or every other week."

"I would actually like that a lot, Danni," affirms Jay. Would you be up for that?"

"I see no problem with it," I assure Jay. "It would actually be my pleasure," I add.

"But, wait a minute; I'm getting this crazy idea," I exclaim. "You have video conferencing through the firm, don't you?

"Yes, of course we do," Jay confirms, with a look of bemusement on his face. "Where is all this going, Danni," he asks.

"Then," I continue, "Why not join our 'Mornings with the Rabbi' sessions each weekday morning at 6:30 a.m.? I'll be glad to set it up on our end. So what do you think, Jay," I probe.

"How will R' Osher Chaimson feel about it," Jay queries.

"I'm quite sure R' Osher would not have a problem with it," I reply. "In fact, I'm just reminded that, on several occasions, we've discussed video recording the sessions and R' Chaimson was all for it. In fact, it was his idea. Well, this sounds like the perfect opportunity. So, Jay, is it a deal?"

"Deal!" says Jay.

SEQUEL

Since his midair encounter with his old college friend, Jay's life substantially changed. On a daily basis, he takes part in the Chassidus study sessions with R' Osher Chaimson, via video conference, and remains in close contact with Danni.

His religious observance continues to grow in many ways. He dons Tefillin daily, keeps a kosher diet, observes Shabbos, and preforms many other Mitzvos.

His family status remains the same, but his wife and children are supportive of his religious endeavor and showing some interest of their own.

"Life is a journey," says Jay, "whose destination is not always known to its traveler, but for each individual soul, there is a road to traverse and a destiny to discover. Finally, the journey is just as important as the destination.

GLOSSARY

A

Ahavah Ela'e'e. Superior love of G-d.

Ahavah Tata'a. Inferior love of G-d.

Aleph Bet. Hebrew alphabet.

Am Yisrael Chai. Nation of Israel is alive.

Assiyah. World of Action, lowest of the four worlds of creation.

Atzilus. World of Emanation, highest of the four worlds of creation.

Atzvus. Depression.

Avoda. (Lit. "service") Formerly, the sacrificial service in the Temple, and later the service of prayer instituted in its stead.

Avodat Hashem. Serving G-d.

Avodat Hatefila. Contemplative prayer.

B

Bar Mitzvah. (Lit. "son of the commandment") A Jewish boy who reaches the age of thirteen, the age of adulthood in Jewish life, thus becoming religiously responsible for his own conduct; the event marking this milestone.

Bat Mitzvah. (Lit. "daughter of the commandment") Jewish girl who reaches the age of twelve, the age of adulthood in Jewish life, thus becoming religiously responsible for her own conduct; the event marking this milestone.

Baruch Hashem. Praise G-d.

Basi L'Gani. (Lit. "I have come to my garden") Last Chasidic discourse written by Rabbi Yosef Yitzchak Schneersohn, before his passing on 10 Shevat, 5710 (January 28, 1950). Each year his successor, the Rebbe, Rabbi Menachem M. Schneerson (1902-1994), explained another of its chapters in depth. This was the inaugural Chassidic discourse delivered by the Rebbe, on 10 Shevat, 5711 (January 17, 1951).

Beis Medrash. Hall of study.

Bereishit. Genesis, the first of the five books of the Pentateuch.

Beriah. World of creation, second of the four worlds of creation.

Binah. (Lit. "comprehension") Second of the three intellective Supernal Sefiros-Divine emanations; second of the human intellectual faculties— the power that develops the abstract conception of seminal intuition, "Chochmah," giving it breadth and depth.

Bittul. Self-nullification.

C

Chabad. Kabbalistic terms for the three intellectual faculties, reflecting the Supernal emanations , namely, Chochmah, Binah, Da'as—Wisdom, Understanding, and Knowledge; name of a Chassidic movement.

Chag. Jewish holiday.

Chagas. Kabbalistic term for the first three of the seven emotive attributes namely, Chesed-benevolence, Gevurah-strength, Tiferes-compassion; Polish Chassidism, known for their emphasis, in serving G-d, with the emotive attributes.

Chakira. Jewish philosophy.

Chassid. (Lit. "pious one") One who goes beyond the letter of the law;

member of the Chassidic community, who follows its ways and adheres to a Chassidic Rebbe.

Chassidus. Jewish mystical theology based on the inner dimension of Torah. Chassidus takes the abstract and often impenetrable principles of classical Kabbalah and distills them into a practical medium, in one's service of the Heavenly Creator.

Chazal. Talmudic Scholars.

Chesed. (Lit. "kindness or grace") Kabbalistic term for the first of the seven emotive Supernal attributes, or Divine emanations, also reflected in the powers of the human soul.

Chochmah. (Lit. "wisdom; conceptual knowledge") Kabbalistic term for the first of the three intellective Supernal attributes, or Divine emanations, which are also reflected in the powers of the human soul.

D

Da'as. (Lit. "knowledge") Kabbalistic term for third of the three intellective Supernal attributes, or Divine emanations. Having proceeded from seminal intuition—Chochmah, through meditative gestation—Binah, it now matures into their corresponding attributes of character.

Derech Mitzvosecha. (Lit. "The way of your commandments") One of earliest works of Rabbi Menachem Mendel, third leader of Chabad-Lubavitch (1789-1866), penned between the years 1814 and 1828, when he was still a young man. It is a Chassidic/Kabbalistic treatment of many of the Torah's Mitzvos, such as belief in G-d, tzitzit, tefillin, prayer, loving a fellow Jew, starting a family and others.

Dirah. Dwelling.

Dirah B'tachtonim. Dwelling place for G-d in this lowest world.

D'rash. Homiletic, expounded interpretation of the Torah, one of the four levels of interpretation known as Pardes.

Dveikus. Fervor.

E

Ein Od Milvado. Nothing beside Him exists.

Ein Sof. (Lit. "without end") Kabbalistic term for the infinite nature of the Divine creative energy.

Emunah. Faith in G-d.

Emunah Ramah. (Lit. "Exalted Faith") Philosophical work written by Rabbi Abraham Ben David in Arabic, translated into Hebrew by Rabbi Solomon ben Labi under the title "Emunah Ramah."

Etz Hachaim. (Lit. "The Tree of Life") Classic Chassidic treatise written by Rabbi Shalom Dov Ber, fifth leader of Chabad, on the mystic core of spiritual vitality.

F

Farbrengen. Heartfelt Chassidic gathering, including words of inspiration, some L'chaim and stirring Chassidic melody.

G

Gam Zu L'tovah. This too is for good.

Gedolei Yisrael. Great Jewish leaders.

Geshmack. Enthusiasm.

Glatt Kosher. Meat from animals with smooth or defect-free lungs.

Gzeyras Tach Vetat. Persecutions of 1648-1649, consisted mainly of attacks by rebels against many Ukrainian, Belorussian, and Eastern Polish towns with large Jewish populations. As many as 20 thousand

Jews were killed. A similar number became refugees and some were forced to convert.

H

Hakadosh Baruch Hu. The Holy one blessed be He.

Halachah. Jewish law.

Halachic. In accordance with Jewish law.

Hashem. (Lit. "the name") Name referring to G-d.

Hashgacha Pratis. Divine Providence.

Haskalah. (Lit. "enlightenment") Jewish Enlightenment, an ideological and social movement that developed in Eastern Europe in the early nineteenth century, active until the rise of the Jewish national movement in the early 1880s. Its partisans were known as maskilim.

Helem. Hidden or concealed.

Hishtalshelus. Cascading order of descent, a Kabbalistic reference to the chain-like descent of the (four)spiritual worlds that exist between G-d and creation. Each spiritual world denotes a complete realm of existence, resulting from its general proximity or distance to Divine revelation.

I

Iggeres Hakodesh. The holy letter.

Ikvesa D'moshichah. (Lit. "Heel of Moshiach") The period immediately before the coming of Moshiach, which, so to speak, hears the approaching "footsteps of Moshiach".

K

Kabbalah. (Lit. "receiving" or "tradition,") Judaism's mystical strand

and related literature. It is an esoteric discipline and school of thought meant to define the existential nature and purpose of the universe and its human inhabitants.

Kabbolas Shabbos. Joyous Friday evening prayers welcoming the Sabbath,

Kabel. To receive.

Kedoshim. (Lit. "holy ones") Name of a Torah portion in Leviticus.

Kegavna. Section of the Zohar recited by Chassidim during Friday night prayers.

Keilim. Vessels.

Ki Sisa. (Lit. "when you uplift") Name of a Torah portion in Exodus containing the sin of the Golden Calf.

Klipah. (Lit. "bark" or "shell") Kabbalistic term for impure coverings that serve as the source of sensual desire in human nature.

Kol Hashviim Chavivim. (Lit. "all sevenths are beloved") Quote from Midrash Rabba (Vayikra 29). The Midrash proceeds to lists an array of generations and sequences that peaked on the seventh. The word Sheva-7 etymologically correlates with the word Sova-satisfaction.

Kol Mah D'ovied Rachmono, l'tav Ovied. Everything that the Merciful-One does is for the good.

Kosel. Western-Wall complex located in the Old City of Jerusalem, a relatively small segment of the structure which originally composed the western retaining wall of the Second Jewish Temple.

Kuntres ha'Avoda. Tract on Avodah-Divine Service. A fundamental treatise on prayer penned at the turn of the 20th century by Rabbi Shalom Dov Ber, fifth Rebbe of Chabad.

Kuntres haTefila. Tract on Prayer. A fundamental treatise, explaining how to refine one's character traits through prayer, penned at the turn of the 20th century by Rabbi Shalom Dov Ber, fifth Rebbe of Chabad.

L

Lechtchila Ariber. (Lit. "to go above in the first place") Famous adage, by Rabbi Shmuel, fourth Rebbe of Chabad: "The world says, 'If you can't crawl under an obstacle, try to climb over,' but I say, 'at the outset, one should climb over!'" This is understood to mean that we should confront challenges with courage and a boldness of spirit, so that they don't become obstacles in our service of G-d.

Lev Nishbar. Contriteness of heart.

Likutei Amarim. (Lit. "Collected Discourses") Also known as *Tanya*. Magnum opus of Rabbi Schneur Zalman of Liadi, first Rebbe of Chabad, *Tanya*, serves as the basis of Chabad Chassidic mysticism.

Likutei Sichos. (Lit. "Collected Talks") Contains both the scope and the core of the late Lubavitcher Rebbe Rabbi Menachem Mendel Schneerson's teachings. It is the most authoritative source text for the Rebbe's unique, original and often revolutionary, explanation of Judaism. These talks represent the legacy of the Rebbe's teachings to the world.

Litvish. (Lit. "of Lithuanian descent") Jews who follow a Lithuanian, non-Chassidic, style of Jewish practice.

M

Maamar. Chassidic discourse.

Maggidim. (Plural for Maggid) traditional, Eastern European, Jewish itinerant preachers, skilled as narrators of Torah and religious stories.

Mamad har Sinai. Presence at Mt. Sinai during the giving of the Torah.

Manna. Food from heaven, provided to the Jews during their 40 year sojourn in the desert, after their exodus from Egypt.

Mashpia. (Lit. "source of influence") Spiritual Chassidic mentor.

Mattan Torah. Giving of the Torah.

Matzliach. Successful.

Menorah. Candelabrum, described in the Torah as the seven-lamp (six branches) lampstand made of pure gold and used in the portable sanctuary set up in the wilderness and later in the Temple in Jerusalem.

Merirus Hanefesh. (Lit. "Bitterness of the soul") Unsatisfying state of mind, due to one's spiritual situation, which spur him to positive growth. One of various terms used in Chassidus, particularly *Tanya*, to describe the state of the human psyche.

Mesirut Nefesh. Personal sacrifice.

Midrash. Classical collection of the Sages' homiletic teachings on the *Torah*.

Mi Kamocha. Who is like you? Referring to G-d. A Biblical passage in Az Yashir-Song of the Sea.

Mikdash. (Lit. "sanctuary") Tabernacle in the desert and subsequent structures built to house G-d's presence, as dictated by Jewish law.

Minyan. (Lit. "number") Quorum of ten adult men necessary for communal prayer.

Misnagdim. (Lit. "opposers") Anti-Chassidic antagonists.

Mochen de'katnus. (Lit. "small-mindedness") A less than stellar spiritual state of mind, which does not allow one to achieve the level of religious pursuit of which he is capable.

Mitzvos. Divine commandments.

Moreh Nevuchim. Guide for the Perplexed. One of the three major works of Rabbi Moshe ben Maimon, primarily known either as Maimonides, in the West, or by the acronym RAMBAM, by the Jewish people. It is the main source of the Rambam's philosophical views, as opposed to his corpus on Jewish law, which is the focus of his other works.

Moshiach. Messiah.

Musar. (Lit. "rebuke") Jewish ethical, educational and cultural ideology, developed in the 19th century in Eastern Europe, popular among Orthodox Lithuanian Jews.

N

Nefesh Bahamis. Mankind's basic animal-like soul.

Nefesh Elokis. Mankind's G-dly soul.

Nemichas Ruach. Lowness of spirit. One of the several terms used in Chassidus, particularly in Tanya, to describe the state of the human psyche.

Neshama. (Lit. "breath of life") Divine soul.

Nigleh. Revealed dimension of the Torah, such as the 24 books of Tanach, the Talmud, and the related commentaries.

O

OBM. Of Blessed Memory.

Ohros. (Lit. "lights") Kabbalistic term for Divine energy.

Olam. World, entomologically related to the word helem-concealment.

P

Pardes. (Lit. "orchard") Acronym of the four levels of Torah expression:

pshat-literal meaning of the text, remez-allusions, derush-homilies that can be derived from it, and sod-mystical secrets.

Parsha. Section of Torah as divided in Jewish tradition into weekly portions.

Peninim. Inner dimension of Torah.

Pintele Yid. Essence of the Jewish soul.

P'shat. Plain meaning of the scriptural passages, one of the four levels of interpretation known as Pardes.

R

Remez. (Lit. "hint") 'Implied' meaning of the Torah, one of the four levels of interpretation known as Pardes. Remez refers to methods such as Gematria—word number values and codes.

S

Schmaltz. Rendered chicken fat; traditional Jewish delicacy.

Satmar. Hungarian/Romanian Chassidic sect.

Sefer HaBahir. Book of Illumination, one of the earliest Kabbalistic works.

Sefer haSichos. Textual recordings of the Lubavitcher Rebbe's talks.

Sefer Yetzirah. Book of Creation, one of the earliest Kabbalistic works.

Sefiros. (Lit. "attributes") ten Divine attributes that are manifested in each of the four worlds of creation and corresponding ten faculties of the soul.

Shabbos. Sabbath.

Shechinah. Feminine aspect of the Divine; manifestation of the Divine presence in this world.

Sheitel. Wig.

Sheva. Seven.

Shiduch. Match, especially for marriage.

Shiurim. Lessons on Torah topics.

Shluchim. (Plural for Shliach, lit. messenger) An emissary of the Chabad movement whose life is devoted to promulgating Judaism and Chasidism in all types of locations around the world.

Shovavim. Period dedicated to repentance and introspection, within certain Chassidic communities.

Shtreiml. Fur hat worn by married men of particular Chassidic circles on Shabbos and Jewish holidays, as well as other festive occasions.

Shulchan Aruch. (Lit. "set table") Code of Jewish law.

Sh'vat. Fifth month on the Jewish calendar, beginning from the month of Tishrei.

Sichah. (Lit. "a talk") One of the thousands of talks delivered by the Lubavitcher Rebbe throughout his 50 years of leadership, during his renowned "farbrengens".

Simcha. Joy, joyous occasion.

Simcha Shel Chaim. Joy of life.

Simcha Shel Mitzvah. Joy of a Mitzvah.

Sod. (Lit. "secret") One of the four levels of Torah expression known as Pardes, particularly, the mystical, esoteric level.

Sova. Satisfaction/satiation.

T

Tallis. Prayer shawl with ritual fringes at the four corners, worn by men during morning prayer services.

Talmud. (Lit. "instruction, learning") Central text of Rabbinic Judaism, comprised of Mishnah and its voluminous commentary Gemara. The term Talmud commonly refers to the Babylonian Talmud, although there is also an earlier compendium known as the Jerusalem Talmud.

Tanach. Acronym for Torah-Pentateuch, Nevi'im-Prophets and Ketuvim-Writings;" i.e., Hagiographa. The books of the Tanach were passed on by each generation.

Tanya. Fundamental text that systematically and comprehensively lays out the principles of Chabad-Chassidic philosophy. Authored by the movement's founder, Rabbi Shneur Zalman of Liadi in the 18th century, Tanya is the initial word of the book. It is also called Likkutei Amarim -Collected Discourses and Sefer Shel Beinonim, the Book of the Intermediates.

Tefillin. (Lit. "phylacteries") Two small black boxes with black leather straps containing parchment scrolls inscribed with the Shema and other biblical passages, that Jewish men are enjoined to place on their left or weaker arm and on the front part of their heads, at the hairline, during weekday morning prayers.

Teshuva. (Lit. "return") Repentance, return to one's true essence.

Tikkun Olam. (Lit. "repair of the world") Variety of meanings are given in medieval Kabbalistic literature, relating to the spiritual correction of the world.

Tinok Shenishba. (Lit. "captured infant") Talmudic term referring to a Jew who inadvertently sins as a result of being raised from infancy among gentiles and therefore has no understanding of Judaism. By Talmudic law one is not held accountable for failing to live in accordance with Torah when raised without Judaism.

Torah. (Lit. "teaching) Five Books of Moses; vast scope of Jewish teachings, encompassing Prophets, Writings, Oral Torah, all commentary, and traditions.

Torah-u'Madda. (Lit. "Torah and secular knowledge") Progressive philosophy of some centrist Orthodox persuasions concerning the Jew's relationship with the secular world, especially regarding the consumption of secular knowledge.

Toras Chaim. Torah of life.

Tzaddik. Righteous person. Described in the Talmud as one whose righteous acts constitute a majority of his actions. In Chassidic literature it relates to one who is wholly righteous—one who has conquered his animal impulses and is filled entirely with love and reverence for G-d.

Tzimtzum. (Lit. "contractions") Process of Divine self-contraction and withdrawal that creates the space, as it were, for physical, worldly existence.

U

Ushpizin. (Aramaic, lit. "honored guests") Seven leading figures in Jewish history who make non-corporeal visits to our Sukkah-hut on the holiday of Sukkos.

V

Vayechi. Name of the final Torah portion in the book of Genesis.

Ve'ata Tetzave. (Lit. "and you shall command") A portion in the Torah in the book of Exodus; title of the last Chassidic discourse-maamar edited by the late Lubavitcher Rebbe before suffering a stroke on Adar 27, 5752-March 10, 1992. Its significance is heightened by the fact that the Rebbe personally handed a copy of the maamar to thousands of men, women, and children, on Purim Katan, less than two weeks before the 27th of Adar.

Y

Y'chida. (Lit. "complete singular unity") Highest and innermost of the five levels of the soul.

Yehudim. (Lit. "Juda-ites") Jewish people. A name that traces back to the father of the tribe of Judah.

Yeshivos. Jewish religious schools.

Yesh m'ayin. Creation ex nihilo.

Yetzer Hara. Animal/evil inclination.

Yetzer Tov. Good inclination.

Yetzirah. (Lit. "formation") Third of the four spiritual worlds of creation, in which created beings take on corporeal form and definition of sorts.

Yibum. Levirate marriage.

Yid. Yiddish term for Jew.

Yiddishkeit. Yiddish term for Judaism.

Yirah. Attribute of awe of the Almighty

Yirah Ela'e'e. Superior awe of G-d.

Yira Tata'a. Inferior awe of G-d.

Z

Zitzfleisch. Yiddish term for patience.

Zohar. Classic text of the Kabbalah, compiled by 2nd century Mishnaic sage Rabbi Shimon bar Yochai.

CHABAD LEADERSHIP

The Chabad movement has been led by a succession of Chassidic Rebbes. The main line of the movement, Chabad-Lubavitch, has had seven Rebbes in total:

Rabbi Shneur Zalman of Liadi

Rabbi Shneur Zalman of Liadi (1745-1812), founded the Chabad movement in the town of Liozna. He later moved the movement's center to the town of Liadi. Rabbi Shneur Zalman was the youngest disciple of Rabbi Dovber of Mezritch, the principal disciple and successor of Rabbi Israel Baal Shem Tov, founder of Chassidism. The Chabad movement began as a separate school of thought within the Chassidic movement, focusing of the spread of Chassidic mystical teachings using logical reasoning (creating a kind of Jewish "rational-mysticism").

R' Shneur Zalman's main work is the *Tanya*, or "Sefer Shel Beinonim,"- Book of the Average Man. The *Tanya* is the central work of Chabad thought and is studied daily by followers of the Chabad movement. R' Shneur Zalman's other works include a collection of writings on Chassidic thought, and the Shulchan Aruch HaRav; a revised version of the code of Jewish law, both of which are studied regularly by followers of Chabad.

R' Shneur Zalman's successors went by last names such as "Shneuri" and "Schneersohn" (later "Schneerson") signifying their descent from the movement's founder. He is commonly referred to as the "Alter Rebbe"- Old Rebbe.

Rabbi Dovber Schneuri

Rabbi Dovber Schneuri (1773–1827), son of Rabbi Shneur Zalman, led the Chabad movement in the town of Lyubavichi (Lubavitch). Rabbi Dovber was generally recognized as his father's rightful successor, and the movement's leader. Rabbi Dovber published a number of his

writings on Chassidic thought, greatly expanding his father's work. He
also published some of his father's writings. Many of Rabbi Dovber's
works have been subsequently republished by the Chabad movement.
He is commonly referred to as the "Mitteler Rebbe"-Middle Rebbe.

Rabbi Menachem Mendel Schneersohn

Rabbi Menachem Mendel Schneersohn (1789–1866), a grandson of
Rabbi Shneur Zalman and son-in-law of Rabbi Dovber. Following his
attempt to persuade the Chabad movement to accept his brother-in-law
or uncle as Rebbe, Rabbi Menachem Mendel assumed the title of Rebbe
of Chabad, also leading the movement from the town of Lubavitch. He
published a number of his works on both Chassidic thought and Jewish
law. Rabbi Menachem Mendel also published some of the works of his
grandfather, Rabbi Shneur Zalman. He is commonly referred to as the
"Tzemach Tzedek," after the title of his responsa.

Rabbi Shmuel Schneersohn

Rabbi Shmuel Schneersohn (1834–1882), was the seventh and youngest
son of Rabbi Menachem Mendel. He assumed the title of Rebbe in town
of Lubavitch, while several of his brothers assumed the title of Rebbe
in other towns, forming groups of their own. Years after his death, his
teachings were published by the Chabad movement. He is commonly
referred to as the Maharash, an acronym for "Moreinu HaRav Shmuel"-
our teacher, Rabbi Shmuel.

Rabbi Sholom Dovber Schneersohn

Rabbi Sholom Dovber Schneersohn (1860–1920), Shmuel's second
son, succeeded his father as Rebbe. Rabbi Shalom Dovber waited some
time before officially accepting the title of Rebbe, as not to offend his
elder brother, Zalman Aaron. He established a yeshiva called Tomchei
Temimim. During World War One, he moved to Rostov-on-Don. Many
of his writings were published after his death, and are studied regularly
in Chabad yeshivas. He is commonly referred to as the "Rashab," an
acronym for Rabbi Shalom Ber.

RABBI YOSEF YITZCHAK SCHNEERSOHN

Rabbi Yosef Yitzchak Schneersohn (1880–1950), the only son of R' Sholom Dovber, succeeded his father as Rebbe of Chabad. Rabbi Yosef Yitzchak was exiled from Russia, following an attempt by the Bolshevik government to have him executed. He led the movement from Warsaw, Poland, until the start of World War Two.

After fleeing the Nazis, Rabbi Yosef Yitzchak lived in Brooklyn, New York until his death. He established much of Chabad's current organizational structure, founding several of its central organizations as well as other Chabad institutions, both local and international. He published a number of his writings, as well as the works of his predecessors. He is commonly referred to as was the "Rayatz," or the "Frierdiker Rebbe"-Previous Rebbe.

RABBI MENACHEM MENDEL SCHNEERSON

Rabbi Menachem Mendel Schneerson (1902–1994), son-in-law of Rabbi Yosef Yitzchak, and a great-grandson of the third Rebbe of Lubavitch, assumed the title of Rebbe one year after his father-in-law's passing. Rabbi Menachem Mendel greatly expanded Chabad's global network, establishing thousands of Chabad centers across the globe. He published many of his own works as well as the works of his predecessors. Rabbi Menachem Mendel's teachings are studied regularly by followers of Chabad. He is commonly referred to as "the Rebbe". Even after his passing, he is revered as the leader of the Chabad movement.